Six Weeks

WILLIAM LEDBETTER

Buswell
— PRESS —

First published by Buswell Press 2026

This book is a work of memoir. It is based on real events to the best of the author's recollection. Some names and identifying details have been changed, and certain scenes may be compressed or reconstructed from memory to protect privacy and improve narrative flow.

First edition
ISBN (paperback): 979-8-9958309-0-0
ISBN (hardcover): 979-8-9958309-1-7
ISBN (EPUB): 979-8-9958309-2-4

To my sweet sister, Nancy.
Siblings through thick and thin.
Best sister ever.

Contents

Prologue

Nancy was my older sister, the best kind. She was sharp, funny, and stubborn in a way that passes for fortitude until you realize it is strength. Her faith ran quietly through her life, more private backbone than performance. She entered hospice as she lived, steadfast, private, proud, determined to endure without turning her pain into another person's burden.

The final six weeks of her life unfolded in a space that was still, technically, someone's home; the ordinary furniture within was pushed aside to make room for a bed, her life narrowing to a small radius. Her days became measured and repetitive from then on, tender and unsentimental, marked by small decisions, constant care, and an intimacy you don't rehearse for and can't fully explain to someone who hasn't lived inside it.

Peace always seemed elusive to us. Nancy and I had faced hard things before and gotten through them together, but whatever calm we earned was always temporary, always borrowed. We were a team, even though we were different kinds of players. I brought steadiness and the business of getting things done: plans, calls, logistics, and the plain language of responsibility to the game. Nancy brought grace and compassion, the human touch that never needed to announce itself. Crucially, we shared one tool that mattered more than people like to admit: humor. We were often sarcastic, sometimes inappropriate. Yet our humor was almost always necessary. It was our common bond, the means by which we stayed ourselves.

This is a story about those last six weeks of Nancy's life. It is also a story about what came before them, because what happened in that room didn't start there; neither the debts we inherited nor the ones we took on over time. We are the sum of the decisions we make and the decisions made upon us by generations before us. People often talk about inheritance as cherished heirlooms, things that are remembered, polished, and kept safe. Some people even look forward to their inheritance, as one might look forward to opening a box and finding something that still smells like home. Sure, Nancy and I ended up with a few sentimental things along the journey. In my case, it was an old clock, one of those objects that looks harmless until you realize it's been keeping time for your family for decades.

The reality, or at least our reality, is that some debts come with those knick-knacks. Some are ordinary, like where we lived, what we could afford, what was said at the table, and what never was. Others are louder, like the ruptures that rearranged a family, leaving everyone improvising around the damage.

Our inheritance didn't just shape us; it strengthened our bond. The patterns we learned to manage it with became our strengths, our ways of buffering, smoothing, solving, and enduring. Though we didn't handle things the same way, together and with the humor we shared, we found a rhythm that carried us through what was given to us over time and what we added along the way. We leaned on each other's strengths until we had forged a bond that held, and we kept showing up for each other when it counted most.

Faced with challenges most of our lives, we did what we'd always done. We brought what each of us had, Nancy's steadiness in one hand, my structure in the other, and supported each other through what could not be fixed. The decisions made upon us did not disappear. But facing this together one last time, we settled what we could, and when there was nothing left to perform, there was still a way to show up and find peace.

This memoir may feel heavy to some, yet it isn't meant to frustrate a reader's hope for a different ending. The outcome is predetermined. Rather, it traces what we inherit and how we face adversity with understanding for what went before us, with forgiveness and clear eyes, with ordinary routines still trying to hold us. Humor is still breaking through at the right moments.

Ultimately, it is a story of finding grace and peace through reconciliation, commitment, redemption, and love, told through the breadth and depth of those precious six weeks.

I
The Promise

1

The Call

The day of Joe's memorial service was an Indian summer day. Warm for early November, but pleasant enough that one did not need a coat yet. It was the kind of day that makes you believe endings can wait their turn.

Family, friends, and acquaintances filed out of the church as the service concluded. Small groups gathered in loose clusters, offered their condolences, then broke apart, hugs ending awkwardly, car doors opening and closing in uneven rhythm.

Inside, placed near the front, was the urn, a maple box with a brass plaque. Joe's name was there on it, plain in its finality. It didn't look like it could hold a person.

I was the second to give a eulogy. Joe's brother-in-law spoke first. He was tall and lean, a lanky, middle-aged Connecticut native with a professional ease about him, the kind that comes from years of speaking in front of people.

The church was small, stone on the outside but remodeled within, with dark wood pews, a simple pulpit, plaster walls, and aged stained glass that held the light in place. He leaned gently into humor, talking of the hard-luck Jets, Joe's loyalty to underdogs, and how he rooted for teams that never quite delivered. People laughed in the way people do when they are grateful for being permitted to breathe. It loosened the room.

As he spoke, I remembered that Joe had been in a nursing home when I visited him last. Ellen, his wife, was already there, sitting close to him like spouses do when they've been pulled into a new reality and don't yet have the language for it.

The gift basket I had sent them sat unopened on a side table.

Joe was brought in on a hospital bed by orderlies. He had no strength left. They used a sling to lift him like cargo, lowering him carefully onto the bed. His left arm was visibly atrophied. His legs were thin and still. The stroke, which had happened during a surgery meant to remove the tumor in his brain, had taken much of his motor function with it.

He looked surprised to see me. But once he had settled back into bed, the covers bunching beneath his hands, we talked as best we could, going through all the old topics we used to discuss. The Jets. Old coworkers. Filling the space with familiar names, trying not to stare directly at what had happened.

After a while, his expression changed. The small talk dropped away.

"Bill," he said.

"I'm screwed. My life is over. I'll never see my daughter walk down the aisle."

He started crying. I silently let him, knowing, as we both did, that this was probably the last time we would see each other, but left it unsaid.

On the drive home from Joe's nursing home that day, just a few short months before the service, I thought about how much Joe had looked forward to retirement, counting down the few years remaining, enduring work for the promise of peace with his family and grandchildren. Life is timed, planned, and scheduled.

It wasn't to be.

That moment stayed with me. It explained why, today at Joe's memorial, I spoke as I did: He could no longer, and because Ellen and the girls needed someone to say aloud what he had carried and what he loved.

When my turn to speak at his eulogy came, I rose from the pew beside my old boss. He gave a slight nod as I stood. It wasn't encouragement precisely, but acknowledgment. Respect.

I told them that Joe and I often spoke about the things you inherit and the things you choose. I had once told him something my sister Nancy and I had been saying for years: *We are the sum of the decisions we make, and the decisions made upon us by generations before.* Joe understood that, and we spoke of it often at tailgates, noting how, as parents, we try to do better than our parents did generations before us. We take shape and manage what was given. Joe did something rare with this by ensuring his next set of decisions was gentler.

I'd known Joe as a coworker and a friend. His wife and daughters had joined us on football game days, Jets games each season, and he often spoke lovingly of Ellen and the girls, looking forward to being a new grandfather and finally spending time focused on them.

My tone grew quieter as I recounted all this. More measured. There was no reach for levity, for this eulogy wasn't a performance. There was no applause afterward, just people blinking, swallowing, and accepting what had been shared with them.

After the service, I stood in the parking lot finishing a conversation with Joe's widow and daughters. There were a few final hugs to keep the line moving. Words that mattered, and that didn't, were offered.

Then I stepped aside and joined a loose circle of former coworkers and old friends we had shared. Old partners. Familiar faces. People I'd spent long days with years earlier.

It was businesslike, as grief among professionals often is: contained, courteous, sincere, yet not intimate. We spoke about Joe. About how unfair this was. About how sudden everything had been. There were quiet nods in my direction for the eulogy. Promises to catch up sometime. We all knew we probably wouldn't.

My old boss, uncomfortable with emotion, always businesslike even when we were close, told me my eulogy was well done and moving. There was no hand on my shoulder. No physical affinity. That just wasn't him.

My phone buzzed then.

It was not a call, I saw.

A text.

The vibration felt louder than it should have. Phones always choose their moment, don't they? I slid it out of my pocket with my thumb still pressed to the screen, how you do when you don't want anyone to notice you're checking your phone.

For a second, I just stared at the lock screen. The parking lot was still full of activity: people folding programs, straightening jackets, searching for keys, pretending their faces weren't wet. Someone laughed too brightly at something that wasn't funny. Somewhere close by, an engine started, and then died, as if the driver needed a moment too.

I unlocked the phone and glanced at the text.

"Uncle Bill, Mom is in the hospital, admitted, and unconscious."

I read it in silence, without interrupting the conversation or my duties as Joe's witness. I kept on talking. I kept shaking hands, doing what I was there to do.

The whole while, something in me tightened, an internal click. A hinge was moving.

In my head, "hospital" still meant tests. Nancy had been acting funny lately. She wasn't eating, she kept stumbling, withdrawing. I thought they were trying to figure out why. I assumed Chelsea did, too. So, I texted back while I was still standing there.

"OK. I'm in Connecticut. I'll drive down as soon as I can."

I didn't call her or follow up. I didn't even send any additional texts.

The sentence sat there, in my mind, like a closed door, the kind that makes you press your ear to the wood and listen for movement on the other side.

People were still moving through the parking lot, drifting off in separate directions. My mind hung onto Nancy, even as my old boss stayed focused on Joe's memorial and catching up on work.

I tucked the phone back away in my pocket and let my expression turn neutral. That was something I'd learned early: how to keep the outside normal while the inside changed.

My boss asked how long I'd been down in Florida. He asked if my commute had been brutal, about a few people we both knew, names that used to matter more than they do when you're outside that world.

I answered automatically. I could hear myself answering. I sounded like myself. That was the strange part.

A gust of warm air pushed through the parking lot, carrying the smell of damp leaves and exhaust. It felt wrong for November. It felt wrong for a memorial. It especially felt wrong for whatever was happening to Nancy now.

We walked to his car. He unlocked it with a beep that sounded too cheerful.

In the car, for the drive back from Connecticut to New Jersey, he just kept talking. I kept answering, though underneath the veneer of the conversation, I was elsewhere.

He drove in the same steady, attentive manner he always did, careful about his mirrors. As the road stretched on, the GPS gave instructions we didn't need. We merged onto the highway with the rest of the late-afternoon traffic, everyone moving as if there was nothing urgent in the world that they needed to get to.

The conversation drifted toward what it always had been between us: to Joe at first, then work. Eventually, my old boss started telling me about a new role he had taken on. There were familiar problems. He asked questions, asking for advice. He listened. He still valued my counsel, and he made that clear without saying it directly.

Hence, I gave him what advice I could, clear and efficient as always, while tracking something else entirely in the background. I could feel it, that familiar split: one part of me present, another already mapping out the logistics, timing, failure points, what mattered most. How far was it to the hospital Nancy was in? Who was with her? How long had she been there? Why did she lose consciousness? Was Chelsea scared and alone?

I checked my phone once when he stopped for gas. There were no new messages. The absence of one was its own message: Nothing had improved or changed.

When my boss got back in the car, he resumed the conversation as if we were still on the same day we'd started. I nodded at all the right places and said the right things. The rhythm of work talk is its own shelter, replete with safe sentences and familiar, solvable problems. You can hide inside it.

Once he dropped me off, said goodbye, and left, I got in my car and headed south. The sun was lower now, making the road glare at me. I gripped the wheel tightly, then deliberately loosened my grip, not for comfort, but for control. I called Chelsea. The phone rang until I heard her voicemail.

I didn't leave a message, but I called again a few minutes later. Again, no response. I stopped after that. I knew how it would feel to pause. I knew because I'd done it before to other people when I was trying to help.

At a red light, I glanced at the text again. *Admitted.* The word pressed on my heart harder each time I read it. *Admitted* is not "we're here for a test." *Admitted* is "you can't leave."

I finally arrived and walked in through the emergency room entrance. The automatic doors breathed open and shut in regular cycles. Inside, the air was colder than outside. Over-conditioned and stale. The floor shone too brightly. A television mounted high in a corner was tuned to a news channel with the sound off. The captions crawled along the bottom like an afterthought. Everyone in the room stared at the screen anyway.

The visitors' window was blocked by glass except for a narrow opening. A tired sign listed the rules in small print, about IDs, visiting hours, and security procedures. Rules that don't stop the world from falling apart but insist on being obeyed anyway. I passed my identification through the gap in the window and asked what room Nancy was staying in. The woman behind the glass looked down at her screen, typed, then looked back up, expressionless.

"Name?"

I repeated it. The woman typed again, her nails clicking like a metronome.

"Third floor," she said finally, sliding my ID back through the slot. "You have to get a visitor's badge."

The sticker printer whined, the badge coming out warm and slightly curled, and the woman behind the glass handed it over as if it were any old receipt.

I stuck it on my shirt and moved toward the elevators. The hallway smelled of disinfectant and microwaved food rising from somewhere behind a door. A man in scrubs walked past me quickly, eyes fixed forward. A woman sat against the wall holding a plastic bag with her purse clutched inside it, as if anything could be stolen at any moment. In the elevator, I watched the numbers change and tried not to think about what each meant. Every floor was a different kind of waiting.

When the doors opened, the third floor was quieter. A nurse's station up ahead glowed with monitors and computer screens. Phones rang and were answered in clipped tones. Someone let out a laugh, just the once, the sound short, surprised. Then the laughter disappeared as if it had been pushed back into a pocket.

I spotted Chelsea there with her husband in Nancy's room. Brian, Nancy's closest friend, was there, too. They were waiting, as people do when they don't yet know what they're waiting for. Nancy was sharing a room with another patient, I saw, their beds separated only by a curtain. The other family spoke in low tones in Spanish. The curtain provided not privacy so much as the idea of it, and everyone acted accordingly, voices dialed down to low tones, bodies angled away from others, eyes averted.

Nancy had been taken for tests, I was informed, so we decided to wait in the hall to give the other family as much privacy as we could. Outside the room, we stood shoulder to shoulder with strangers, each of us trying to occupy as little space as possible. The hospital made a kind of democracy out of everyone pressed into the same narrow lanes, reducing everyone to a sticker on their chest. A custodian pushed a mop bucket past us and apologized, as if he were the one who had interrupted us.

We could still hear the Spanish family murmuring behind the curtain. Every so often, I caught a word that rose above the rest, soft laughter once, then a hushing sound, followed by a woman's voice that sounded like prayer. I didn't understand the language that was being spoken, but I understood its cadence: people trying to be brave for the person in the bed.

Chelsea leaned against the wall with her arms folded, phone in her hand, as though it might ring with some explanation. She was in her glasses, hair pulled back off her face, the phone resting in her palm like it had weight beyond its weight. When she shifted one foot angled out and her shoulder set against the wall, I caught a trace of Nancy in her, not in looks exactly, but in the way she held herself, the same contained patience, the same habit of bracing without announcing it. Brian stood a few feet away, hands clasped in front of him, over six feet tall and lean, staring at a distinct spot on the linoleum floor. He had a long, narrow frame, a straight posture, and a stillness that looked rehearsed, as if he had decided that if he did not move, nothing else would move or change.

We could only visit rooms two at a time, so Chelsea's husband offered to stay back while Chelsea, Brian, and I rotated into the room in fifteen-minute shifts. Brian was posted near the doorway like a bracket holding the hall together. None of us wanted to leave the orbit of that room in case Nancy returned.

A nurse came by later and said they were delayed because Nancy needed further testing. "We'll bring her back," she added. It was meant as reassurance, but it sounded more like a promise no one could guarantee. We nodded anyway. We always nod in hospitals. It's a way of saying we're cooperating with reality.

Chelsea filled me in on what had happened. Nancy had come in for tests because she kept falling over and wasn't eating. They scanned her, found nothing, and discharged her anyway, even though Chelsea insisted on further testing. Brian had been helping Nancy into the car when she collapsed outside the emergency room. Because she passed out on hospital grounds, the hospital had to readmit her. Brian said they'd keep her now until they figured it out. They seemed puzzled.

As Chelsea talked, I listened intently, pulling out the valuable bits, discarding the rest, trying to keep the fear from turning into noise. I looked down the hallway, toward the closed doors, and thought about how many lives were changing behind them at the same time.

A cart rolled past us, its wheels squeaking softly. A nurse stepped into a room and closed the door behind her. Somewhere, a monitor was chirping in a steady rhythm that was almost calming until you remembered what it was counting. As I listened to the hospital sounds around us, the diner came into my mind without invitation.

Not because I was hungry, but because it marked how, just this past June, my sister was still alive, and we were both pretending that meant we still had time.

2

The Diner

The diner had been chosen because I had told Nancy I was returning from Florida via Trenton, near Mercer. She suggested it as an opportunity for us to say hello to one another. We weren't meeting for food. We were meeting to keep the word "later" from swallowing us whole. Chelsea was still engaged then, and with the wedding so close at hand, everything in Nancy's life felt like it had a countdown.

The week before, I had gone to Clearwater to see some friends for a long June weekend. It was an easy flight in and out, and the airport always felt less like a fight than Newark. From Tampa, I could be back home in central New Jersey without losing the whole day. There were no long parking shuttles, no snarled exits, and no extra friction that makes travel feel like punishment.

On the flight home, I tried to keep my mind in check. I'd been gone a week, surrounded by sun and salt air and the easy laughter of old friends, working remotely but still feeling, for once, a different pace, a slower tempo that made the days seem negotiable. It was the sort of week that makes you believe, briefly, that life is manageable.

Then I landed, walked those fluorescent corridors, waited at baggage claim with everyone else pretending they weren't tired, and felt the familiar pressure reappear, not as a mood shift but as a list running through my mind, going over the commute I still had to endure. The meetings I need to take in the coming days. The pace in New Jersey was quickening already on all fronts.

My inbox was already refilling, as was my calendar. Beneath the weight of my professional responsibilities, though, there was a quieter burden, one of personal obligations, that did not pause just because a plane touched down. Already, the ongoing management of everything outside the office, which still depended on me, thrummed in the background, alongside the constant effort I had to keep up to prevent my two worlds from colliding and everything else from tipping over.

Once in the car, I texted Nancy that I was back in New Jersey: "Home. Want to meet?" She replied quickly, she always did when something mattered, and suggested a diner not far from her, a place neutral enough that we could talk without announcing to the world what we were talking about.

I got there first.

The diner itself was smaller than most, but packed so tightly that the room felt hot even before the food arrived. People had wedged themselves into booths, their voices layered on top of each other, coffee cups clicking against saucers. A waitress cut through the aisle carrying a ridiculous load, six plates balanced along her arms like she'd been built for it. I watched her pass and thought, without any real reason, that it was something I could never do. I saved the observation for Nancy, like a harmless coin I could put on the table before we spent the larger ones.

I scanned the menu and almost ordered breakfast because it looked so good on other tables: eggs, toast, pancakes, the comfort-food version of safety. Then I decided that chicken was the better choice, since it felt more honest for dinner.

When Nancy arrived, she struggled to get up the stairs with her cane. I got up from where I was sitting, and we moved toward each other in the doorway, pretending that we had done this a thousand times, that we were always meeting halfway.

"Hey, Nant," I said. When I was a kid, I couldn't say the word "Nancy," and the nickname had stuck.

She smiled. "Hey."

Nancy was my height and frame, unmistakably my sister even before she moved. Up close, the family resemblance was almost blunt. We shared the same build and the same set of eyes, but she carried more of Dad in her jawline, with a firmer edge, while my face has always favored Mom. She had the cane in one hand, but it was her face that told the story first. She had just turned sixty, and the last year had rearranged her. The chemo had thinned her hair and changed her skin tone, pulling color from places that used to hold it. Her eyes looked tired now, and the wrinkles and furrows around them were more plainly visible, as if the year had pressed itself into her face and decided to stay. Even when she smiled, it arrived with effort, brave and practiced, a familiar expression on a face that had aged quickly since the double mastectomy the year before.

While we waited for the waitress to return, we made the usual small talk to maintain the illusion that we were just two people meeting for dinner. I told her how work had changed. I'd taken a new job in Warren, New Jersey, after months of commuting to a role in Rochester that required me to fly out every other week. The shorter commute allowed me to get hours back of my life, which I appreciated.

I asked after Chelsea, how she was holding up, and how the wedding plans with her fiancé were going. Nancy's face softened at that. Chelsea was looking at a home in Roebling, something bigger where she could finally have a room of her own. She had been living with Nancy in a one-bedroom rental till then, and the apartment was cramped in a way you stopped noticing only because you had to. I told her I was happy for Chelsea and meant it, glad that she and Nancy both would now have the simple dignity of space.

"Roebling?" I then asked. I'd never heard of the town.

"Old manufacturing town," Nancy explained. "The townhouses were built for the workers."

It was now dinner time. The waitress finally came over, and I ordered half a chicken with stuffing and vegetables that had caught my eye when I sat down. I told Nancy not to worry about the cost. I didn't want her to think about the bill. She ordered a simple sandwich and water.

The waitress didn't write anything down, not needing to. Her attention was steady, practiced in a way that made you feel both cared for and managed. As she turned, the same waitress from before, with the six plates, passed by again. I nodded toward her.

"Seriously," I said to Nancy, "I could never do that."

Nancy glanced up, followed my eyes, and gave me a half smile. "You can barely carry a coffee and your dignity at the same time," she quipped.

It was a small line, yet it was classic Nancy: light enough to be a joke and sharp enough to be true. I laughed once, grateful for the familiar blade.

Our waitress turned out to be kind and unhurried. The menu looked as if it had been printed decades ago, its laminate worn smooth, newer prices taped over old ones like quiet revisions. I caught myself squaring the menu against the table edge, measuring nothing, just making it a straight edge.

"You know Dad never used a ruler," she said, noticing what I was doing. "Tape measure only."

"Yeah," I said. "It was a pain in grade school looking for one for our pencil box. Not one in the whole house. Like rulers offended him."

When the waitress walked away, I watched the other tables as one would observe the tide. A couple across from us was quietly arguing about something small, like who forgot to pay a bill, then softened when their food arrived. At the counter, a man in a work jacket sat eating alone, staring at his phone between bites. It struck me that everyone in the room was carrying something, and most of it was invisible.

"How are you doing?" I finally asked Nancy, having finished catching her up on the goings-on of my life.

"Checkup tests," she said with a wave of her hand. "They keep looking for something even though they say I'm fine. The AFP scores are sometimes high, they say, and maybe something on the other side. I don't know. I always feel off, even though they say I'm cured."

"Well, it's probably just routine testing," I said.

She looked down for a moment.

"I hope they don't find anything."

For a few seconds, neither of us spoke. The word "hope" hung between us, feeling heavier than it should have, like a note in a familiar song that lands just off key. Around us, the diner kept moving as if nothing had changed. A waitress slid past with a pot of coffee and refilled a stranger's cup without looking up. The kitchen bell rang, announcing the arrival of more food. It was the old miracle of public places: Your private fear gets no special accommodation.

Nancy's fingers worried the edge of the paper menu. Her hands were small, but the motion there was restless, like she could smooth the future if she pressed hard enough. I watched her and waited. With Nancy, waiting was part of the conversation. If you rushed her, she'd turn what she wanted to say into humor. If you gave her room, on the other hand, she might step into it.

The pause stretched, seemingly for an eternity, as Nancy's eyes cast down at the table, and then she finally spoke.

"Well…I'm going to need you to…It would be too much for Chelsea… I'm asking if you…"

She couldn't get the words out cleanly.

I didn't fill the silence now, either. I didn't rescue Nancy from the words she was trying to say. I knew what she was trying to ask and why it was hard. Asking for help is one thing. Asking for that kind of help is another. You can't dress it up. I felt it before she said it, the way you recognize a tune even when someone only hums the melody. I knew the words. And underneath the ask, I heard what I had heard in her for years: Chelsea. Not panic, not drama. I took it as Nancy being worn down by the treatments, in one of those melancholy blue stretches, wanting assurance, a safety net, something that would let her exhale.

Across the aisle, a man tore open a packet of ketchup with his teeth and squeezed it onto his fries as if it were the only urgent thing in the world. The normality of it made me feel briefly insane.

"So, what you want to have done if it's needed and the time it does come…" I said, leaving the sentence unfinished at the exact point where our mutual cadence could sense the prompt. She opened her mouth, then stopped, stuck at the same ledge as before, where the words wouldn't carry.

I finally said, "You want me to be your caretaker?"

She looked at me with relief and nodded.

"Yes," she said quietly. "If it comes back. If it gets bad."

I didn't hesitate.

"Of course," I said.

She exhaled, like she'd been holding that breath for weeks. Then she did what Nancy always did when something got too heavy. She found a way to light up things without denying them.

"You realize," I said, "I feel like, after everything I've been through, I'm becoming 'Doctor Death' now. I'm getting way too experienced. More than I'd like."

Nancy laughed. I smiled.

Before we stood up to leave, Nancy looked down at the table like she was checking an invisible list. I subtly shifted the topic to our dad just then, and the plans Nancy and I made after his passing, and she lifted her eyes. "And we still have to go see Grandma Rita's grave," she said. "Do you still have the small box of Dad's ashes, the ones you saved?"

"Not on me," I said, and she almost smiled at the absurdity of how literal that sounded. "But yes. I've still got them. I've had them for a while already. We'll make plans."

She held the look I gave her for a beat, relieved that there had been no theatrics, like crossing one more thing off meant she could breathe again. Finally, she pushed herself back from the table, and we went back to being just us, walking out into the parking lot like the world hadn't just changed.

I looked toward the next booth and lowered my voice, as if we were coconspirators.

"The people in the next booth must think we're the Addams Family."

My words made her laugh again, and for a moment, the smiles came back into the room. At that diner, I promised her she had nothing to worry about. At the time, I believed that. I was planning for contingencies that would endure, after all. So, she finished her meal, boxed my leftovers into a container, and we sat together in front of our empty plates. Together, we shared a silence that was not awkward. She took all my leftovers.

The thing about Nancy was that she always ordered dessert without exception. And if rice pudding was on the menu, she chose it as if it were an old rule. Looking at the menu now, she gravitated toward rice pudding at once, feeling like the diner had just offered her proof it knew her. Normally, she'd take it to go in one of those cheap paper coffee cups, she said, the kind with the plastic lid that never quite sealed, and ask for cinnamon on top.

This preference went back to Grandma Arline. Rice pudding was comfort food: hers, Dad's, mine. It was something warm and sweet from a house that could be cold in every other way, the one dessert that felt less like indulgence than belonging.

When the pudding finally came, Nancy didn't immediately pull it toward herself the way she would ordinarily have done. Instead, she looked at the cup as if she couldn't quite recognize it.

"Do you want this?" she then asked, turning to me.

I hesitated, ignoring the way my stomach dropped at this simple question, and asked if she was sure.

"I ordered it out of habit," she explained, almost apologetically, as if habit was something you could get caught doing. She slid it toward me across the table.

Unwilling to say anything more about it, I took it to go. And thus, we parted ways.

I noticed the necklace around Nancy's throat, the one Grandma Arline left her, just as she was turning to go. It was one of the few things she had inherited from her. As I got into the car, though, I began to think that the things we "inherit" weren't just money or physical items. Sometimes they were just a way of being.

II
The Dawn

3

Generations

Flying into Trenton airport just before stopping by the diner meant catching cheap flights in and out of the place, but the trip was longer once you counted the driving. I didn't mind this. It gave me time to myself and was less stressful overall. It gave me time to ruminate. Hence, as I drove, I began to wonder how Nancy and I had gotten here, this place in our lives where we needed to meet like this, in stolen pockets of time, in out-of-the-way places, always overloaded and catching our breath. We always seemed to be picking up the pieces of ourselves, reconnecting, healing for a bit, before we had to leave and brace for the next thing.

In the past, I've told people that in life, we're all passengers on a train. Some folks climb on for a few stops and step off. Others stay longer, interacting with you along the way. Still others get off early. Lives thus intersect and overlap. I often wonder how many riders have come before us, leaving behind legacies we never asked for but still must carry.

Nancy had been tired when I saw her at the diner, but she was still Nancy, as quick with the deflection as she was with the line that kept things moving. I walked her to her car, hugged her, and made sure she was steady, then watched her pull out before heading to my car. When she disappeared from the lot, the diner's neon lights felt a little louder than they had an hour earlier.

The road now was familiar, and that should have comforted me. The thing about it, however, is that it doesn't always calm you. Sometimes it just gives your mind more room to run on and on. Especially when traffic moves in the slow, obedient way it always does after a meal, the way it was doing now, headlights, brake lights, the steady hum of other people living their evenings all melding together as if nothing urgent had been introduced into the day.

At the first red light, I glanced down at the digital clock on the dashboard. Blue numbers. Block-like. Unromantic. I blinked at the lateness the clock denoted, but it wasn't really time itself that caught me. It was the fact that time was still passing, still measuring, still indifferent. The day had shifted, and the clock didn't care. It kept ticking on.

That fact caused my mind to hook onto something far older.

I asked myself the question again: How did we get here? By "this," I didn't just mean a diner on this night, with Nancy looking tired across a table, both of us pretending we were only talking about what we could name out loud. I meant the longer question: how our lives came to be what they are. What had been chosen along the way? What had been inherited? What had been imposed, and later renamed as "normal."

Nancy and I used to talk about it sometimes, usually in passing, as if we didn't want to give it too much ceremony.

"We are the sum of decisions made by us, and decisions made upon us by generations before us."

This wasn't just us philosophizing. It was something we had learned the hard way, namely by watching adults make choices and then call them fate. Watching family stories harden into rules and kindness show up in the wrong places, and cruelty in the places that were supposed to be havens.

The light changed, and I drove on. The blue numbers shifted again, minute feeding into minute, steady and indifferent. A measurement. A reminder. Time passes whether you are ready for it or not.

The blue dashboard clock didn't just move forward into the future, though. It was connected to an older clock, in the past, to another way of counting.

The clock was of German make. Dad had brought a clock back when he was stationed there in the army. Specifically, it was a mantle clock that he had gotten as a gift for his father on his return from Germany. It ended up sitting on Grandpa Alfred's television, like a strange kind of offering. A piece of Dad's adult life was thus stationed inside Grandpa Alfred's house like a flag that still had to bow.

That clock told a different kind of time. It had a winding mechanism and brass balls that moved as a horizontal pendulum, swinging left, then right, both patient and relentless. It chimed on the hour, a sound you felt in your chest when the room was quiet enough, turning waiting into something physical.

I could still see it there, on top of the television at Grandpa's house, as if it belonged there.

Nancy and I were sent there whenever Dad and Mom went on vacation. We didn't go with them. Vacations didn't mean beaches or amusement parks for us. Instead, they were times we spent with Grandpa Alfred and Grandma Arline. We'd arrive with our bags and our forced politeness and settle into that house like it was a sentence we hadn't earned.

I watched the minutes tick by on that clock because they were the only honest thing in that living room. The brass balls swung left, swung right, and the clock kept proving what Grandpa Alfred never had to say out loud: You'll leave when I'm done with you.

After Grandpa Alfred died, Nancy gave me that clock. Not as an inheritance, but more like a correction of an old wrong. I'd been left out of the will for Grandpa Alfred, for I didn't get along with him. In fact, I avoided him whenever I could, and he returned the favor in ink. Nancy knew I'd want the clock, though, as proof that I had survived him. She knew what it represented: me staring at it, waiting to go.

Now, the blue numbers on the dashboard kept staring at me as the highway carried me home. Years later, when Grandpa Alfred had gone, and Nancy had gifted me the clock, I placed it on the mantel of my family home. It didn't last, though, as someone broke that clock. It happened when my girls were playing with Pepito, our dog. Pepito was the only dog I ever had. He was a smart little black schnoodle, playful and quick. My girls, toddlers at the time, were playing catch with him in the house. One of them threw a ball, which bounced into Grandpa Alfred's clock. Pepito took the rap, and in that moment, the clock finally took the physical hit it had already been metaphysically taking for years. The excuse was funnier than the reality of what the clock represented. I laughed at my girl's attempt at selling the reason for the accident and the irony of the moment as I gazed at the shattered clock on the floor. It was fitting. The clock was broken even when it worked. It kept time still rather than telling it. Now, its purpose was done. The fitting end to release the clock's anxious spell over Dad's parents' house, where it lorded as a pall over any visitor's time, and its breaking there would not be met with any hilarity.

Grandpa Alfred wouldn't have appreciated Pepito, the humor of the moment, or the dry jokes surrounding his feats. In contrast, Mom's parents, Grandpap Shem and Grandmam Cathryn, would have. They would have appreciated the humor of blaming Pepito and the innocent excuses of a toddler trying to explain what happened. They lived in an old coal-mining town, a world away. They insisted on being called Grandpap Shem and Grandmam Cathryn. They always had dogs, and no matter what dog it was, regardless of its breed, size, or gender, all the dogs only ever had one name:

Princess.

When I first heard them call one of their very obviously male dogs Princess, the same name they had given their previous, deceased dog, I thought I had misheard them. I was just a kid. Adults said things, and you assumed you were the one missing the nuance. I remember standing in their yard, looking at a dog that didn't match my mental picture of the last "Princess," and feeling a mild panic about whether to correct them. Kids don't correct grandparents, after all. They don't correct anyone older than them, not when they speak with certainty, even if that certainty makes no sense.

"Grandpap Shem," I asked once, carefully, because even then I knew there were ways to ask questions that didn't invite embarrassment. "Is that… the same Princess?"

He looked at me like I was asking whether the sky was still up there. "Sure," he shrugged.

Then, after a beat, the smallest smile pulled at one corner of his mouth, like he couldn't help himself.

"Made it easier to remember," the explanation came soon after.

That was his sense of humor: dry, flat, and always delivered like instruction after the fact. I never knew if he was pulling my leg, and that was part of the joke.

Years later, I'd realize something: That kind of humor is a form of generosity. It ensures the other person can keep up with you. It invites you into the game without telling you. It doesn't need to win. It just wants the room to stay light.

Whatever room Grandmam and Grandpap were in was always light. Their house, even their town, in fact, was like a fun house to me. The floors in their place weren't level, not in the way houses in brochures are. The walls leaned. The door-frames looked tired. Everything carried that old coal-town wear, which made a house feel like it had its own posture.

We used it to our advantage. Like a kid would. We raced toy cars from the living room to the kitchen, reveling in the fact that they didn't roll straight. They drifted, veered, and found grooves in the floor like a river finds channels. We'd see them off and run ahead to watch the finish, laughing when one hit a chair leg and spun out as if it had been decided.

It was play, but it was also training. You learned the house's physics in this way. You learned what you learned and what you didn't. You came to understand that things can still work even when they're crooked.

When I asked Mom about why the house leaned, she explained that the town of Shenandoah was built atop a coal vein. During the Great Depression, illegal miners had tunneled under the city, leading to a sudden, massive cave-in sometime in 1940. The row homes aboveground had shifted as a result. The one at the end of the line had collapsed. The rest had stayed standing, and, instead of moving to safer ground, their inhabitants had adjusted what they could. They reset the window level and just lived with the tilt.

So, inside, Grandpap's place was like a fun-house. It reminded me of the nursery rhyme about the man who lived in a crooked house. Walls didn't meet where they should. Stairways always felt slightly off, like your body had to learn the house's rules. You could feel it in your knees if you stood still long enough, the way the floor told the truth even when the window frame tried to pretend otherwise.

And then, there was always heat. This was not the clean, invisible heat of artificially warmed air, but the honest heat of a solid iron coal stove. Heat that had to be earned by tending to the fire and feeding it.

Looking to keep me out of her hair in the kitchen, Grandmam Cathryn once sent me out on a snipe hunt. Saying she needed more coal, she sent me downstairs with an iron bucket to get some. I was glad to help. I eagerly lifted the heavy bucket, legs wobbling at age five beneath the weight as I trod to the stairs, proud of my accomplishment. I can still feel the weight of it in my hands, the cold metal against my fingers, as my child's grip tightens the way it does when something feels too heavy, and you don't want to ask for help. I remember how Grandmam Cathryn smiled as I left, pleased with her cleverness, while I was blissfully unaware that filling the bucket would make it impossible for me to return to her.

The basement steps were steep. The walls weren't square. Everything smelled like coal, damp, and old paint. The light was dim as if the house was trying to keep its secrets. The coal bin sat there, a little way away from the stairs, like a shadow you could touch.

I remember looking at the coal and thinking it looked like black rocks from another planet. I remember the sound of the bucket scraping the floor as I dragged it to the staircase after filling it up. I remember the moment I realized the physics of the whole thing didn't work, how the bucket alone was heavy. Now, it would be impossible for me to lift and carry, and understanding, slowly, that this had been Grandmam's version of sending me on this fool's errand.

Still, I was determined. I struggled down there for what felt like forever, trying to lift the thing and failing, and then trying again because that's what you do when you're five and proud and being watched by your own imagination. When the grown-ups had finished cooking, they eventually came down to "help," as though this had been a real assignment and I'd encountered an unexpected complication.

By that time, I had resolved on a plan: to carry the empty bucket back up, iron—cold in my palms. When I got back up the stairs, the heat felt like a reward for my long hours of labor. I basked in it for a moment, then went back down to take handfuls of coal. I moved the coal upward in stages, chunk by chunk.

When I finally arrived at the top of the stairs with just a single piece of coal in my hands, the adults laughed at the sight I made, even as I went back a score of times, determined to complete the task I'd been given, bringing up one piece of coal at a time. This seemed to keep me busy and determined.

Grandpap and Grandmam adapted humor to offset the challenges of their lives and rolled with it. That, more than anything, was the difference between the two worlds of my two sets of grandparents. Grandpa Alfred's house had rules that made you smaller. There, time pressed on your chest, and the clock chimed like a sentence that was being carried out. Grandpap Shem and Grandmam Cathryn's place had work, crooked floors, jokes you had to catch on your own, and warmth that came from effort. There was poverty, yes, but there was also competence, pride. There was no arrogance there and no feeling that you needed an audience to feel accomplished. Hence, what they didn't have in riches, they made up for in love and sarcastic wit.

Grandpap Shem had been a slate picker at eight and worked the mines until they closed. He coughed a miner's cough, because the job never really ends, even after you've left it, and still he laughed till he got his jokes off, like they cost him nothing and saved everyone something.

Grandpap Shem used to say, "Doctors are different now than when I was your age. Once, when I went to the doctor with a headache, he gave me a mustard plaster. When it got hot, it hurt my elbow. When I told the doctor that my elbow hurt, he said, 'Yeah, but yer headaches are now gone!'" In his Welsh accent.

Continuing on home, it occurred to me how much of Nancy and me came from that contrast between our grandparents: much of our shared language, our sarcasm, our ability to carry something hard without collapsing, had been learned in rooms like Grandpap Shem's, where humor wasn't cruelty and survival wasn't performed.

Much of it came from the fact that "Princess" wasn't just a dog name, but a way of saying: Don't overcomplicate things, kid. Put another way, a lot of it came from how this was a way of making scarcity feel less sharp and of reminding you that the world could be crooked and still be livable, and that laughter could be a kind of heat.

Grandmam Cathryn always laughed at Grandpap Shem's jokes. After a while, I started catching the beat of his dry wit by listening for her laugh, as if she were the translation. When I thought of Grandmam Cathryn, always sewing, always making things stretch, my mind turned to the next layer: how she could take one dress and make it last four years, taking advantage of the creativity of inserting a ribbon at the waist and calling it practical.

Frugality was a survival skill, and in this case, the key tool for its power was sewing. Grandmam Cathryn didn't just sew. She made everyone's clothes and remade them when necessity called. Nancy and I grew up with evidence of her hands in the ordinary parts of our lives like the crocheted sweaters and socks we wore—things you don't think about until you realize someone had to make them—and the little covers you put on doorknobs, which were meant to protect you from touching cold metal while adding a softer look and feel. Such things, we came to understand without anyone saying it, were meant to protect you from the world's roughness.

In Shenandoah, frugality wasn't a choice. It was in the air. You learned it as one would learn gravity. Mom used to say Christmas wasn't about piles of gifts. It was about a rag-doll and an orange because that was what she'd get. The orange mattered because it was bright and rare and smelled like somewhere else. You didn't devour it. You held it. You kept it as long as you could, like you could stretch joy in it the same way Grandmam Cathryn could stretch a dress.

In this town, people's roles were stitched into everything, too. Women didn't go to college. They didn't "have careers." They cooked, sewed, and kept the house running. The whole place felt older than its calendar, with its coal-stove heat and a push-pedal sewing machine working like a heart in the corner. This way of living wasn't nostalgia; it was just how things still were.

Yet Grandmam Cathryn herself wasn't only that. She'd had a rebel streak in her time and had been a flapper. I didn't understand what that meant until later, when "flapper" stopped being a costume term and became a clue instead. She could be anxious and still defiant; I came to realize that once the word's meaning fully sank in. She could be old world and still want to watch women fly around a roller derby track as if they owned the place.

She died when I was young. What I remember most about her is how nervous she always seemed, how her worry always ran ahead of her. Grandmam Cathryn used to watch Grandpap Shem's health like it was a job she couldn't clock out of. She didn't watch her own the same way.

Still, she introduced us to small pleasures of life as if they were sacred: ice cream and pretzels, shoo-fly pie, Lebanon bologna, goods that felt like artifacts from another country, Pennsylvania coal-town taste, old recipes, old smoke, old habits. Somehow, it was warm in her home, and being with her felt like being let into a room you didn't know existed.

Driving home from the diner, the contrast between the two sides of the family only kept sharpening. Decisions about how each home's essence was impressed upon my parents, each coming with its own benefits and deficits. The home Mom had grown up in was poorer and humbler than Dad's, but love and joy had been ever-present there. Family compensated for lack with frugality, humor, and compassion. The air she grew up in was therefore lighter, and time passed more freely in her home.

Grandpa Alfred's house, on the other hand, made you feel measured and judged. The rooms were heavier there, and time moved by the metronome of the clock, slowly marking each second. So, when Nancy and I said we were the sum of decisions we made and those made upon us, that was part of what we meant. Not just the obvious fractures, but the quiet shaping. The domestic inheritance. The way frugality turns into ethics, how humor becomes air, how a woman sewing a doorknob cover can leave her fingerprints on children who won't even understand what they've been handed until decades later.

It was only a year later, when Mom's hands began to fail, when her sewing slowed, then stopped, that I understood that those fingerprints weren't sentimental. They were practical. They created things meant for overcoming hardship. They were shaped by people and places even as they shaped things themselves.

Shenandoah itself was poor and hard, but Mom's side had adapted to it by creating a world that felt crooked and warm at the same time, just like the floors, the house, and the whole town. The ground itself felt different here. It was warmer in some places, even when the season was cold. The town was marked with cracked pavement that didn't look new enough to be breaking. There were spots where the street dipped slightly, like the earth had exhaled and never fully inhaled again.

"Why is there smoke coming from the ground?" I asked Grandpap Shem once.

"Just stay away from that, Billy. The coal under the town is on fire, and you may fall in," he said.

What kind of playground was this? One that was built over the underworld of the Greek gods, clearly. Still, we kept playing. We played how kids play when adults are near but not hovering, when the warning is casual enough to become part of the game. We tested the edges of what we were told not to do, because danger is sometimes just another kind of adventure.

The adults would call out to us from a porch or doorway without any urgency, like they were reminding you of some rule you already knew.

Stay where we can see you.

Don't go down there.

Yeah, it's warm, don't worry about it.

That was the strange lesson they taught us: Home can have perils that, over time, become normalized, for no one panicked. No one packed up and left. They lived on top of the danger, making dinner, telling jokes, and sending you down for coal with an iron bucket, as if the impossible were just another chore.

Since this was Shenandoah, Grandpap Shem and Grandmam Cathryn's world, time moved differently there, too. It flew by. There was always something new to look at, something odd, something funny. A dog named Princess. Pretzels. Shoo fly pie. Grandpap Shem's cough and jokes. Grandmam Cathryn's nervous energy still making room for roller derby on television. The crookedness made it all enjoyable. The warmth made it feel safe. When we were there, we were free.

Then we would have to go back to Grandpa Alfred's, and time would stop.

At Grandpa Alfred's, you didn't feel curious. You felt measured. The atmosphere was thick with its edges. The rules weren't about comfort, but they were about approval. The clock sat there, chiming, brass balls swinging left and right, counting out visits as a judge counts out a sentence.

Grandpa Alfred could be good with us in flashes. That was part of the confusion. He'd make root beer floats like it was an event: cold sweetness in a tall glass, the ice cream rising and melting into foam. There were afternoons he'd take us out to a movie, like *The Pink Panther*, as if he were performing grandfatherhood the way he believed it should look from the outside.

Then you'd be back in the house, and the mood would turn without warning. The same man who could lift you could cut you down in an instant. The sweetness didn't cancel out the cruelty. It just made it harder to name, because you'd be holding both versions of him at once.

He'd be having fun and offering piggyback rides to Nancy, and when I'd ask, he'd say, "No, you are too fat! You'll wreck my back," and all would go quiet. The fun would be over.

Grandma Arline was there too: quiet, efficient, continually moving. She cooked, served, and absorbed. Grandpa Alfred treated her like an appliance with a pulse. I felt sorry for her long before I ever understood why.

Nancy and I would often visit the cemetery across the street. This wasn't some desperate escape for us. It was just a place where we could breathe a little freer. We'd walk the rows, step between stones, let the quiet settle onto our shoulders. We didn't have language for what we were doing, but we were doing it all the same: finding peace and choosing it, taking it when we could.

Only later would I recognize the echo in what we were doing and what it was borrowing from: history, for Dad and his brother used to escape their own version of Grandpa Alfred. They would do so by finding a pond, though, not a cemetery. Nancy and I did not call what we did an escape. We did not narrate it. Instead, we just crossed the street and took the quiet when it was available.

The cemetery was plain and still. The headstones were the kind with inlaid portraits of the deceased, staring back at us. The air smelled like damp dirt and old leaves, and the stones stood in rows like they had been waiting longer than anyone inside that house had patience for. We walked until we no longer felt watched. Sometimes we read names and dates without meaning to. Sometimes we just stood there, letting the quiet reset our faces before we went back.

When we went back to the house, the door closed behind us, and the air thickened again. The television glow and the kitchen smell returned, and the clock kept its slow rhythm. Grandpa Alfred did not raise his voice upon our return. He did not need to. He dropped his lines like utensils on a plate, casual and sharp, meant to make noise and then sit there.

"Billy, don't marry anyone stupider than you, like your grandmother is over there," he said to me once, in such a moment.

Another time, when Nancy and I were visiting with some of our friends in tow, after Grandma Arline was finished cooking a meal, Grandpa Alfred said, without an ounce of shame, "Your grandmother will serve us."

He pointed at her, a subtle but noticeable enough gesture. Grandma Arline, without a word, did what she always did. She brought coffee. She brought plates. Then Grandpa made her sit in the chair in the corner, as if she were an object returned to its shelf.

Nancy and I were wary of bringing outsiders there because of stuff like this. I could feel our friends trying to stay polite, trying to keep their faces neutral, trying to pretend they had not just seen what they had seen. Usually, Nancy would go still beside me. Then, she'd stand and move toward Grandma Arline, the kitchen, the work, toward the one person in that house whose dignity needed defending. Nancy would sit with Grandma Arline whenever she could and ask her to show her something or other, pull her into a task. In doing so, she would comfort and spend time with her. She would increasingly avoid Grandpa Alfred. This was Nancy's defense mechanism. Mine was sarcasm, which I learned to use over time, thanks to Grandpap Shem, and which constituted the only way I could hold Grandpa Alfred in check without starting a war. My routine was simple. I kept him occupied. I fed him questions. I let him talk. I then redirected his attention just enough to keep him from circling back and landing another cut where it would do the most damage.

So, Grandpa Alfred's house was part of the decisions we made and ones made for us, which contained not just his cruelty, but the duality of his nature: the floats and the cuts. The way a child can be given a treat and still needs to stay wary on the same afternoon.

4

Rita

I rolled down the car window to let the mild June air in and turned off the air conditioning, my mind still on Nancy, continuing my drive back from the diner. I was glad Brian was there for her, close enough to help with the commute, the distance, the ordinary burdens that were no longer ordinary.

Nancy and Brian were both people of faith, though Nancy was a member of the Lutheran Church–Missouri Synod and Brian was Roman Catholic. Nancy was deeply faithful, as religion was one of the ways she steadied herself. Brian's devotion matched hers in spirit, even if the language and rituals weren't identical. Mine was real, too, but it always carried a hint of Dad's: It was less about doctrine and more about practicality.

Dad's religion was and had always been pragmatism. It was the one faith he practiced consistently. When Nancy and I were kids, Mom and Dad treated religion as they treated everything else: as a solution. We went to a Methodist church, not because Dad believed in Methodism, but because it was an agreed-upon middle ground. A truce you could drive to.

Dad was the only one who could drive in our household. So, every Sunday, he'd pull up out front, open the door, and send us out to church like he was sending us out on a delivery run.

"You need to get some religion in ya!" he'd say, and then he'd drive off, leaving Nancy and me standing on the sidewalk in our Sunday best, the church doors ahead of us, his car already shrinking away.

There's a particular feeling I had in that moment, being left at the curb with my clothes too clean and my choices too small. For a second, we'd stand there, not quite sure what to do with ourselves. I'd glance at Nancy and think, *We could go to the diner.* I could already taste the freedom of it, the stolen normalcy.

"Let's go to the diner, Nant," I'd whisper sometimes as we started toward the steps, half testing her, half pleading.

Nancy would give me that look: all patience, amusement, and determination. Then, she'd turn around and walk into the church, head held high as she kept going. So, I would follow. My impulse, back then, was to escape. Her instinct, on the other hand, was to commit, yet the two of us still moved together anyway.

That was our version of religion for a while: dropped off, sent in, and expected to absorb something helpful. It took years for Dad to admit he was raised Catholic, not because anyone around him was, but because his birth mother, Rita, was devout. After she died, that thread was cut. Alfred and Arline were Protestants, as were the rest of his family, and Alfred's people came from England with old country reflexes about Irish Catholics, the kind of bias that was more common in turn-of-the-century life than it reads today.

In the States, it softened over time, but in some families, it lingered as a quiet rule about what you did not claim out loud. Nobody else in our family was Catholic. We were not even aware we had Irish ancestry growing up. So when Dad finally said the word "Catholic", it didn't fit anything we understood about our family. That clue puzzled Nancy and me even more.

Grandma Arline didn't offer us clues. She offered dinner. She offered quiet. She offered survival. For years, knowing Grandpa Alfred and Grandma Arline as "Grandma and Grandpa," we learned not to ask questions. Dad was always evasive when it came to talking about his parents.

This was partly because Dad always had his guard up around Grandpa Alfred. I certainly would.

Then, one day, Nancy found out the truth and told me about Rita.

"Rita?" I asked when she mentioned the name. "Rita? Who the heck is Rita?"

"You up for a road trip to Scranton?" Nancy countered.

Dad had always been an evasive man; his stories were filled with many gaps, leaving many mysteries. As a result, Nancy and I had learned to become sleuths so we could fill in those gaps where we could. A decade earlier, Nancy cracked one of those mysteries when she figured out who Dad's birth mother truly was and where she was buried.

Nancy said, "Before Alfred and Arline, there was our real grandmother, who died when Dad was just a boy. According to Arline's sister, Blanche Roselle, she said they were friends, and Rita was sweet, but she died less than a decade after Dad was born." And then her voice trailed off, as if the trailing off was part of what she inherited, too.

We were in the car in Scranton when she said it, idling at the edge of a Catholic church that looked older than our questions. Stone, steep roof, dark windows. The kind of place that feels like it has been standing there long enough to watch families forget and then come back, decades later, pretending it is only curiosity that brought them. Nancy had a legal pad in her lap, and on it she'd built directions the way she built everything once she decided it mattered. Over the years, she had written them, corrected them, rewritten them again, adding small notes in the margins as new clues arrived, as if our history could be navigated if you took the right turn at the right street. The pages had started as directions. Somewhere along the way, they became a map. Not a metaphorical one. A real map, drawn by hand, with arrows, little blocks, and names that stood in for landmarks.

I parked and turned the key until the engine fell quiet. For a moment, we just sat there, the hush of the car making room for what she had said. Then I got out and walked around to her side. Nancy already had the cane angled toward the door, ready. When I opened it, she shifted forward carefully, swung her legs out, and set the cane down like a third foot. I offered my hand, and she took my forearm instead, firm, familiar, the way she always did when she needed steadiness but didn't want it announced. Nancy rose in stages, pausing when upright, letting her balance settle before she moved again. The treatments had changed her tempo. The cane made it official.

She stood there for a second, half in and half out of the car, and looked past me toward the cemetery behind the church. Then she looked back down at her paper. She held it up between us and unfolded the crude drawing she'd made, the cemetery reduced to a few rectangles and lines, little markers labeled with names as if they were street signs. She traced a path with her finger, stopping at a corner, then starting again, her fingertip moving as though she could feel the ground through the page. I watched her concentrate, watched the set of her mouth, the way her eyes narrowed as if she could will the place to give up what it had kept.

There was something tender and fierce in it, this careful cartography of grief and omission. Nancy wasn't looking for a view. She was looking for proof. For confirmation that Rita existed in more than a story told sideways by an old sister-in-law. For a plot of ground, a name, a date. Something you could point to and say, "There. That's her. That's real." And if you could make that real, maybe the rest of the story could stop slipping through your fingers every time you tried to hold it.

Rita Rosemary Banks. That was her name. Irish Catholic. The type of Catholic that wasn't decorative, as in not the Christmas-and-Easter badge-wearing type. Instead, Rita was the kind of Catholic who adopted her religion as a daily posture: She'd make the sign of the cross without thinking, always keep her rosary close. She held on to the quiet belief that if you carried your burdens correctly, God would recognize the effort.

When I try to picture her, I don't start with her face. I begin with a church.

A neighborhood church. Old wood and old varnish. Wax, incense, damp coats, hymnals that have absorbed generations of hands. I see a line for confession, people waiting with their eyes down, shifting their weight on scuffed floorboards, keeping their distance as if shame were contagious. The priest behind the screen. The soft murmur of voices that were never meant to be overheard.

Grandma Rita went to confession a lot.

Years later, one of Dad's cousins said this was a mystery she couldn't stop turning over in her mind. "Rita was the sweetest person I ever met," she said. "Why would she need to go to confession?"

That question lodged itself in my mind because it was the first time I understood something adult: Sweetness doesn't protect you from guilt. It doesn't protect you from the compromises you make to keep life running or from the things you're forced to do, or whatever you do to survive, which you then must carry like a stone in your pocket.

Maybe confession wasn't proof she'd done something wrong. Perhaps it was proof she was trying to stay clean in a world that kept smearing grime on her hands.

Sometimes, Nancy and I would press Dad for details about Rita, looking for scraps of stories, anything human. Dad would shrug and toss out a line with that dry edge to his tone that he used whenever his pain was too exposed.

"She probably went to confession over a desire to kill Grandpa Al," he'd say, like it was only a joke. Like it wasn't.

Dad showed us almost nothing. We saw a picture once, but then it disappeared. This was not done out of sensitivity but a sense of control. Those were his few moments with his mom that hadn't been taken from him, and he kept them as one would keep a match dry when you're not sure you'll ever be allowed to light it.

Still, I did manage to learn that Grandma Rita worked as a clerk at the *Scranton Times*. That was apparently where she met Grandpa Alfred, young, working, trying to assemble a life that would hold. Soon after, she got pregnant. Thus, "holding" became something else, transforming from something romantic into pressure, crafting a marriage made less by love than by gravity, by family expectation, Catholic discipline, and the insistence that the story look correct from the outside.

Grandpa Alfred brought hierarchy into the rooms he inhabited. You could feel it before he spoke. He carried himself as if life owed him a softer landing, and everyone else was responsible for providing it. Rita's pride ran quieter with Irish Catholic dignity in scarcity: apologize for nothing, ask God's forgiveness for everything.

I picture her in small rituals: her hands dipped in holy water, holding a rosary, making the sign of the cross without thinking, to keep her insides from falling apart. Dad carried her that way: not as a person he could describe, but as a before-and-after inside him.

Somewhere under all of that was the simplest thing: a mother trying to stay alive long enough to raise her boys. They were living in Lyndhurst at that point, in a small house enshrouded in quiet that didn't denote peace. Within this shroud, the adults carried stress like a second coat. The boys learned early how to read a room before they spoke in it.

Rita tried to keep softness alive inside a narrowing life, doing the laundry and the dishes, and going to confession as a form of maintenance. Blanche was her friend, and in her, she found the one person she didn't have to perform for.

Then, the illness arrived. It didn't happen overnight, arriving as a sudden spectacle, the way you see in the movies. Rather, it came as a drain, one that sapped her strength every day until doctors had to be called. Soon enough, a diagnosis was made: Rita had contracted tuberculosis.

By the time Dad's brother was born in 1938, the illness had already taken a foothold in her body. It wasn't histrionic, like Hollywood makes sickness out to be. There was no single night when everyone ran into the street shouting for help. Things progressed more quietly than that. The ailment was the way adults lowered their voices when Grandma Rita entered a room. It lived in how a bedroom door started staying shut a little longer than it used to. It lived in objects: a handkerchief being folded and refolded, a bottle on a nightstand, a faint medicinal smell that doesn't belong in a young home.

They called it consumption back then, which is almost too honest a word for what it does. It consumes time first. It consumes attention. It saps a household's confidence. And then, slowly, it consumes the person.

Grandma Rita had been the kind of woman people remembered as sweet. Sweet in demeanor that can be mistaken for simple, when it was really discipline. A way of keeping your edges smooth so you don't cut anyone while you are bleeding. If she complained, her words didn't travel. If she felt afraid, she tamped it down where only God could hear it. Even as she weakened, she kept her posture so as not to be a problem.

But the body doesn't negotiate.

The boys weren't told what was happening, not in plain terms. They were "protected" by silence and choreography.

They would be dressed in their Sunday clothes. Their hair would be combed. "Keep your hands clean," they were told. "Be good. Don't upset your mother."

The first lesson they thus learned wasn't death itself. It was how to perform.

By the early 1940s, the household could no longer pretend things were normal. Grandma Rita was sent away to Bergen Pines. "Sent away" is the phrase families use when they don't have a better one, not when the truth is that someone has been taken out of the center of the family and placed behind rules, glass, and institutional hours.

I've tried to imagine what those drives must have been like. A windshield framing the road, as a picture frame holds a photograph, everything moving forward while you're trying to keep one thing from disappearing, the radio in the background on low. The children are quiet because quiet is what you do when adults are tense. Tires humming. The faint sensation, even if you can't name it yet, that this isn't just a drive. It's a transfer. A hand off.

Afterward, the boys were shuttled among relatives. They learned early that home could become a plural, temporary, and conditional concept.

Then there were the visits from behind glass.

The glass is what stays with me when I picture it, because the image repeated itself in our family in different forms, in other decades, with different names. I see it as a pane separating the sick from the living. A barrier meant to protect ends up teaching the same lesson the family would learn anyway: Closeness has limits.

I imagine my father and his brother all lined up, coached, dressed up, brought in like small visitors to a museum exhibit that just so happened to be their mother. Someone saying, "Smile for her," like they were telling the kids to smile for a photo. The boys are trying to obey because obedience is what children have when they don't have control.

What do you say through a glass wall when you're a child?

And the worst part, the part that doesn't sound like the worst part until you sit with it, is that leaving that place is what opens up the wound, not arriving there. Arriving is hope. Arriving is the belief that love still has a place to land. But leaving, walking back down the corridor, the echo of your shoes, the moment the door closes behind you, is where a child learns what the adult already knows.

She stays.

You go.

You go because someone tells you to. You go because visiting hours are over. You go because the world demands it. You carry that instruction for the rest of your life: When things are unbearable, you still leave the room or want to.

Rita carried her own version of the same instruction. She worried about the boys from where she was. Blanche would later say she worried constantly, afraid in that way a mother worries when she can't do anything useful with the worry. Fear would be a steady pressure on her, the fear that her sons would grow up without being held. That her other son, Dad's brother, especially, born into the illness, would never know what it was like to have her at full strength. Conversations between friends and Rita's family took on a somber urgency and a sense of noise.

That noise cut off with the ringing of a phone, sharp and out of place. Someone answered, and the entire room changed. You could feel it without being told. A voice lowered. A single "yes" was spoken far too quickly. The receiver hung up, and for a moment, no one could look each other in the eye.

A drawer opened hard. A closet door thumped closed. The Sunday clothes came out again. Shoes appeared at the edge of the room. Buttons were fastened with hands that didn't quite work smoothly.

No one explained anything to the kids. Adults didn't have to. Children don't need the words to know something has happened that cannot be undone.

They drove to a place the boys knew in the general sense, a church, a cemetery, but not ever like this. This trip wasn't a typical excursion to Sunday church service, nor was it a ritual you could lean on like a habit. This moment was adults crying while still trying to behave. It was grief dressed up as correctness.

The cemetery had that distinct smell of grass, damp earth, and the faint, sweet rot of old flowers. People stood in small clusters close enough to look united, but far enough apart to be able to breathe.

Somewhere in that cemetery, in the Banks plot, a tombstone had been prepared. It did not read "Rita Leadbeater." Not "Beloved Wife" or "Mother." It was just…"Rita."

I didn't understand it as a kid, but I know now how a single word on stone can serve as erasure rather than a remembrance.

At the diner, I recognized Nancy's mind because it matched mine. We spoke of Rita then and how she was left incomplete, both in name and in her last words. Even her funeral must have been rushed. The details Nancy had chosen for the marker of her grave would never allow anyone else to guess who she was or had been. I was certain in that moment that she had already chosen Psalm 27 as her marker, the words she had carried with her for years.

Unlike Rita, Nancy would make sure she got in the last word. She always did.

It's a small thing, a name. A single word. Yet it still contains an entire argument. A decision made by adults that a child would only understand later: Names are not just names. Names are claims. Names are sides.

At the funeral, everyone likely performed the correct moves while carrying their private contempt, like stones in their pockets. Someone held a prayer book. Someone tried to keep the boys quiet and still. Someone else said "poor thing" in a voice that didn't sound purely sad.

Because the world is cruel in its timing, World War II was still on the radio when they got back in the car, spewing words like "D-Day" and naming places people had never heard of until they had to. The announcer's voice didn't soften because one woman in New Jersey had died. The world kept going, loud and indifferent. That contrast teaches a child something: Your grief is private. Your grief does not stop the day.

At some point, maybe that day, maybe in the days that followed, the boys would understand that their mother wasn't coming back from behind the glass. That the visits were over and the drives were done.

The consequences of that loss, however, weren't.

Death doesn't just remove a person from your life. It rearranges power.

It exposes who decides what gets written down. Even a name on stone can become a victory lap for one side and a slap to the other.

So, my father and his brother became the casualties of this shift, not because they did anything wrong, but because they were the only ones small enough to be moved without explanation. Rita's death did not end the conflict; it simplified the board. One burden removed, one problem left behind. The adults kept writing, kept deciding, and the boys became the paper on which it was written.

It took Nancy and me finally asking Blanche directly for the truth for the truth to come out. She told us what no one else would: Arline wasn't our real grandmother. Rita was.

The detective work then began in earnest. Nancy and I went to the Scranton public library, where Rita had been buried. There, we sat down with old newspapers on microfiche, sliding the reels under the lens until names and dates stopped being vague and turned into concrete coordinates.

Those in hand, we drove out to the cemetery listed in the obituary.

We found it there, that plain stone. Cold. Not softened by language and not helped by sentiment.

Rita.

Nancy stood close to the marker and said the prayer she carried, Psalm 27:1–14, in that steady, soft voice of hers, like the words were a handrail.

She held flowers in her hands and laid them down. They looked as though they belonged there, even if the story had never made room for them. When she finally spoke, it wasn't as a performance or in outrage. It was only the simplest verdict.

"How sad," she said.

I took a picture of the grave because no matter whose plot she lay in, no matter what surname was spoken or omitted, the truth remained merciless and straightforward: She was our father's mother, even if she was now only a word on stone.

Sometimes, things get left incomplete for generations. Unfinished. As I thought about Nancy and our plan, I thought about what we ourselves had left unfinished. A few years had passed since Dad had died, and Nancy and I still hadn't taken Dad, or rather the vial of ashes I had saved for this purpose, back to Grandma Rita.

I did, however, send a picture of his mother's grave to Dad when he was still alive.

His reply came back without ceremony. He said it was the first time he'd seen the grave since the day she was buried. Grandpa Alfred never took them back there.

The truth snapped into place for us, then, not as theory, but as evidence. In Grandpa Alfred's house, Rita's existence had been erased. After her death, there were no pictures of her on the mantel. No wedding photo. No portrait. Nothing to point at and say, "This was your mother."

Not a single object was left behind to insist that she had been real. Instead, the slate had been wiped clean, and she had been erased.

Grandpa Alfred erased the inconvenience of a forced marriage from his life as he did with any challenge he found difficult to face. Thus, the only thing that was left of Rita was that single marker in that Scranton cemetery. For him, it was "one difficult time down."

That and a question, one of logistics rather than poetry: What about the boys?

5

What About the Boys

Later, in the car, the to-go cup of rice pudding tipped in the console for half a second, just long enough for the lid to burp loose and a little warm pudding to spill out, cinnamon-smelling, onto my fingers. I opened the glove box for a napkin and wiped it off as I kept driving.

The spill made irritation bubble inside me, not because it made a mess, but because it reminded me that Nancy hadn't wanted it. Nancy always ordered dessert. Always. Now she had ordered it out of *habit*, she had said, then pushed it away.

While I enjoyed the rice pudding, Nancy loved it, especially Grandma Arline's, as it was her go-to comfort food when we visited in our youth.

I thought of Nancy's throwaway line from the table then: Dad never used a ruler. Tape measure only. Like rulers offended him.

Later, when I finally understood why, it made perfect sense. A ruler hadn't been a tool of measurement in his childhood. It was a tool of discipline instead. It was a hand. Authority. The sound of metal on skin. The road fell away the moment that thought landed, and in a blink, I was back with the boys, my father and uncle as the kids they used to be, in that place where rules replaced love and "good" meant quiet and invisible.

I had driven past it once, that place Dad and his brother had been sent to after Rita's passing, where the ruler came to take on new meaning for them. Nancy made sure that we did. We only knew enough about the place to be unsettled by it, which is to say, not a lot. Later, Aunt Blanche would name it, only the once, in passing, as if naming it quickly could soften it.

Dad, Nancy, and I were in the car together, the day we passed it, and Nancy had angled us onto a road she scrutinized with intent. That was Nancy's style: Give someone a door they could walk through without admitting you built it.

She looked out the window and said, lightly, "Hey, what's that creepy place?"

The building she was pointing at was back from the road, standing tall in an institutional posture. A castle-like, dead-eyed structure, built to outlast the people inside it. Even from the car, you could feel the schedule in it. You could feel the rules.

Dad didn't look over right away. His jaw tightened.

"If I had a bazooka," he said, "I'd take a bazooka to that place."

He tried to make it sound like a joke, like a man keeping the car's temperature from changing. But the sentence carried something old with it. Then he added, quieter, like it had slipped past him before he could stop it: "My knuckles still ache from those damn metal rulers," he said. "We used to have to stand there with our hands out. Not flinch. Flinch, and they hit you harder."

The words hung in the air for a beat, like a smell you can't pretend you don't notice. Then Dad tried to shake the moment off and move past it.

That was when Nancy and I understood not just what that place was but why Dad never used a ruler in his adult life. Tape measure only.

So, in the end, the boys were put in a Catholic boys' home.

It sounds like a solution when you say it quickly, like something practical people do when they don't know what else to do. But if you slow down and live inside it, you can feel the cruelty in it.

Because a boys' home isn't a home; it's a place where order stands in for intimacy, where rules become love's substitute because rules are what an institution can afford.

The things you remember from such a place and carry with you are always small. Like rules. Or a metal bunk.

The sound it makes when you climb up the side of the bed spring and frame, letting out an unwilling squeak that announces you. A thin blanket that won't stay tucked. A mattress pressed flat by other bodies, the dip already shaped for a boy who isn't you. A sheet that smells like bleach and old sleep.

In winter, the air was too cold. In the summer, it was too hot. Comfort wasn't the point here. The point was compliance.

There's always a bell in places like this. A sound that cuts through whatever you were doing, thinking, or hoping, and tells you that your body belongs to the schedule now. Meals. Prayers. Sleeping. Waking. The day is chopped into segments so no one has to wonder what a child might be feeling in the spaces between.

Quickly, you learn to move when told. You learn to speak when spoken to. You know that questions can be read as disrespect, and come to understand that silence is safer than explaining yourself. You learn to keep your wants small.

Years later, my mother mentioned it in a way that sounded almost casual. Grandpa Alfred was the youngest of eleven. Mom said he had been spoiled, that his sisters had babied him. They had been like proxy mothers to him, though they were young themselves, not much more experienced than he was. Still, they doted on him. There had always been someone else to take care of things.

At the time, it didn't feel like it explained anything. It was just something my mother said. But it stayed.

By the time Dad learned what it took to survive in a place like that, the lessons had already sunk into his muscles. They didn't leave when he did, either. Instead, they became him.

They became how he stood in a room. The way he spoke to authority. The means by which he reached for approval, and never reasonably believed that it was real. Decades later, they became the small adult choices he made, which looked like personality until you realized they were actually scar tissue.

Remembering this made me wonder again what would have happened if someone had checked in on those boys back then. Someone did, albeit too late: Blanche.

Nancy found out from Blanche that she had been Grandma Rita's best friend. She learned from her that whatever promises women make to each other at the edge of death don't always die when the Grim Reaper finally calls. They carried beyond, and so did the one that Blanche made. Blanche had pledged to Rita she'd help the boys. This was not empty sentiment. It was the kind of promise that necessitated taking actual action, which she did.

Blanche checked in on the boys when she could. Quietly, but persistently. When it became clear the boys weren't going to be rescued by Alfred's conscience, she realized that something else would be needed for this, or rather, someone else. Thus, she reached for the only lever she had at her disposal: family.

Thus, she introduced her sister to Grandpa Alfred:

Arline.

6

It Happened on Scrivens Street

I sometimes catch it by accident, the way a house can look occupied and withholding at the same time, with the porch light off. The front windows are dark, but there's a faint spill of light from somewhere behind, as if the life of the place has retreated to its back rooms and left the front to stand guard.

Scrivens Street had that kind of feeling.

Grandma Arline kept it that way on purpose. The back of the house could glow while the front stayed unwelcome; the porch had a blank face. Everyone came to the front door because that was the rule. There was an order to it, and a kind of superstition dressed up as common sense.

"Evil and salespeople come in the front door," she'd always say.

She said it lightly, like she was joking, and it didn't matter. But it did. The line had teeth. It revealed a larger belief: The front of the house was where the world made demands, and you met them on your feet.

The house itself helped. It had a narrow hallway. Rooms arranged so you could be seen as you passed through. A staircase that didn't feel like a path so much as a funnel. Even the basement stairs were particularly steep, as if they were designed for quiet exits. There were places you could go, but none of them felt private. The walls didn't keep secrets. They held sound.

On the outside, the place was ordinary. Totowa, New Jersey, is a working street with small lots; other houses were close enough to one another that you could hear the overlap of neighbors' chatter when you opened your windows. But inside, Scrivens was its own climate, governed by Grandpa Alfred's moods and rules, his unspoken preferences made visible through other people's behaviors.

When Dad went there, he did not go casually. He dressed up as if he were going there to be evaluated, because he was. He didn't always wear a suit. Sometimes, it was just slacks and a pressed shirt, a jacket that had lived too long in a closet. Whatever he wore, it was always deliberate. Clean. Correct. A version of himself that was assembled for inspection. His hair was combed. His shoes were shone or wiped down so they didn't look careless. His tie pulled tighter around his neck than comfort required.

He had learned young that clothing could be a shield, and that looking "right" could buy you a few inches of acceptance. It didn't stop Grandpa Alfred, but it reduced the surface area of his attacks. It gave him fewer openings. Dad made those choices like a person moving through a checklist: If everything were correct, nothing else would be singled out.

We saw that same instinct resurface later in churches, weddings, and the office, really in any environment that smelled even faintly of authority. Dad entered those rooms as if someone might decide, without warning, that he didn't belong there.

This was the skill he learned and practiced on Scrivens Street.

You pulled up, parked, and sat for a moment longer in your car than necessary to steady yourself. You looked at the dark porch and the front door, trying to remember which version of you was acceptable inside. Dad could do that in silence. He would shift, shoulders becoming squared, his expression turning neutral, his voice already lowered before anyone had spoken.

Then you went in.

The porch step was a slight rise, but in memory it feels like a threshold to a holiday you dread and rituals you can't refuse, where everyone insists there isn't a problem until the problem announces itself anyway. You show up because you're supposed to. You bring something, flowers, dessert, politeness, and you hope the offering will count. Dad's offering was himself, all cleaned up.

Seeking approval can look like respect from the outside. From the inside, it feels like you're bracing for impact.

Grandma Arline would open the door. Sometimes she smiled as if warmth alone could soften the moment. Sometimes the smile was thinner, already a measure of Grandpa Alfred's temperature behind her. Her goodness didn't remove the danger from the situation, but it tried to buffer it. She stood in the doorway like a small mercy you could pass through.

Behind her, the hallway ran straight back like a line you were meant to walk without wavering. Grandpa Alfred didn't always appear immediately. Sometimes he made you wait, just long enough to establish that you were entering his time, not yours. You could hear him in another room: a chair shifting, the scrape of newspaper, a cough that sounded like judgment.

Dad would stand still and let the house settle around him. He did not fidget. He did not look as if he were waiting. Waiting, in that house, was another way of being accused.

He stood as if he'd already been spoken to.

That was the stage: a front door reserved for evil and salespeople, a hallway built for surveillance, a man dressing himself into acceptance and walking in anyway, hoping, as you wish before a holiday you dread, that this time the cost might be smaller.

If Grandpa Alfred was the law of that house, Grandma Arline was the faith and the soul. She was not soft, never that, but steady, like a person becomes steady when there's no other way to be. She moved through Scrivens Street with practiced quiet, as if noise could invite trouble. She cooked. She cleaned. She kept the house's rhythm. And in the middle of all that, she did something that still matters to me: She mothered two boys who hadn't been hers, and she did it so completely that they called her "Mom."

They didn't do so out of politeness. They called Grandma Arline "Mom" because it was true. For loving them, for saving them, they would say.

I grew up hearing that with the type of awe a family reserves for one of its few unambiguous heroes. In the story of Scrivens Street, Grandma Arline isn't a footnote. She's the only warmth in the entire place that doesn't feel borrowed.

She was a great cook, great in the old, practical way women become when food is one of the only forms of care they're allowed to practice without being punished for it. The kitchen was where Arline had power. Not the political or marital kind, but the power to make something better than it had been a moment ago, like through rice pudding; comfort food that is never skipped.

In hospice, when Nancy's appetite was fading, and even a few bites felt like negotiation, she still was able to make this one strange exception for rice pudding. If a diner had rice pudding, she wanted it. She never said it out loud, but I knew: In those moments, she was reaching for comfort she didn't have words for anymore.

And still, the dessert was never better than Grandma Arline's rice pudding. Nothing was. Arline's was homemade; patience, milk watched instead of boiled, rice tended until it gave up its hardness, and cinnamon and sugar measured by instinct. It was the type of dessert that tells you, without any speeches, that someone has been paying attention to you all day.

Grandma Arline wasn't as educated as Grandpa Alfred was, and he used education as a weapon, as he did with anything he could, a ladder, a way to feel superior. Grandma Arline wasn't academic. But she was educated in faith the way some people are educated in survival.

When Nancy and I were little, we'd sometimes sleep over there, lying on the floor or on an old army cot Dad had brought home from his army days. These weren't planned sleepovers with matching pajamas and storybooks. They happened when our parents needed an emergency babysitter, and the children had learned to adapt. Blankets were found. Pillows were borrowed. The cot squeaked beneath one body, while the other curled on the rug.

In the dark, then, Grandma Arline would teach us the Lord's Prayer. She wouldn't do so with a lesson or a lecture. She'd do so gently, like she was handing us a set of words we might need later. She'd say a line, and we'd repeat it. Sometimes we got the cadence wrong. Sometimes we mumbled because we were half-asleep. She never scolded me when I did either. She just kept going, line by line, soft repetition that felt less like religion than belonging. That's how her faith worked: practical and straightforward, bearing words you could hold.

Dad, by contrast, had no time for religion. After the boys' home, after what life had done to him, he didn't have much patience for anything that required trust. His version of faith was to show up, endure, and keep moving. When Nancy and I were young, he dropped us off at the Morristown Methodist Church "to get some religion in us," as if religion were vitamins that you could take once a week, and it would cover whatever was missing.

He wasn't cruel about it. Just distant. Religion wasn't his language.

It was Arline's. She gave it to us the way she gave food: as comfort, as grounding, as a small assurance that the world had order even when adults didn't. And that's where the captivity came in because Arline's kindness cost her something.

You could feel the cost in how her goodness never turned performative. She never stormed or threatened. She never left. She learned, instead, to keep turning the other cheek, not because she was weak, but because the culture she lived in didn't offer her many other exits. Back then, you didn't divorce. You endured. You kept the house running. Dinner still had to appear, even if the room felt unsafe. And she saved the boys the only way she could, by staying close enough to catch the worst of Grandpa Alfred before it landed, by putting herself between his mood and their faces.

She supported Dad and his brother. She buffered them. She gave them a mother they hadn't had. She did it while still feeding her husband, too, because that was the bargain.

In later years, when the checks began to run out, she sat in silence. This wasn't sulking, but the quiet of a woman who has learned that words can change the temperature. Because silence was sometimes the only way to keep the room from exploding, her restraint was less about passivity and more about strategy. It was what people develop when they are trying to protect children inside an unstable marriage without making themselves the next target.

That's what I mean when I say goodness inside captivity. Arline's goodness wasn't naivete. It knew exactly what it was up against. It fed people anyway. It prayed regardless. It mothered despite the circumstances.

And decades later, in a diner, watching my sister order rice pudding in a Styrofoam cup like it was the last good thing left on earth, I could feel the thread of her reaching back for Arline's particular kind of care, laden with quiet and competence, costly and real.

In that house, food was how Grandma Arline owned something. Everything else-time, mood, movement, the emotional temperature of the room-belonged to Grandpa Alfred. He set them. He enforced them. He made the rules without ever having to announce them, because everyone learned them as people learn gravity: by falling.

Hence, Grandpa Alfred's cruelty wasn't occasional. It was a system. He didn't have to hit anyone to make the house feel dangerous. He could do it with language. Tone. The pause before answering, as if he were deciding whether you deserved to be spoken to at all. Teasing that was really humiliation packaged as a joke, so that if you reacted, you were the problem.

He could make you doubt your own memory of a moment that had just happened. He could turn a simple question into evidence of your incompetence. He could create a trap where every response was wrong, too eager, too quiet, too defensive, too slow. There was no correct posture. The point was the accusation itself: to keep everyone just off-balance enough that they were always seeking the approval he never intended to give.

That's how a house becomes a tribunal. For Dad and his brother, this created a nervous system reality that lasted long after Scrivens Street. Stillness, to them, felt like idleness. Idleness felt like danger. Even much later, in rooms where Grandpa Alfred wasn't, their bodies stayed slightly braced, as if he might appear in a doorway and demand to know what they thought they were doing.

For Arline, it was worse because she lived there full-time.

And she endured…Until she broke.

People say that as if breaking is a single momentary event, like a glass slipping off a counter. But a person doesn't break all at once. They break by degrees. By erosion. By being told, day after day, that their thoughts are unreliable, their feelings are excessive, their reactions are proof of weakness, their needs are selfish, and their exhaustion is "craziness."

Arline's mind didn't fail her. It defended her. It tried to find an exit from a room that had none. Meanwhile, the house kept asking for the same performance, the same meals, the same quiet, the same swallowing. Then one day her hands stopped cooperating. A pot boiled over. A spoon clattered against the sink. She stood in the kitchen as if she'd forgotten what came next, blinking at her own countertops as if they belonged to someone else. When she finally spoke, it didn't land in the room as a conversation. It landed as an alarm.

Later, the family would call it a "breakdown." The word is convenient. It lets everyone keep their grammar clean because naming what happened would require naming its cause. In that era, in that household, the remedy was not gentleness. The remedy was containment.

Electroshock treatments.

I didn't grow up knowing the medical details. No one explained the procedure or its timeline to me. What I grew up with instead was the family version of the story, the one that keeps its distance from the actual events and turns a human emergency into a sentence you can say at the table. Arline was "sent away" until she was "better." Grandpa Alfred repeated it like a verdict, and the way he said it made the point clear: He didn't treat it as a tragedy. He treated it as confirmation that he had been right about her all along

"Leave until you aren't crazy anymore," he told her.

As if her suffering were a behavioral problem. As if she were misbehaving. As if the house itself hadn't been the instrument that pushed her there. That sentence tells you everything you need to know about him: Go away, and come back fixed. Make your pain disappear so it doesn't inconvenience me.

So…Arline ran away.

It wasn't some cinematic moment of escape. No suitcases were thrown, no doors were slammed hard enough to shake the walls. It was more like someone slipped out of a burning room when no one was watching. Grandma Arline got herself to Blanche. To the one place she believed might hold her without judging her, might listen without turning her pain into a defect.

Blanche Rozelle. In the family's vocabulary, her name carried a particular meaning: refuge.

Arline ran to Blanche, and Blanche took her in. Fed her. Let her sit. Let her breathe. Let her be a person again for a while, not just a wife under a life sentence. But then Blanche's husband did the part nobody wanted to do, the part that required standing before a man like Grandpa Alfred and negotiating with him as if he were a reasonable person.

He meant to convince him. Not because Grandpa Alfred had earned his gentleness or because Arline had any obligation to return to his cruelty, but because that era had its own law too, and it was heavier than individual will: divorce wasn't a possibility then, not a realistic one, not an allowed one, not one a woman like Arline could choose without becoming, in everyone's eyes, the problem.

And then, there were the boys.

Dad and his brother were now twelve and eight years old, respectively. For the boys' sake, Blanche's husband would try to convince Grandpa Alfred to allow Arline back, and convince Arline, too, that returning was the least bad option available. That staying gone would mean leaving Dad and his brother alone in the house with Grandpa Alfred. That her presence, however costly, was a shield to them. That shield mattered.

In a better story, that would have been the moment the family broke apart and rebuilt itself around decency. A sister. A friend. A minister. A doctor who recognized what was happening. But Scrivens Street wasn't a better story. It was a common one, written in a time when women were told to endure, men were excused for the damage they caused, and the medical system often served the household's need for quiet more than the person's need for healing.

So, the interventions were temporary. Human. Limited. Consequently, Arline went back. She kept cooking. She kept praying. She kept buffering the boys.

Something in the household changed after that, even if no one spoke of it, and not for the better.

From then on, Grandpa Alfred, rather than shrinking from what he'd done, used it as further authority. Once a person has been labeled "crazy," you can dismiss anything they say. You can rewrite the past. You can make your own cruelty disappear under the cover of their diagnosis.

That was the household law: Grandpa Alfred could do anything, and if you reacted, your reaction proved that you deserved what he'd done.

People think cruelty is loud. Often it isn't. Often, it's just constant. It's the daily insistence that everyone else is wrong and you are right. It's the quiet turning of love into leverage. It's how a man can sit at a table, reading his paper, and still govern the entire nervous system of the room.

Once more, Arline's desserts were hers; everything else belonged to Grandpa Alfred.

And in that ownership, he took not only comfort and dignity, but sanity itself until the family's goodness had to live inside captivity, because there was nowhere else for it to go.

7

No Loitering

"Just don't get arrested."

This was my standard reply to Nancy whenever she asked for advice, and it would always make her laugh, just as it did at the diner.

It was part of our lexicon of humor and sarcasm that helped us with the more difficult asks to come. It was shorthand for the longer phrase that Dad gave me upon my turning eighteen:

"Billy, don't ever get arrested because I am not bailing you out."

Then again, when Dad turned eighteen, Grandpa Alfred threw him out. In that house, standing still could be interpreted as guilt. Movement was the closest thing to permission.

People tell stories like this as if it's a rite of passage, older generations shrugging and labeling exile "independence." But when you've grown up in a house where stillness is treated like a crime, being told to leave doesn't feel like freedom. It feels like a verdict finally delivered.

The object in my mind as I continued my drive home from the diner was small: a suitcase. Something scuffed and cheap that you can carry in one hand while the other steadies you on the front steps. And maybe a tie. Because Dad still dressed how he'd been trained to dress, as if looking correct might save him even then.

He stepped out into the world without making any theatrical goodbye to anyone. Just a step and the door closing shut behind him, the night stretching in front of him, and the knowledge, deep and physical, that there would be no soft place to land unless he built one.

He found a job as a dishwasher. That detail has always stuck with me because it's so raw in its practicality. It was not a job that looked good on paper. Not one that promised a future either. But it was a job that kept Dad alive and ultimately earned him the right to come back for the night.

Hence, that was one of Grandpa Alfred's rules, the kind that pretends to teach character while just asserting power: You can return if you can prove you aren't loitering. You can exist if you can show receipts.

So, Dad washed dishes in hot water to the tune of clattering plates, with steam rising and grease on his forearms, doing the kind of work that leaves you tired enough to collapse but not enough to relax. Then he came back, not as a son, but as a temporary tenant, permitted back into the house because he had produced evidence of his usefulness.

Something happened to Dad at that time, though, and it matters: He learned. He finally saw how the system's mechanism worked. When you're forced out of your home early, you start paying attention to what makes the world move. You notice that some men sit at desks and other men wash the plates that those men eat from. You see that the people who get invited indoors don't just work hard; they work differently. They understand systems. They speak a language that buys them shelter.

Dad realized then that education wasn't just a school thing. It was survival, a way to stop being handled like disposable labor. After that, he started angling toward training in business and insurance. That word, "insurance", feels almost funny in the context of Scrivens Street, because everything about that house was risk. But it makes sense. Insurance is a world where rules exist on paper, where you can build a life by understanding the fine print. For someone raised under a man whose rules changed with his mood, written rules would have felt like relief.

He was getting trained in this way, building a foothold. But then came the draft, or, more accurately, the shadow of it. The knowledge that the government could do to him what Grandpa Alfred had always done: make his decisions for him and call it duty.

Dad didn't wait to be taken. He joined the army before he was ever drafted. That choice mattered because it marked the first time Dad grabbed the steering wheel of life himself. If he were forced into something, he would choose the version that offered structure, pay, and a path. Not to mention a way out of Scrivens Street that didn't require Grandpa Alfred's permission.

The uniform becomes the new object here.

A uniform is an identity. A uniform is protection. It is permission to belong somewhere that isn't your own family's house. The army gave Dad rules, which were harsh but consistent. He could handle harshness. It was the inconsistency that broke people, he knew.

He was sent overseas in late 1958 to Germany and England. He served at the same time Elvis did. He landed a supply job and learned what he already suspected: Working in an office suited him better.

The army didn't heal him; it hardened him into a functional adult and called it success. At the same time, it gave him something Grandpa Alfred never did: a story he could tell about himself that didn't begin and end at Scrivens Street.

Leadbeater thus became Ledbetter.

This was a slight change in spelling but a massive shift in meaning. People who haven't lived under a family name like that might not understand why a man would make such a seemingly small change. They'll assume it's cosmetic, or done out of shame, or vanity. But name changes like that are often a form of witness protection, a way of stepping out from under the file folder someone else keeps on you.

The new signature was a way of taking action, but it was also a ritual: The moment you say, in ink, "I am not the version of me that you made."

Ledbetter.

When he came home, Dad was a new man. At least on the surface. New name. New posture. New way of speaking. His discipline looked like maturity from the outside. Underneath, the bigger change he had undergone was quieter: He had discovered a doorway that didn't require Grandpa Alfred's approval.

He had discovered that you could leave. And stay gone.

So, Dad had grown and tried to rebel by surprising everyone with a name change and a new commitment to a fiancée. Grandpa Alfred had other plans. There's a particular kind of waiting that feels like being watched. As I got closer to home, I stopped near a train station. The gate was down. The lights flashed. I paused, waiting, abiding by rules made by someone else, holding me in place. And I thought of Dad waiting for his bride.

The one that wasn't my mother.

She came to the train station with her wedding dress.

That detail sits in my mind as inevitable humiliations do, bright, undeniable, impossible to soften with later explanations. A woman stepping off a train with her future folded in white fabric, believing she is arriving in her life. Believing she is being welcomed into love.

Only for Grandpa Alfred to send her right back.

Not with a conversation. Not with a debate. With the blunt authority of a man who considered himself the final gatekeeper of what was acceptable. This girl was "unacceptable." He didn't explain why. He didn't have to. In that house, his disapproval was treated as self-evident.

So, the bride turned around. The wedding dress went back with her.

And Dad? Dad spiraled.

It was a quiet kind of collapse. Depression that looked like emptiness that turned Dad into a man moving through days as if the verdict had finally arrived in its clearest form: You don't get to choose your own life.

You can almost see him in the hallway, not sitting because sitting feels like loitering, not moving because moving feels pointless, already carrying the weight of a childhood that trained him to see hope as temporary, something you pay for later.

Another humiliation followed soon after, one smaller on paper but sharper in the nervous system: the loitering arrest.

The word mattered because it was one that Grandpa Alfred could and would use like a weapon. It didn't mean standing around. It meant being useless. Taking up space you hadn't earned. Existing without producing something he respected.

So, for Dad to be arrested for loitering outside a shop, near a station, wherever a cop decided his presence looked wrong? It wasn't just a legal moment. It was Grandpa Alfred's worldview being echoed back to him by the outside world. Proof that even strangers could look at him and decide he didn't belong.

It was Grandma Arline who saw the spiral. She watched Dad as one would watch the weather you can't control. From the kitchen doorway, she tracked him without staring. He moved from room to room and never landed anywhere, as if the furniture might accuse him. He stopped once near the hallway mirror, then kept going. His hands opened and closed at his sides, empty, restless. No cigarettes, no coffee, nothing to do with them.

Grandpa Alfred's chair creaked in the next room. The newspaper made its dry, deliberate sound. Dad flinched, then pretended he hadn't.

Arline wiped her hands on her clean apron. She looked at Dad's face as a mother looks at a child who is too old to be held and too young to be left alone.

She didn't say anything at first. She waited until Grandpa Alfred coughed, as if clearing the air of Dad's presence, and then she stepped closer, close enough that Dad could hear her without Grandpa Alfred having to.

"Go out," she told him.

Two words, said softly, like a door being unlatched. Not permission from Grandpa Alfred. Permission from someone who knew what it cost to stay.

Dad looked at her as if he hadn't understood the language at first. Then his shoulders dropped a fraction. He nodded once, small. He grabbed his coat from the hook and moved toward the front door like a man trying not to make noise.

Arline didn't follow after him. She didn't even watch him leave. She went back to the sink and turned on the water. In that house, even mercy had to look ordinary.

So, go out, Dad did. He went back to work at his old insurance company in the city. And here is where the story takes one of its quiet turns, the kind that looks like a coincidence until you notice how often survival depends on timing. Because Mom had temporarily taken over his job. That line always makes me pause. Dad spirals. The world fills the vacancy, and in the filling of it, two lives intersect.

Mom trained Dad on insurance before he left for the army and filled in for him until he returned. The office smelled like paper and carbon and whatever coffee had been sitting too long on the warmer. Metal desks sat in rows. Fans clicked overhead in a tired rhythm. Somewhere down the aisle, a typewriter kept pecking at the day.

Mom slid a file across to him.

"Start here," she said.

Dad opened the folder as though it might bite him. He read a line, then read it again. His finger traced the paragraph as if he didn't trust his own eyes.

"What does this mean?" he asked, and his voice carried the same caution he used in Scrivens Street. Careful. Prepared to be corrected.

Mom didn't look at him like she was a judge tasked with carrying out a verdict. She looked up at him like he was a coworker.

"It means the policy pays if the loss fits the definition," she said. She tapped the page with the end of her pencil.

"Here's the definition. Here's the exception. Here's the form that proves it."

She pulled a blank document from the stack and laid it beside the file.

"This goes here. You write it this way. If you don't know, you ask," she explained as she demonstrated. Dad nodded, once, as if by receiving instructions, he could finally follow without guessing someone's mood. He tried the next line. He stumbled. Mom corrected him without any heat, steadily transferring a system from one head to another.

By the time they got to the third file, Dad had stopped bracing for an impact that wasn't coming. His shoulders dropped a fraction. He wasn't being tested. He was being trained. Competence has a sound when it lands, the quiet relief of knowing what comes next.

Mom never had to be approved by Grandpa Alfred. She didn't enter through the front door of Scrivens Street to be measured. She entered a workplace where rules lived on paper, and the only thing that mattered was whether you could do the job.

She met Dad on the ground that wasn't poisoned. And for him, that mattered more than comfort ever could.

Dorothy.

Her name still looks formal to me on the page sometimes, like it belongs to a different era. She wasn't formal in spirit, though. She was sharp. She had learned the codes. Had received charm school training instead of college, the version of preparation her era offered. She knew how to move around rooms. How to speak. How to present herself to others so a man like Grandpa Alfred wouldn't immediately dismiss her.

And it worked.

Soon, Dorothy had become Grandpa Alfred-approved.

That phrase lands as quietly as a chill. Because we understand what "approval" costs; approval meant you wouldn't threaten Grandpa Alfred. Approval meant you'd fit inside his idea of respectability. Approval meant you would not embarrass him, or confront him, or make him feel small.

Dad brought Mom to Grandpa Alfred, and he approved her as "his kind." Not because she was weak but because she could perform the acceptable version of womanhood that Grandpa Alfred believed in: composed, socially trained, not asking for more than the era allowed. She was soft-spoken and always arrived punctually. Time and measure went together.

Dad married her as she measured up to Grandpa Alfred's measuring.

Then came the children, meaning Nancy and me, arriving in a life that, from the outside, could look like stability: work, marriage, two kids, and the typical architecture of a normal family.

But the foundation beneath it was older and darker than first impressions would have it believe, built of verdicts and approvals, and the sort of endurance that gets mistaken for strength.

Soon, the apartment was too small, and Mom said she needed a bigger place, a house.

8

Mom's House

The first house Mom and Dad lived in was big. Our world wasn't small back then, but the rooms were. The world was small because our perimeter was.

Before Nancy's hospice bed came to sit beside a dining table, this was the house that taught us how close life and loss could be.

Nancy and I moved into Hillview Terrace in Morristown in the mid-1960s, when Dad had a house built on property he'd purchased from a man eager to sell because he was terminally ill. The home was shoehorned onto the end of a dead-end street, next to a brook that flooded when it rained hard.

Mom was shy and agoraphobic, meaning she was afraid to leave the house, even if she never used the term. Dad and Mom lived the classic model: Dad worked, and Mom stayed home. She didn't leave the house much. She never learned to drive. The house was quaint and remote, for we lived on a dead-end road. The outside world wasn't. Our home was quiet and peaceful, a small bi-level with three bedrooms, each small but larger than the apartment Dad and Mom left. Brick-faced cinder-block foundation with siding; Dad oddly picked orange. The neighborhood was suburban, and the location meant we had only a few close friends nearby.

Nancy and I lived on that dead-end road, inside a small, close, intimate circle. It was contained and familiar. We knew everyone there and everyone, in turn, knew us.

Surrounded by county-owned woodland, it was an excellent place for young kids looking to build tree forts and play adventure games. The house's location limited the number of playmates we could have over, since Mom didn't drive, but we found our own entertainment.

In the woods, there were trees with low branches, the kind that invited a kid to climb. We'd drag fallen limbs into piles and call it a fort, then argue about whether it needed walls or whether walls were for cowards. Nancy was the planner; she wanted a name for everything, a purpose, a set of rules. I was the builder, the fixer, and made things stand by my own means.

One afternoon, we found a length of old rope half-buried under leaves. Nancy held one end as if it were a treasure while I pulled and pulled the other until it came free, damp and smelling of earth. We tied it between two trunks to mark the boundary line. A drawbridge. A trap. It didn't matter what we called it. It mattered that we could make something out of what we found.

We came home with our hands dirty and our clothes dripping, and Mom looked up from the kitchen table, taking us in with a quiet attention that was both love and inventory. She didn't scold us, nor did she ask where we had been. She just checked for blood, then went back to what she was doing. That was our arrangement. The woods gave us freedom. The house gave her control. Everyone pretended it worked.

Mom and Dad were always punctual. Knowing the time and where one had to be was a must. Nancy and I have always been known for rigid punctuality, as our parents demanded it. Time for meals. Time for play. Plenty of time for study.

Dad didn't counterbalance our isolation in the house. He didn't invite Nancy and me to any social events. There were no team sports. No clubs. No insistence that we widen our perimeter. Both Mom and Dad emphasized school and homework. They were strongly aligned in their belief in the importance of constant learning.

Mom was brilliant, but she was denied admission to college because she was a woman. She had graduated from high school as salutatorian, but only men went on to college back then. So, she was sent to charm school instead. She didn't get over this denial and move on. Instead, that loss stayed with her. It became fuel.

She tutored us constantly, giving us lessons and reviewing our homework at night. She aligned herself to ensure Nancy and me would never miss an opportunity that had been denied her. At times, Nancy struggled with math but excelled in every other subject, and my parents focused more on her, believing I wasn't as capable. When our testing scores showed otherwise, the focus shifted. Eventually, both of us lived inside a full-time education system: formal school by day, reinforced at home by Mom.

Neither Nancy nor I had much time for socializing beyond the studying we were assigned. We carved out personal time for ourselves. School always came first. Mom took over after school, then Dad on weekends. Come evenings, they took shifts to tutor us constantly, much like sports parents today watch over and live through their children to ensure success, ours and theirs intertwined.

There was a benefit to it, in a way. Being raised with limited exposure makes you into an observer. It did with us as well. We learned to watch. We learned how to scan a room. We learned motivation without ever being taught the word. We knew what was expected without anyone needing to say it.

There was a lot of quiet in our house. Not the peaceful kind that settles when nothing is being addressed directly, or the forced silence of Grandpa Alfred's house to avoid unexpected shifts in his mood. Our home was more like a library or an after-school program. My mother read frequently and encouraged Nancy and me to focus on schoolwork. We played quietly with our projects, did our homework, and watched television.

Nancy filled this quiet by organizing. We both learned to use binders, but Nancy took it to extremes. For her, everything in her life lived inside binders: vacations, finances, and plans. Meanwhile, I filled my binders as I filled up life by observing, anticipating challenges before they happened, and planning action. It worked until high school, at least. Then Dad left.

Mom found out the same way I did. It was night. The porch light threw a weak circle onto the front lawn, and everything outside that circle went dark. Our street ended in a brook at the dead end, and in the dark, you could hear it if you listened, a soft, constant sound beneath everything else. That night, I heard tires first. Not the usual slow roll of a neighbor coming home, but the hard rush of a car coming too fast down a road with nowhere to go. Gravel spat. Then a sharp screech, the sound of someone braking late, as if they had remembered the brook at the last second.

A door slammed. Then another. Voices rose immediately, too sharp and too fast to be mistaken for company. They were close enough that the words blurred, but the intent behind them was clear. There was a clear accusation in them. Heat. The kind of tone that does not ask to be let inside.

Liz, Dad's secretary, husband was there. In the porch light, he looked squared toward the house, planted in place as if he had arrived with a plan. Liz's husband, shoulders hunched forward, chin lifted, already moving as though the argument had started before the car stopped. Mom stayed near the doorway, half inside and half out, as if the threshold could act like a shield. She did not step onto the lawn. She held the door frame with one hand. Her posture said she was trying to keep the house from being contaminated by whatever was coming.

I was downstairs when the voices hit that pitch. I remember the garage door was already open, its black rectangle framing the yard. I ran out through it because it was faster than going through the front, and I wanted to get outside before Mom did, before she was fully pulled into it. I wanted, even then, to contain it. To keep it from waking her all the way up. To keep it from becoming the kind of memory that never leaves.

The argument did not stay an argument. It tipped into bodies physically, fast.

Liz's husband lunged first, a sudden forward surge. Dad met him with a preemptive block-and-tackle, a blunt collision that stopped the momentum cold. It was immediate, almost practiced. My father moved with calm skill, not rage. He had always told me he learned to fight young, from the daily fights he got into with bullies at the boys' home. In that second, I believed him in a way I hadn't before. Liz's husband brought passionate aggression to the fight. Dad brought something else. Timing. Control. The mismatch was obvious even to me as I ran toward them.

They grappled. Someone shoved someone, and they stumbled in the gravel. Dad had him then, turned him around, pulled him down, and put him in a hold. It happened quickly, like a mechanism clicking into place. Dad got an arm around his neck and locked it, a headlock tight enough to subdue, tight enough to make the fight one-sided. It should have ended there. It could have ended there.

It did not.

By the time I reached the lawn, Dad was on top of him, straddling him, driving his fist down in short, hard punches like a machine that had been switched on. Liz's husband's face was already a mess, blood staining his lips, smeared on his cheek. The sound those punches made was nothing like what you would hear in a movie. It was wet and close and final, skin and bone and breath. The porch light caught the shine of it, bright in that weak circle, and everything beyond it stayed dark.

For a moment, I stood there, stunned by the speed of it, by the fact that it was my father, by the fact that he looked so composed while doing something so violent. Then the shock was replaced by something sharper. A need. A decision. I had to stop it, not only because it was wrong, not only because it was too much, but because I could feel Mom behind me at the doorway, half inside and half out, and I wanted to spare her the rest of it. I wanted to push the scene back into darkness where it belonged. I wanted, futilely, to keep the house asleep.

I did not think. I just moved. I grabbed Dad by the shoulders and hauled him back, bracing my feet in the grass, pulling as if I were trying to separate two parts of the same wreck. He fought the pull for a second, still trapped within the rage, then turned just enough for me to get between them. I held him off with both arms and a voice that did not sound like mine, shouting, "Stop," like the word could build a wall.

As I yelled, Mom stood there, rooted to the spot, watching the life she thought she had collapse on her own front lawn. Nancy was not home. She was out on a date, safe in a different version of the night.

In the end, I broke up the fight. Dad did the other thing, the one you cannot break up. He broke Mom's heart.

Mom was forced to face the world head-on after that. She learned to drive. She got a job. She did all this even when doing so tore at her. Later, progressive, crippling rheumatoid arthritis arrived, and she struggled with that, too.

Our world changed after that incident.

Not long after Dad left, Mom was still learning to drive, practicing the turn signals and the mirrors like they were a foreign language, and the house felt unmoored. Even the ordinary things seemed to move around, like furniture after a storm. The place had lost its old rhythm. Doors closed differently. Footsteps sounded louder. Quiet no longer meant restful. It meant listening.

We had a cat named Mittens who was a great mouser and always sought me out for a warm lap to curl up on. Nancy would include Mittens in tea parties, while my action figures had a pretend antagonist for my adventures. We had fun growing up, but we were also always on the clock. During the day, Mittens ruled our home, basking in the sunlit window, in quiet slumber. But she was never only a decoration.

Our house backed up to the woods, and she took that border seriously. If a field mouse made the mistake of crossing into our world, Mittens would present it with stiff-legged pride, the prize set down like an offering that demanded recognition. Nancy and Mom would recoil, shocked and unhappy, and Mittens would stand there anyway, unbothered, as if she had done her job and we were the ones being ungrateful. And when the house began to feel less like a home and more like a waiting room, Mittens started drifting to the edges, taking her naps in back rooms, choosing distance the way animals do when something in the pack has changed.

Even when Mittens got older, and the sunny spots became her favorite address, she still had that playful, sharp-edged streak. A piece of string dragged across the carpet, a shoelace flicked at the edge of a doorway, a pinch of catnip, and she would snap awake, batting and pouncing with a focus that made you forget she'd been asleep a second earlier.

Then Mittens got sick.

It happened quickly, as first real emergencies do. One minute, Mittens was there, quiet and watchful, a small warm presence that belonged to the house. The next, she was gone, not out playing, not asleep in a closet, but hidden in that animal way of slipping off to suffer alone. When we found her, she was on her side, one eye half-open, her body trying to move and not obeying. Her breath was shallow. Her legs twitched once, then went still.

Mom knelt beside her and made a sound I had never heard from her, not a cry, not a scream, but something smaller, as her throat had locked around the grief. She touched the cat's fur with the pads of her fingers, careful, as if touch could bruise her.

Mittens couldn't eat. She couldn't stand. She just looked at us and then looked away, like even her eyes were tired.

The nearest vet was about a mile away, past the Seton Hackney horse farm, down South Street. I wasn't of driving age yet as I was only a freshman in high school. Mom could drive in theory now, but not in practice, not in crisis, not with her hands shaking and her confidence still new and brittle. So, the job fell to me, as all jobs seemingly had started falling to me since Dad left.

I found a pillowcase. The cotton was thin and smelled like the linen closet. I slid it open on the floor and eased Mittens inside, trying to keep her body straight, trying to be gentle and fast at the same time. She was limp in a way that frightened me, heavier than she should have been because she wasn't helping me at all. I knotted the end, not tight, just enough to keep her from slipping out, and lifted the sack like it contained something fragile I didn't know how to carry.

As soon as I stepped outside, she began to howl.

It wasn't a meow. It was a long, broken sound that kept repeating, muffled by fabric but still sharp enough to cut. It rose and fell with each step, her voice pushed up against the pillowcase, her body shifting inside it as if she were trying to crawl back into a life that had already started leaving her. The sound made my stomach turn. It made my throat burn.

I walked down South Street, past the farm, past the quiet stretch of road where the world kept looking normal. Horses behind fences. The smell of wet earth and manure. The sky is doing what it always does. The pillowcase swung against my leg, and every time it bumped, I adjusted my grip, whispering, "Okay, okay," like she could understand. Like I could fix it by saying the right words.

By the time I reached the vet's office, my arms ached. My hands were damp from gripping the cloth too hard. The howling had gone on so long it felt like it had moved into my bones.

Inside, the place smelled like disinfectant and animals and a kind of sadness that is always present in rooms where mercy is sold. The waiting area was quiet. I walked up to the counter with the pillowcase in my arms and tried to look like someone who knew what he was doing.

The vet came out and looked at the sack, then at me, and his face softened in a way I couldn't stand.

I followed him into the back room. He opened the pillowcase and slid Mittens out onto the metal table. Her fur was flattened where it had pressed against the cloth. Her eyes were wide, her body slack. She made a small sound, weaker now, and I felt something in me panic because she was still alive and I was the one who had brought her here.

I didn't have the right words. I only had the feeling.

"Please," I said, and my voice cracked on the first syllable. "Please, it's time. Please."

I pressed what money I had into his hand, a wad of bills that suddenly looked ridiculous, like an offering a child makes when he doesn't know what things cost. I wanted to make it enough. I wanted to buy mercy as one would buy shoes. I wanted to pay my way out of guilt.

I remember standing there, too young for the job I was doing, watching the vet prepare the needle, watching Mittens's chest rise and fall. I remember my anger arriving like heat, not at the vet, not even at the cat, but at Dad, at the absence of him, at the means by which the world had re-balanced itself so that I was the one standing in this room making an adult decision.

And I remember Mom's face when I left the house, the way she couldn't come with me, and how she stood behind the window like she was already learning what it meant to be trapped inside a life that kept demanding things anyway.

When it was over, the room was suddenly too quiet. Mittens was still. The vet's hands were practiced, gentle, done with this part of the world.

I carried the empty pillowcase home.

After Dad left, we all had to grow up fast. Mom was learning to drive, getting back into work, and learning to exist in public again. And I was learning that the task of covering the gaps and being a responsible adult would be hard on me while I was still a late teen.

Watching Mom improvise survival taught me something I didn't name until hospice: When you can't stop the damage, you manage it.

When we sold the old house and moved into a smaller one, I started working. After my shift in retail sales, I would come back home to do some chores and run errands. By June, I was taking seasonal jobs regularly enough that they had become an assumed fact, just as mowing the lawn had become my task.

June meant mowing the lawn, one of the things Mom, I saw, could no longer do as her arthritis progressed, but still would notice if it wasn't done.

The television stayed on all day, keeping the house from turning entirely silent.

Soon, Mom's hands became crippled by arthritis. She could no longer sew, the thing she loved most. I still have her sewing machine.

Sewing, as Grandmam Cathryn taught Mom, had been more than a pastime for Mom over the years. It was one of the ways she made my childhood home feel bigger than just a dead-end road. Fabric became something you could transform. You could take a flat, plain thing and make it functional or beautiful. As the arthritis progressed and her fingers became gnarled and distorted, the loss wasn't only physical. It was personal, for it was the loss of something she loved that was being taken from her in slow motion.

Afterward, the sewing machine sat in its usual place like an animal at rest. When Mom could still use it, the room would fill with that steady hum, needle rising and falling, the smallest kind of industry. Later, the machine stayed quiet, and its silence was an insult. She'd run her hand over the metal as if touching it might bring back the old order.

I would sit with her and thread the needle for her. The sewing machine was a small object, with a metal thread and a hole you could barely see. I would sit there, steadying my hands while hers betrayed her. For all that the sewing machine was small, its emotional beat was large: watching her try to hold onto these last pieces of herself, and realizing I couldn't fix what was happening, only help her keep doing what she loved for as long as possible.

When the thread finally slid through the hole, she'd exhale like I'd solved something. Then she'd try to stitch for a few minutes, her fingers pinching the fabric with effort, her jaw set. Sometimes she'd stop and stare at her hands as if they belonged to someone else. I learned to keep my face neutral in those moments. I learned not to pity her out loud. Pity would have made it worse.

Before Dad left, Mom couldn't drive, but she still found ways to move through the world.

She walked everywhere. Birthdays meant cupcakes, carefully balanced in boxes, as she walked miles and miles to make sure class parties were supplied. At the time, we were embarrassed about this. Now, I see it differently: how her fear was held in one hand, her duty in the other, and how she chose duty and love every time.

I remember one set of cupcakes in particular: the cardboard box softening at the corners from the heat of her hands, the smell of sugar and vanilla following her into the classroom. She'd stand there a little too long, too proud and too exposed, while the teacher thanked her and kids reached in with greedy, unfiltered joy. I wanted to disappear just then. I wanted her to disappear. That's what shame feels like when you're young: You confuse your own discomfort for other people's faults.

It would be years before I truly understood what she was doing in those moments. Mom was repeatedly crossing her own line. She didn't drive, so she walked. She was afraid, but she went anyway. The cupcakes weren't the point. The point was that she kept showing up.

Our childhood home was sold the day I graduated from high school. After that, Mom, Nancy, and I moved into a much smaller place, something Mom could afford, a little Cape Cod with two bedrooms and one bathroom.

It was simple and contained, with rooms close enough that you were always aware of each other in the ordinary ways, a kettle starting, a cabinet closing, the television murmuring in the background, footsteps moving from kitchen to hallway. The kitchen was near the living room, and the house had a steady, lived-in rhythm, the kind of rhythm you feel more than you describe.

Mom bought a futon and set it up in the living room so that Nancy and I could have the bedrooms. She did this how she did everything, not as a speech, not as a gesture that needed applause, just as an arrangement that made the most sense.

At night, she unfolded it with practiced ease, smoothed the bedding, set her book or glasses within reach, and made a small space for herself that worked. In the morning, she folded it back up, squared the blanket, put the pillow aside, and the living room returned to being a living room, ready for the day.

With one bathroom, we learned to coordinate quietly. Someone would knock, someone would answer, and the morning moved forward by habit and courtesy. It was not dramatic. It was just life, shared.

What stays with me is not hardship, but the shape of Mom's choices at the time. Two doors for her kids, and she took the open room for herself. She never called it an inconvenience. She never treated it like a loss. She treated it as one does when you love people, trying to keep their world intact.

That futon became a kind of altar to sacrifice. It sat in the living room, folded and unfolded like a daily reminder that comfort was negotiable, but duty wasn't. Mom never complained about it, which somehow made it worse. If she had complained, it would have been nothing out of the ordinary. Instead, she treated it like a reasonable arrangement, as if shrinking herself was simply what mothers did.

In due time, Nancy finished college, married her first real boyfriend from high school, and moved away. The smaller house made the timing of it all feel inevitable. The wedding offered Nancy an exit. Nancy took it.

I stayed.

Dad wanted my college money to be redirected elsewhere, not toward tuition or books, but toward the life he was building with Liz. He framed it as practicality, as need, as his money being "better used" somewhere else. What he meant was simple, even if he never said it plainly. He wanted the funds available to him for his personal use, for their household, for whatever pressure or plan came next.

By then, my relationship with Dad had shifted into something more controlled and more surface level. We saw him for dinner every few weeks. We talked about school, sports, weather, and the safe topics that didn't require depth. He could be friendly in that lane, almost normal, as long as nothing threatened his choices or forced him into accountability. Our visits had a neutral feel, not an intimate one. Two separate worlds meeting for an hour, then parting again.

Sometimes, at the end of a dinner, he would slide an envelope across the table for me to take to Mom. It was usually a letter, sometimes paperwork, sometimes something he wanted delivered without the discomfort of delivering it himself. He used me as a courier. Mom never used me that way. She never passed her pain through my hands to reach him. She carried her own messages to him herself, or she chose silence. In any case, she left me out of it.

I learned what was inside those envelopes anyway.

One night, I came into the kitchen and saw one of Dad's letters lying open on the dining room table, the paper flattened as if it had been read and left there on purpose. Mom was nearby, moving quietly, but with that clipped precision she got when she was trying to keep herself from shaking. I shouldn't have read it. I did.

Dad had written that the tuition money should only be used for "practical" majors. According to him, a business major was practical. So was accounting. Anything else was indulgence. He wrote it like a rule he still had the right to enforce, even from a distance.

Mom did not answer him in rule language. She answered like a woman who had spent years building that money in small, invisible ways. Through coupons and scrimping. By stretching meals and making those careful, careful choices that turn into a fund only if you repeat them a thousand times. She reminded him, plainly, that she had done the saving and that the money existed because she had made it exist. She had her own idea of practicality, too, but hers was about outcome, not control. She wanted my education to buy security. She even researched careers with the shortest runway, the most direct path to stability, as if she could reduce my risk the way she reduced everything else. If we were going to fight over the money, she wanted it to at least purchase something real.

I didn't have to announce what I wanted to study. Dad found ways to make it clear what he would permit.

He came with me to college admissions interviews at Stevens Institute and the New Jersey Institute of Technology, sitting beside me in waiting rooms and office chairs, looking, from the outside, like an engaged father doing the right thing. But the moment an interviewer tried to widen the conversation, the moment anyone suggested a school with a stronger price tag or a major that wasn't business, Dad would scoff. Sometimes it was a sound. Sometimes it was a look. Sometimes it was the little dismissive comment he dropped as if it were harmless. It never felt harmless. It felt like a thumb on the scale.

He would downplay my abilities in front of them, or talk over the possibilities, steering the conversation back toward what he called practical, as if any other path was vanity. I could feel the interviewers recalibrating around him, pausing, then returning their gaze to me, trying to figure out whether I was being supported or managed. In those rooms, with the brochures on the desk and the polite smiles, it was a quiet form of sabotage, delivered with a calm face and plausible deniability.

Dad wanted me to attend the cheapest state school I could get into, where I could earn a practical business degree that would "yield something." The less I spent on my education, the more remained for him and Liz so they could live their second childhood and spend it on their own interests. Mom objected to this because the money in question was not his to guard. It was money she had saved, and she wanted it spent on the one thing that could not be taken back once given: an education that opened doors instead of narrowing them.

So when Dad tried to steer my education, he wasn't offering guidance from a stable place. He was posturing, wielding authority without closeness, expressing preference without investment. Since accounting became the only avenue that felt allowed, I made the most of it, first as a major and later as a career.

I figured I should graduate from college as early as possible. So, I took night classes and loaded up my schedule, often coming to college in my work uniform. I wanted to fast-track to a full-time job, rely on my own initiative, and be powered by my own steam. Accounting came easily to me because I had the knack for it, so I loaded up my classes with a plan in mind.

I learned business drive and skills from Dad. From Mom, both Nancy and I learned how to face our limitations with dignity and determination. One of my jobs was selling ladies' shoes at a local department store. I got Nancy a job there, too. The shop had that department-store smell to it, all leather and perfume, since the carpet had absorbed decades of footsteps. The stockroom was a wall of shoe boxes stacked like a library, where every title was a size. Women sat on padded benches and held out their feet like offerings. I'd kneel, slide on a shoe, check the fit, then stand back as if I were a specialist, not a kid trying to keep the lights on.

Selling ladies' shoes was a unique experience. You learned quickly how people moved, what they noticed, what made them comfortable, and what made them impatient. And you learned something else, too: when the discount ladies' shoe sales were happening.

Knowing when sales happened became a great pickup gimmick for me, letting me talk to girls and score dates. It was one of the few places in my life then where something light could still happen.

When Nancy started working there before her wedding, she quickly learned the rhythms, too. She was good with people. She could soothe a frustrated customer, find the right size for them, and sell them things without seeming to be trying to sell anything. One night we closed together, and she counted the register with careful hands, then looked up and said, "This is ridiculous, isn't it?" She meant our lives, not the shoes. I just shrugged in response.

Later, when I started working as a first-year accountant, I passed the CPA exam. Entry-level accounting positions were manual grunt work, but I needed work experience to qualify. The lowest guy on the rung was responsible for travel and out-of-state inventory.

In the meantime, I had already started caring for my increasingly disabled mom, now racked with progressive rheumatoid arthritis, while I was working two jobs and going to college. The caretaking years came early, and I juggled as best I could, traveling to hotels for work weekdays, then visiting Mom's house on weekends to do errands and care between workweek obligations.

My business trips took me to various client warehouses, which were always cold in winter and hot in summer, the fluorescent lights flattening everything. You'd count for hours, then recount because someone above you didn't trust the numbers or didn't trust you. I didn't resent this. I accepted it as the price I had to pay to reach the next level in life. But it made my caretaking duties harder, because you can't be in two places at once and still pretend you are.

One weekend, I had to run errands, take care of things, and do chores before the remote workweek. I told Mom I would be returning the following weekend so I could set her up for the coming week.

That weekend was in June, which meant mowing the lawn. The mower was loud and heavy and stubborn, and it pulled at my arms as I tried to get through it as quickly as I could, as if speed could reduce fatigue. When I finished, I came inside all sweaty and grass-stained to find Mom examining the yard through the window like it was a report card.

Before I left for the week, she said, "See you soon, Billy." I said, "Yep, Mom, I'll be back Saturday. See you soon."

"See you soon" turned out to be her last words to me.

I drove out for my work trip and settled into the familiar rhythm of it: the road, the client site, the cheap hotel light, the stiff shirt hanging from the closet rod. At some point, I did what I always did. Responsibility and checking in were always on my mind. As the responsibility for work was trumped by this commitment, I stepped away from whatever I was doing and called Mom.

The phone rang.

One ring. Two. Three.

I pictured her in the small house, the television on, the sound turned low, the curtains half drawn. I pictured her on the futon, at the kitchen table, or asleep in the chair, her hands folded in her lap. The medication could knock her out like that. It had before. The silence on the line did not panic me at first. It fit the pattern.

I kept calling. The phone kept ringing. At the end of it, there was no click. No shuffle. No irritated "Hello?" No small sigh of inconvenience. Just the same hollow ringing, steady and patient, as if the house itself were answering for her.

I hung up and told myself what I always told myself: Mom is asleep. She is fine. She will call back when she wakes up.

I called again later. Same thing.

The longer the phone rang, the more my mind began doing what my mind always does when something is fragile. It ran scenarios without permission. It started measuring time.

I watched the clock. I did the work in front of me. I talked to people. I nodded. I wrote things down. And under all of it, there was the quiet thought, a thin wire pulled tight: *I am not there.*

When the trip was over, I drove back on schedule, as I always did. I told myself the schedule was responsible. I told myself that being steady mattered. The closer I got, the less I believed my own narration.

When I pulled up, nothing looked wrong from the outside. No sirens. No lights. No neighbors on the lawn. Just the house, still, as if it were doing its job. I unlocked the door. The air inside was different. Not dramatic. Just wrong. A stillness that was not ordinary quiet. The television was not on. The room did not feel lived in.

I walked in and said, "Mom?"

No answer.

I found her right where she should not have been, and the moment I saw her, I understood before I touched her. Her eyes were open. The expression was not one of sleep. It was of absence.

For a second, everything narrowed.

The room went quiet in the wrong way, like the sound had been pulled out of it. A high ringing settled in, steady and thin, and the edges of things slowed just enough to feel off.

I stood there, aware of it, and then it passed.

There were things to do.

I stood there, unable to do anything but take in the fact that I had arrived on time, right on schedule, and she had passed.

The stillness of that moment was immediate and complete. Mom's eyes were open. As I looked into them, I understood in an instant what had happened.

That shock stayed with me for a lifetime.

Nancy and I didn't inherit a clean story as we grew into adulthood. We became wiser through the formal and informal education we received in the crucible of adaptation. When things broke, I didn't react first. I moved. Nancy did something else. She steadied what I didn't. Between us, we inherited strategies.

9

Patterns

"Billy, you have to forgive yourself for Mom's death."

Nancy's words hung heavy as I sat quietly.

This wasn't a sit-down talk at a kitchen table. I was on the phone at home, and Nancy was in Texas, teaching outside Fort Hood while her husband was in the army. I called her once a week, a routine check-in that had become part update and part lifeline. Her life was a struggle then, trying to build a career, pay bills, and make a home in a place that still felt temporary. Her focus, even in that season, stayed fixed on forgiveness, on faith, on the belief that people could be carried through.

We didn't always start the call with Dad and Liz. We started the way siblings do when there is distance between them. How are you? How was school? How was work? What broke this week? What bill surprised you? Then we would run out of the safe subjects and let the real ones rise. Sooner or later, almost without deciding to, we would arrive at Dad and Liz. Had we heard from them? Had they called? Had they sent anything?

And if we had, it was rarely about us. It was Liz wrecking her new car from her poor driving, or the facelift she'd just had, or a trip they were planning, details delivered like dispatches from a different world, as if our lives were the background noise and theirs was the only story still being told.

So it came out the way hard truths often do, midstream and quiet, as if Nancy had been holding it for a while and decided it was time to set it down.

"Dad left us all," she said. "And when it mattered most, he didn't face responsibility as he should have. You have to forgive him and yourself. He fell short, but that's on him, not you. You need to find peace."

I stared ahead for a moment, trying to answer the way a grown man would instead of a son.

"Yeah," I said. "Dad did the best he could with what he was given."

Nancy didn't argue with that. She didn't need to. She just kept quietly listening and accepting the sentence for what it was: not a defense, but a way to keep the truth from turning into poison.

Nancy and I were both competent and well-educated, both at school and at home. That mattered because people often assign roles in families: the strong one, the fragile one, the caretaker, the dependent. That wasn't us. We were both capable. We just worked differently.

Nancy managed people by anticipating their emotions. She could assess quickly and decide what was needed to keep moving. She wasn't manipulative. She was protective. She carried the weight of other people's comfort quietly, automatically, without thinking it was remarkable.

I, on the other hand, managed systems by removing variables. I didn't soothe; I stabilized. I identified potential failure points and built redundancies. Where Nancy caught problems in the air, I tried to make sure they couldn't fall in the first place.

You could see the division of labor early, even when we were kids.

When we visited Grandpa Alfred, we knew the whole mood of a room could change without warning. If he was badgering Grandma Arline, Nancy and I didn't discuss what either of us would do; we just moved. I kept Grandpa busy with business and his ego, feeding him questions that let him talk and talk, ensuring he forgot the target he'd been circling. Meanwhile, Nancy pulled Grandma Arline into the kitchen and asked her to teach her how to make rice pudding. Arline couldn't read or write, and Nancy had a gift for making her feel special anyway, like what she knew mattered, like her hands were worth watching.

The kitchen softened, then even as the living room would stay occupied. A small rescue, executed quietly, was how we always did things.

Years later, we executed the same choreography in reverse with Dad and Liz. I'd talk sports or business with Dad while giving him something practical to hold on to. With him, you could always find a handhold. A game, a deal, a plan. Something factual enough to keep him from drifting into the parts of himself he didn't want to face.

Nancy paired up with Liz for a different reason. Liz had no filter and no instinct for what a room could tolerate. If friends or family visited, she could look them up and down, comment on their clothes, name discount stores with a smirk, then name her own high-end places as if they were a credential. She would offer "advice" that landed like a slap. "You'd look better if you waxed your mustache," she once told a woman, as casually as if she were recommending a restaurant, and then she'd pivot to her own cosmetic work the way some people talk about a new haircut. And she didn't modulate for children. She would make sexual, charged remarks in front of teenagers, laughing at her own boldness, oblivious to the way the adults stiffened and the kids stared at their shoes.

So, Nancy stepped in beside Liz and stayed there, offering a line and a smile at the exact moments things were about to splinter. She redirected. She softened. She made small talk that wasn't really small talk, more like a buffer. It wasn't charm for its own sake. It was containment. She smoothed the sharp edges without announcing that she was smoothing anything at all.

In keeping with our respective strengths and strategies, I handled money the same way we handled most things, without discussion. If you watched the two of us long enough, you could see it in the objects we reached for, in what we fixed first, in what we ignored, and in what we joked about to stay steady.

Once, when Nancy was struggling financially, I met her in a parking lot halfway between where she was and where I was. We both knew what the meeting was for, but we approached it as we did everything: indirectly, with as little friction as possible.

I was sending her a check regularly by that point, and I made it a point to always have cash on hand. I would strictly manage my weekly withdrawals for lunch, errands, and sundries, scrimping just as our mother taught us to ensure I always had extra money set aside.

I'd arrive early and sit in my car with the engine off, watching people pushing carts across the lot, ordinary life in motion. I'd take out the envelope, count the bills once, then slide them back in. The counting was how I kept whatever emotions I was feeling from turning into panic. It was a small ritual. A way to make help feel like a task rather than a confession.

I'd have the envelope ready before I saw her, folded flat in my jacket like a boarding pass.

When she got in the car, she'd try to start with small talk: Chelsea, work, news, anything that wasn't the thing. I'd let her say a few sentences because Nancy needed to feel like she was still a person and not a problem. She would talk about something harmless, like how cold the mornings were, how Chelsea was working too much, how the car was "making a noise," and I could hear the underlying strain, the effort to keep the moment normal.

Then I'd gently put the envelope in her lap as it belonged there.

She'd look down at it, then up at me, eyes narrowed a fraction as they did when she was trying to calculate the hidden cost.

"Are you sure?" she'd always say.

"Yeah," I'd say. "I just won big."

She knew what I was actually doing in those moments. I knew she knew. Yet we both agreed to the lie because it preserved our dignity. It allowed her to receive help without turning into "a crisis." It allowed me to give her help without becoming "a rescuer." It kept things simple and clean.

Sometimes she'd touch the corner of the envelope with two fingers, like it was hot, then pull it toward her purse and tuck it in without opening it. She never counted the money, and once the envelope disappeared into her purse, we didn't discuss it. She wouldn't let me watch her need. She wouldn't let herself watch it, either.

We wouldn't say any other word. Just a hug across the console, awkward and quick, Nancy's arms surprisingly strong for how tired she often was.

"Love you," she would say.

Then she'd get out and walk back across the asphalt with her shoulders held a little straighter, as if the envelope weighed nothing.

The first signs did not arrive as a diagnosis. They arrived as interruptions. A headache that wouldn't let go. A day when her balance went strange for a second, and she stopped mid-step, blinking, waiting for the floor to stop moving. Then another day. Then another. She went to doctors the way responsible people do, expecting that if you kept showing up, someone would name the thing and hand you a plan. Instead, she collected tests, referrals, and careful non answers. One doctor suggested stress. Another suggested something else. Nothing landed cleanly. She was left with chronic pain that didn't announce itself as dramatic, only persistent. Left with dizzy spells that could turn a normal day into something she had to negotiate carefully.

It was elusive for me, too. I couldn't explain it to myself any better than Nancy could get answers for it. The slow progression was easy to misread. I told myself it was stress. Constant pressure. A life lived with no slack. At first, that explanation felt reasonable. It was easier than accepting that something was moving through her that none of us could name.

And the life she was carrying did not pause while she tried to figure out what was happening inside her body. She was building a new life, supporting a spouse through law school, then the army, then deployments. She was raising Chelsea. She was keeping the household afloat. She was the person who ate last, if she ate at all. Frugality and habit blurred into self-neglect. She stayed faithful, stayed in church, kept praying, kept trying to believe there was a reason it would lift. She would come home with another inconclusive report and set it aside the way she set aside so many things, as if it could be managed by being endured.

I started to see it in small scenes that never resolved. Nancy would stand up from a chair and pause, one hand on the table longer than necessary. She would reach for the back of a counter as she walked through her own kitchen, not grabbing it like someone in trouble, just touching it, lightly, as if the contact reassured her. Once, in a parking lot, she stepped off a curb and her foot didn't find the ground the way she expected. She caught herself, laughed it off, and kept walking, but her eyes flicked to me for a fraction of a second, checking whether I had seen. I had.

Over time, the difference became visible. We were only two years apart, but those years seemed to hit Nancy harder. The strain showed in her face and in her pace, and there were moments when she looked older than me in a way that startled me, not because age is a crime, but because it felt earned too early.

Eventually, she needed more than me to steady her. She needed a cane to stand upright. She treated it like a practical tool, not a symbol, and she made it look almost ordinary. But I noticed how her gait changed. Slower. More careful. A life lived with a hand on the rail, even when there was no rail.

When I stopped by briefly at her place around this time, I stood too close to the door because small places don't give you many options. The apartment smelled faintly of laundry detergent and whatever Nancy had cooked last. The heat was always a little too high, the air soft and drowsy, as if she wanted anyone who entered to feel held. Chelsea's things were everywhere in small ways: a pair of shoes by the wall, a hoodie thrown over a chair. They were proof that Nancy was still doing what she always did by making room.

Nancy was shrinking her own footprint so everyone else could fit. Even as the dizziness and pain progressed, even as the cane became part of her, the unresolved doctor visits stacked up like unopened mail, she kept arranging the room. Keeping the household afloat. Keeping the mood afloat. Keeping the fear from taking up too much space.

I couldn't visit her as much as I wanted to during the worst of those years. I could call, though, so I did. Again. Regularly. Intentionally. Not just when something was wrong, but as a practice, like checking a vital sign, like keeping a line of connection open so Nancy wouldn't feel abandoned.

And every time I called, I did the same thing: I tried to make her laugh. That was my role with Nancy. Humor was the rope we used to climb through hard rooms, after all, always had been. If I could get Nancy to smile, if I could hear even a thin little laugh at the end of a sentence, it meant she was still herself.

Nancy knew I would only feel secure if I could check in by phone after Mom's passing. When she answered the phone, she'd try to sound normal for the first few seconds, "Hey, Billy!" Then, fatigue would claim the rest of the sentence. I'd hear the TV on in the background, a steady noise to keep the room from going silent, and I'd picture her on the couch, eyes closed, phone pressed to her ear like it weighed a pound. I'd say, "Just checking in," and she'd say, "I'm okay," the way people say it when they're not.

So, I kept doing whatever I could. I kept the system running. I made sure money arrived without histrionics. I kept the story simple. I kept an envelope on hand at all times. I was the only one to do so, it seemed. My father didn't help her; that was for sure. He only offered the occasional gift card and, of course, the many explanations about Liz's expenses. Eventually, I bought Nancy's house outright so the payments would no longer be a question.

As for Grandpa Alfred? Well, he solved things by removing them. Dad solved things by not looking. I learned to solve challenges and crises by walking straight at them.

The assistance wasn't seen as a rescue. In truth, it was continuity. Together, we covered more ground than either of us could manage alone. In this way, we complemented each other. When one of us was tired, the other adjusted. When one of us couldn't speak, the other translated. We didn't discuss it. We just did it. People later called it a strength. To us, it was familiarity. And an agreement, made long ago, not to leave each other alone in it. Sticking by each other through thick and thin.

III
The Afternoon

10

The Diagnosis

All the patterns and skills we had learned over the years helped us plan and prepare for what was to come, at least to some degree. But sometimes, whatever skills you have don't matter in the room or, in my case, the office you are in.

I had a plan to navigate the daily backlog while Brian was with Nancy in the hospital during the day, still undergoing tests. Using time effectively at my office versus the waiting room with Brian as my eyes and ears. I would then drive down to visit and catch up with Chelsea and Brian when the night shift came on, when the hospital staff rotated, and the latest updates could be heard. Until then, Brian was on relay duty for any information.

Brian texted me the doctor's diagnosis he overheard and said, "Nancy would want you to research this."

I scribbled it down on the back of Joe's eulogy, which I had in my coat pocket.

"Bill, doctors say she most likely has LMD," the text said.

Dutifully, I looked it up while at work. I needed to be ready. I then drove to the hospital, long after the diner, after Nancy had been admitted, with information already in hand. The scans confirmed it: leptomeningeal disease (LMD).

The acronym was used, even as the doctor struggled to pronounce the diagnosis's long form; he was trying to say it as I tried to comprehend its meaning.

The doctor spoke carefully, aiming for precision as it mattered more than comfort. He explained what the images showed, how the cancer had spread, and what that meant for treatment options. His voice stayed even. His eyes moved between us, checking that we understood, checking for a fracture.

We were in one of those small exam rooms that try to be blank and never quite succeed. The lights were too bright, the corners too clean, the air cool in that institutional way that makes your skin notice itself. The paper on the exam table crinkled whenever someone shifted, as if the room wanted to record every movement. Chelsea sat closest to the screen. I sat beside her, turned toward the wall monitor, close enough to see the shapes, the shadows, the places the doctor would point.

The scans were already up when he came in. He didn't offer a warm-up. He didn't pretend this was a routine visit that had gone long. He sat down, pulled his chair a little closer to the monitor, and held a pen in his hand. Not like a weapon. More like a baton. Something to conduct the facts.

He pointed with the tip of the pen and then pulled his hand back, as if he did not want to press too hard on what was already true. He traced a path across the screen in short, deliberate movements. Stop. Explain. Pause. Move again. Each time he paused, it felt like the story shifted. His voice stayed level, almost practiced, but his eyes kept returning to us, Chelsea first, then me, then back again, watching our faces the way people watch glass when they set it down.

He explained what the pictures meant in plain terms, where they began, and where they traveled, what they had reached, and what they were beginning to touch. He laid out what it had changed and what it had not. When he said certain words, he slowed down, not to cushion them, but to make sure we received them cleanly. I watched his mouth more than his eyes. The cadence.

The small pauses where he chose a softer word without altering the meaning. He spoke the way people speak when they are carrying something fragile and sharp at the same time, careful not to drop it or cut anyone with it.

As he talked, a new understanding formed for me, not in medical terms, but in the simple logic of cause and effect. This conversation wasn't only about where the cancer had gone. It was about what it was interfering with. When it reaches the delicate layers around the brain and spine, it can foul the normal flow of fluid, the quiet circulation that helps the brain stay clear. When that flow is disrupted, the mind can cloud. Not because the person is gone, but because the signal is being muffled. Lucidity can become a scarce resource, coming and going like a weak radio station.

I didn't have the language for any of this then. I only had the pattern in front of me. Nancy was slipping away in the middle of sentences. Her eyes were turning distant. Whole minutes lost. Later, when a spinal tap was proposed, I did not hear it as only a test. I heard it as a chance. A way to relieve what might be building up. A way, maybe, to give her a clearer hour, a cleaner conversation, a small return of herself.

Chelsea asked questions as they surfaced, one and then another, her voice steady until the last few syllables, where it would thin slightly as if she were stepping onto ice and listening for the crack. The doctor answered each one without rushing. He did not fill the silences between them. He let the silences stand, as if he understood that our minds needed room to catch up to what our ears had already heard. When he finished an explanation, he looked at us again, not impatient, not distracted, checking comprehension the way you check a pulse.

I could feel myself trying to organize his words into something usable. Options. Time. Next steps. The part of me that solves problems kept searching for a hinge, a place where effort could change the direction of the story. But the doctor's calm was not the calm of reassurance. It was the calm of gravity. It was the calm of a man describing what the images already insisted on.

Nancy wasn't lucid by that point. She wasn't in the room with us the way she should have been. She was somewhere else inside her own body, drifting in and out. Chelsea and I sat under fluorescent light while a stranger with a pen showed us, point by point, what was already happening within her.

Her eyes were open but not quite there, bright in the way a hallway light stays on after everyone has gone to bed. The blanket had been folded and tucked so tight over her legs that it made her look smaller, pinned in place. Plastic bands circled her wrist, one with her name printed in black, another with a warning color and a fall-risk code, as if the hospital needed a label for what her body was already doing. A thin alarm cord was clipped to the sheet, ready to shriek if she moved the wrong way. The bed rails were up. The IV pump gave a small mechanical click. The monitor kept printing its calm little evidence. Everything around her had a tag, a sticker, a barcode, and a job. Everything was being tracked.

I stood close enough to hear the doctor but far enough to see the door. I let the extra words slide off and kept only the pieces that changed decisions. I asked the questions in the order they mattered, not the order they were offered. Options first. Timelines next. Then the hard boundary: what could be done, what could not, and what would only look like doing something.

The room moved how hospital rooms move when they've been doing this all day: a steady, rehearsed tempo that doesn't stop just because your life has. The IV pump kept time with small, patient clicks, delivering its measured drops like it had authority over the minutes. The monitor glowed at Nancy's bedside, throwing soft light across the sheets, lines rising and falling, numbers updating without emotion, as if the machine were politely insisting that the body was still participating. Every few seconds, it refreshed itself-oxygen, pulse, blood pressure-each reading a quiet receipt that something inside her was still working, still complying.

On the wall, a whiteboard sat in plain view like a control panel for the day. Names were written in dry-erase marker: the nurse, the tech, the date, and beneath them a short plan, tests, and tasks stacked like ordinary errands. The writing was casual and blocky, the same handwriting you'd use for groceries, and that was the strange part. In this room, the most terrifying reality of our lives was being managed in the same format as chores.

Chelsea stood close to Nancy's shoulder, watching her face for any flicker. Not just information, but recognition. I stood closer to the door, where I could see the whole room and the hallway at the same time. That's where I always stand when the stakes are high. You can't manage what you can't see.

The doctor talked us through our options: drilling into her skull, chemotherapy injected directly into her brain. Everything Nancy would have hated: Prolongation without dignity. Intervention without cure.

The doctor kept offering words like "aggressive," "options," "pathways," but every sentence brought us back to the same place. Soon, the conversation narrowed until it had drained out of the room.

A silence opened between the doctor's words, just long enough to feel the shape of what he was not saying. His eyes shifted from the screen to us and back again, checking whether we were still with him, checking whether we were about to break.

That's when the word arrived, not thrown, not dropped, just placed: "Terminal."

He said the word as if it were a box to be checked after everything else had finally failed to fit. His voice stayed professional, but the room changed anyway, the air tightening as if the word had weight.

I felt Chelsea's body go still beside the bed. In one easy motion, just a small locking up, shoulders held in place. Her hand stayed on Nancy, but her grip changed. She wasn't smoothing Nancy's hair anymore. She was holding on.

I kept my face neutral because if you react, people start managing your feelings instead of giving you facts. I stared at the doctor's mouth, watched him finish the thought he'd been building toward, watched him reach the end of it without giving us a place to stand.

Then I asked the question that had been sitting in my throat the whole time.

"And if we don't treat it," I said, keeping my tone flat, factual, how one speaks when you need the answer more than you need comfort. "If we move to hospice."

The doctor didn't answer immediately.

He looked down at the chart, then back up, as if he were making sure we understood what that choice meant, or buying a second to find a way to say it that wouldn't sound like scheduling.

His lips parted, closed again.

He hesitated. "About…" A pause. "About six weeks."

He didn't sound cruel. That was the worst part. It sounded like he was scheduling it.

"You're thinking in the right direction," he said, and it sounded like relief that someone else had said the hard part.

Chelsea's shoulders tightened as if she'd been bracing for a hit and finally felt it. I nodded once, not because I accepted it, but because I needed him to keep talking.

Hospice entered the conversation immediately after I mentioned it, as if it were a secret code to unlock an option in the clocked-in protocol. The conversation's sudden shift from intervention to hospice was earlier than I expected. There were forms to fill out. Signatures to give. Decisions to make that usually belonged to later days now sat squarely in front of us.

Paperwork arrived like a second diagnosis. A clipboard. Consent forms. The nurse explained the steps with the same tone she would use to describe a diet order. It wasn't cold. It was practiced.

Nancy's Spanish roommate's daughter arrived and, not noticing the room, walked past the doorway as if she belonged to the hallway—as if she'd already learned the hospital's rhythm. Not rushing, but not lingering either, she moved with the practiced caution people develop after living under fluorescent light for too many hours.

She took two steps beyond the room, then slowed.

Not because we called her. Not because she was looking for directions. Something in the sound, or the stillness, or the shape of us stopped her. She turned her head and looked in, and I could tell immediately she wasn't seeing "a patient" as staff do. She was seeing the whole tableau in a single intake of breath, the way a family sees it when you've been doing this long enough.

Nancy was lying in that bed, swallowed by hospital white, not quite present, the room making decisions around her. Chelsea at her shoulder, trying to be close enough to matter. I moved nearer the edge, as if proximity to the door could keep my mind functional.

The young woman didn't stare at us. Her eyes moved once, quickly, across the bed, then to my face, and stopped there, like she was checking whether we were alone in it or whether we had backup.

Her mouth opened slightly, then closed again, as people do when they're deciding whether they're allowed to speak in someone else's grief.

"Excuse me," she said, and her voice was quiet, careful, the same tone you'd use in a church.

I stepped into the doorway a fraction, instinctively, not blocking her, just meeting her, like how you meet anyone in a corridor when you don't know whether they're about to ask for help or deliver bad news.

She nodded toward the bed, her chin barely moving.

"What's her name?" she asked.

It wasn't curiosity. It was a request, a permission to hold the situation with us for a second.

I lowered my voice automatically, as if Nancy could hear the name even if she couldn't answer.

"Nancy," I whispered.

The young woman repeated it silently at first, shaping it with her lips as if she wanted to get it right. Then she nodded once, a small, decisive motion that felt like a promise.

Her face didn't change much, but something softened around her eyes, the way it does when a person stops being "the lady in 412" and becomes a person with a name, someone who belongs to someone.

"Nancy will be in my prayer chain tonight," she said.

Prayer chain. The phrase landed strangely in that room full of monitors and protocols, like someone had brought in an older kind of care, the kind that doesn't require authorization or a badge.

It caught me off guard, not because I suddenly converted in the hallway, but because it was kindness offered from inside her own burden. Her mother was behind a curtain in that same room, sick enough to need a roommate, sick enough to require a daughter's vigilance. She had every reason to keep walking. Instead, she stopped, asked a name, and carried it away with her.

I nodded once because that was all I could manage without my voice changing.

"Thank you," I said, and the words sounded thin, but they were real.

She gave me one more look, her eyes brimming with recognition, then turned and continued down the hallway, disappearing back into whatever worry she was already carrying.

And for a moment after she left, the corridor felt different. Not lighter, exactly. Just reminded of the fact that even here, even now, a stranger could still reach across the line and offer something clean.

Later, I walked with her toward the exit through corridors that felt like a maze, buildings stitched together with turns and connectors that made you doubt your own direction. Signs pointed in one direction and then another, as if the hospital itself couldn't make up its mind.

She hesitated near the door, uncomfortable, like she wanted to apologize for something she couldn't control.

"I heard the doctors," she said. "Talking about Nancy being terminal. I didn't want to eavesdrop, but…the room…"

"It's okay," I said. Because what else do you say?

She thanked me again, and then she was gone.

I stood there a second longer than I needed to, thinking about a hand on my arm, a prayer chain I would never be part of, and the odd fact that even here, in the middle of all this, a stranger could still be kind.

Then I turned back into the maze and went to rejoin Chelsea.

Doctors were gathered outside Nancy's room, and I took the opportunity to discuss options to ease her suffering. Not to save her, but to wake her. To give her clarity. To let her know what was happening and allow her to say goodbye on her own terms.

The doctor hesitated, then mentioned a spinal tap. It would provide her with temporary lucidity. A brief window of relief.

Nancy struggled and moaned, unconscious, as if in a fever. The sounds she made weren't words. They were her body, protesting. Chelsea stayed close to her, smoothing her hair, talking softly even when Nancy couldn't answer.

The doctor didn't promise the spinal tap. He offered it as you might offer a tool you're not sure will work: "Sometimes," he said, "it can help for a bit."

Just then, I remembered waking my father up in the ICU years before, out of a coma, terminal as well.

It had been seven years, to be exact. Dad had sent me a certified letter before then. In it were his DNR, living will, and a cover letter for emergencies. Dad had heart failure because of a rheumatic fever he had suffered in the orphanage, which had led to an enlarged heart. He had already undergone a septuple bypass, but now his heart was failing. These instructions were mine alone. They were proof that, when it came down to the last decisions, he trusted me over Liz.

At the time, I didn't fully understand why he had done it that way. The letter had seemed abrupt, almost random, arriving like a task dropped on my doorstep. But when I called Liz on his birthday that year and found, to my surprise, that he was in the ICU, the puzzle began to make sense. Dad could coddle Liz. He could protect her from discomfort. But he could not ask her to carry something like this. He needed my strength to override his inability to let her suffer, and he needed someone who would do what had to be done without collapsing under it.

I assumed heart attack until the duty nurse used a different phrase, the phrase that changed everything.

"Your father is on life support," she said.

Her voice stayed professional, but her eyes didn't. There is a look nurses get when they're trying to warn you without editorializing. I knew what it meant. I knew this was the moment.

Something in me snapped into a familiar setting. Not numbness exactly. More like a switch to analysis. Adrenaline came first, then the urge to gather facts. How bad is he? What exactly happened? What have they tried thus far? What is left that could be done? He had survived heart attacks before. He had recovered before. Doctors are trained to offer paths, to keep doors cracked open, and families cling to those cracks because they have to. I felt myself fighting for something else, for clarity, for a real answer that could not be softened into false hope.

I flew to the hospital in Atlanta immediately, and Nancy met me there. It smelled like antiseptic and overworked air conditioning. The fluorescent lights made everyone look slightly unreal, like we'd been moved into a place where time ran on machinery instead of sunlight. The ICU doors opened with a hush, and a wave of noise met us, not loud exactly, but constant. Beeps, alarms at a distance, the thin squeak of shoes on waxed tiles.

I walked faster than I meant to. My body was moving with urgency, but my mind was already building a checklist. I asked questions of anyone who looked like they might know something. Nurses. Doctors. Even people from

Dad's church, trying to understand what led up to this, what had changed, what I had missed. Underneath it all was exhaustion, the sense that I had been drafted again into a role I did not volunteer for, and fear, too, a quieter fear that I would commit to a permanent mistake. Our family had trained me to override emotion and find the answer, but the stakes made that training feel like both a strength and a trap.

Before we even reached Dad's room, we found Liz. And in that instant, before she spoke, I felt the familiar, sour mix of sadness and frustration. Not at her exactly. At the burden itself. The fact that, in the end, Dad had no one else to ask.

You could hear her first. Her voice was sharp and high, breaking in the middle of sentences, then surging again, louder, as if volume could force the world to obey. She stood in the hall near the nurses' station, half-turned toward the counter as if trying to occupy the space physically, her purse clutched under one arm, her other hand cutting the air in short, angry motions. Her face was wet. Not soft crying. Something messier. Tears mixed with rage, mascara starting to travel, her mouth pulled tight as if she were biting down on panic.

A nurse tried to speak calmly, palms open, the posture of de-escalation. Liz didn't let her finish.

"You don't understand," Liz snapped. "You don't understand anything. You people are not killing him."

Another staff member stepped in, voice lowered, trying again. Liz swung toward him like a switchblade.

"Don't you tell me what to do," she said. "I'm his wife."

A clipboard hit the counter with a slap. Something plastic, a cup lid maybe, got knocked sideways and skittered on the tile. The sound was small, but it made every head in the area tilt toward us for half a second.

The nurses looked worn out as we approached. When they saw Nancy and me, their expressions shifted into something else, a kind of sympathy that had nothing to do with Dad's prognosis and everything to do with the fact that we had arrived to inherit the chaos.

One of them leaned slightly toward me, not whispering but lowering her voice in that practiced ICU way.

"She's been like this," she said, and didn't have to add "all day."

Dad was in a private room down the hall, the kind of room hospitals reserve for endings. A door that closed. A curtain you could pull. Space to die without witnesses who weren't invited.

I found the doctor and staff and asked the question in the way I ask questions when I can't afford emotion.

"Why is he on life support?" I asked. "He has a DNR, and you have it. He didn't want this."

The doctor's mouth tightened into a line, just briefly, morphing into the expression of a man who already knew the answer and didn't like it.

"Liz denied it," he said.

We stood there for a beat, as if the sentence needed time to land.

In the hallway behind us, Liz's voice rose again, the rant continuing in waves, wailing now, then turning nasty, then collapsing into sobs that didn't soften her posture, only sharpened it. She was fighting the staff and the situation, but not for Dad. She was fighting for herself.

Nancy moved before I did.

That was always Nancy. When something becomes unbearable in a public place, she instinctively tries to protect the room from additional damage, even when the room doesn't deserve it.

She walked to Liz and touched her arm gently, firm enough that it wasn't optional.

"Come on," Nancy said in the tone that made children stop crying. "Not here."

Liz jerked away at first, eyes wild, but Nancy stayed steady, speaking softly, guiding her as if guiding an injured animal.

"Come with me," Nancy said again. "We're going to sit down."

Liz kept rambling as she walked, her sentences snapping in half.

"They're trying to," she said. "They're trying to…" And then, louder, "I'm not letting them do this. Do you hear me? I'm not letting them."

Nancy got her into a small family break room, the kind with a table bolted to the floor and a coffee machine whose coffee tasted like old pennies. The door closed, and the hallway quieted by a few degrees. Even the nurses seemed to exhale.

A nurse looked at me, almost apologetically.

"I'm sorry," she said.

I nodded once. The apology wasn't necessary, but it was human, and I accepted it like a small mercy.

Inside the break room, Liz's focus narrowed to its true center.

"Who is going to take care of me?" she demanded, as if the question were the most obvious thing in the world. "Who is going to take care of me if he goes?"

Nancy sat with her. She neither agreed with Liz nor argued with her. She only listened with empathy and contained Liz's outbursts. Liz's hands trembled. She wiped her face hard, not tenderly. Her eyes darted toward the door as if she expected someone to come in and take something from her.

"I don't care what he wants," Liz said, the line stripped of any shame. "What about me?"

I walked back to the doctor then.

"Dad doesn't want this," I told him point-blank. In my pocket, I could feel the edges of the documents that had been sent to me years before, the means by which Dad and I sometimes interacted, business-like even in intimacy. Certified letter. Instructions. Power was given to me because he trusted me more than he trusted her.

The doctor's voice lowered.

"The only way I can solve this matter," he said, interjecting, "is to wake him."

It didn't sound like hope. It was pure procedure, like the last clean step before the machines could be turned off without war. But it also felt like a hurdle, placed there to slow us down, to see if we would flinch. Almost a bluff. As if the inconvenience of waking him might make us accept something less direct, something safer for everyone else.

"Then wake my dad," I said. The words were simple, but my chest was full. I was angry at Liz, at the selfishness and helplessness she brought into every room, and sad at the world Dad had built where his last, lone hope of mercy depended on my fortitude. I was frustrated that I was the one left to sort out a problem created by years of cloaking and indulgence, and now I was being handed a process that felt designed to protect the hospital as much as it protected him. If this was a bluff, I was going to call it. My drive to settle what was right overrode everything else.

They adjusted the medication soon after I made the demand. Buttons were pressed. Numbers slowly changed. Tubing was checked, and someone kept their eyes on the monitor as if they were in a tight negotiation with it. I watched the staff move with practiced calm and felt the friction of it, the way caution can masquerade as care. Dad had already made his wishes plain, and still the machinery of procedure had to grind forward, as if the people in white coats needed permission from the machines before they could honor what he had already decided. And I could feel it again, that stark fact he had mailed to me in a certified envelope years earlier: He trusted me over her.

When Dad began to stir, it was ugly. He was pale, waxy, his face pulled thinner than I remembered. His eyes fluttered and then opened halfway, unfocused, fighting for coherence. A low moan came out of him, not language, but a sound. His hands moved, weak but urgent, grabbing at the tubes in his throat and the lines in his arms as if his body knew something foreign had been installed and was trying, instinctively, to reject it.

"Easy," a nurse said, and placed a hand on his wrist, not restraining, just anchoring.

Dad's mouth worked around the ventilator. His brow knotted. The effort looked like pain. My anger sharpened again, not at him, but at the arrangement of it all. The fact that he had made a life where, at the end, there was no trusted circle, only me.

I leaned in close enough that he could see me.

"Dad," I said. "I'm here to do as you asked."

His eyes moved, sluggish but real, tracking. Finding.

"Do you still want me to..." I started, and I didn't finish the sentence because I didn't have to.

Dad nodded emphatically, or as emphatically as a dying man could. There was not a hint of confusion or hesitation in his eyes. His hands, now becoming mobile enough to attempt taking the tubes out himself, were restrained. I turned my head toward the doorway, making sure Liz saw it too, even if she didn't want to.

"You saw that," I said.

Liz's face tightened, the expression of a person *now* cornered by the truth. She didn't respond. The room held a brief, brutal quiet. I went back to the doctor and the staff.

"You have twenty-four hours to shut these machines off," I said, and my voice had that flat edge it gets when it becomes an instrument. "Or you will hear from my attorney."

They complied.

Afterward, the monitor still traced its lines, still reported numbers, but the feeling in the air shifted, as a room shifts when everyone understands they are now inside the last hour. Dad's breathing became its own thing, no longer assisted, the inhale arriving like work and the exhale leaving like surrender. The sound was rough, wet in places, and it struck Nancy hard, the animal reality of it, the body trying to do one final task on its own.

Nancy and I sat with him. He was still pale. Still restless. Then, slowly, that restlessness began to drain away as his hands stopped trying to pull the tubes out. The moans thinned, then ended. The color left his face in stages, as if the body were powering down. His tense hands softened. We held them anyway.

Dad's eyes went unfocused again, then closed. And when the last breath came, it didn't arrive like punctuation. It arrived like the end of a long, exhausting sentence, the last exhale leaving him and not returning.

Nancy's hand tightened on his for a moment before loosening.

In the break room down the hall, Liz stayed away from the bed. Nancy had moved her there because someone had to protect the room from her, and because Dad deserved to die without being used as a stage.

Afterward, there were tasks to be taken care of. Promises to be kept. The kind you make in the aftermath when you don't yet understand what you're agreeing to.

Before he was sedated again, I promised Dad that I would care for Liz after he was gone, which I did. I created a trust for her, using the accounting skills he'd wanted me to have, supported Liz as Liz demanded to be supported, and made sure that when she passed, Nancy would finally be cared for with what remained.

This time was different, very different from what happened back then. Nancy deserved to know the truth, I felt. She deserved to leave awake. Time wasn't something to waste. I knew by then. If Nancy could sign the forms, then we could get the process in motion while she was still herself. If she couldn't, everything would become harder: more phone calls to make, more approvals to get, more layers between us and what needed to happen.

I laid out what I could in my head as I always do when something is breaking, not as feelings, but as steps. The hospital had already handed me a clipboard. The pen felt like a toy. The forms felt like concrete.

Chelsea handed me Nancy's wallet, and I opened it on the small rolling tray table like I was sorting evidence. Plastic cards, insurance, the worn edges of her driver's license, and a few receipts folded too many times. Her life had been reduced to what fit behind glass and laminated plastic. I slid the ID free, checked the name and the photo, then looked at Nancy in the bed. The mismatch was unbearable: the official version of her smiling calmly from a card while the real her lay strapped to a medical bed.

On the wall, the whiteboard still pretended the day was normal. Date. Nurse name. Tech name. Tests are scheduled like chores. Someone had written "MRI" in neat block letters, the same kind of handwriting you'd use on a grocery list. The bed alarm cord was clipped to the sheet like a leash. The monitor pulsed and clicked in a steady cadence, announcing numbers that belonged to the staff more than they belonged to us.

We needed to put some power in place before she woke. By this, I did not mean power as domination, but power as permission. Permission to move Nancy out. Permission to sign. Permission to protect her from whatever bureaucracy would appear next, hungry and procedural.

Chelsea needed a power of attorney. If she couldn't sign quickly, we would lose time, and time was the only currency left that mattered. Brian could be a backup if something happened, if Chelsea's hands shook, if I were on the road when the next decision arrived. Hospice would need authorizations, calls, confirmations, and the kind of phone conversations where you repeat the same sentence to three different people because no one system speaks to another. Equipment would have to arrive at a house that had never imagined itself a hospital. A bed that wouldn't fit through a doorway without turning it sideways. Oxygen tanks. Medication lists. Instructions. Schedules. Deliveries timed like an invasion.

I could already see it, the way a house changes when a dying person moves in, not poetically, but practically. Furniture pushed aside. The living room was converted into a space made for living, repurposed for decline. Soon, people were stepping carefully around the equipment as if not to offend it.

I didn't know whether Nancy would wake. I didn't know how long she would stay present if she did. I didn't know what she would understand when she opened her eyes and saw our faces arranged how people arrange themselves at a bedside when they're trying not to cry.

But my focus stayed where it always had: on the execution of the tasks that needed to be done. After all, I knew how fear could be a window of opportunity. Fear often makes you stand in the doorway and stare. Preparation is what gets you inside.

A nurse came in later and adjusted something at the IV. Her hands moved with practiced ease, the sort of speed you develop when you've done the same task in a hundred rooms, a thousand times, and your body knows what to do even if your mind is tired. She didn't meet our eyes for long. She checked the clip, the tubing, and the rate. She checked the bracelet on Nancy's wrist as if it were the truth and Nancy herself the variable.

Then the room held, waiting.

Minutes stretched on. The clock on the wall moved as if it were doing it on purpose. The monitor kept time with its quiet insistence. Somewhere outside the door, a cart rolled past, wheels rattling, life continuing with hospital indifference.

Finally, the change came, small at first. A shift. A breath that sounded less trapped. A subtle tension was leaving Nancy's face. Her eyelids fluttered like she was climbing up from deep water. Chelsea leaned forward so fast her chair squeaked…and Nancy's eyes opened.

For a moment, they were unfixed, searching, how eyes look when the mind hasn't caught up yet. Then they found us. Then they held.

Her gaze sharpened, not wide, not panicked, just suddenly there. Tracking. Recognizing. Present in her own face again. The most ordinary thing in the world, a person looking at her brother and knowing who he is, except that it didn't feel ordinary. It felt like the first clean air we'd breathed in days.

Chelsea made a small sound, half a sob, half a laugh she couldn't afford. I didn't move much. I didn't want to spook the moment, like it was a shy animal that might bolt if the room got too loud.

The doctor came in then and stopped just inside the doorway, as if he hadn't expected to meet Nancy looking back at him. His posture changed. His professional tone tried to assemble itself, and then you could hear it falter, just slightly, because now he wasn't speaking about a patient in a bed. He was speaking to a person.

His voice softened. He explained what could not be fixed, what could not be reversed, and what time would do, whether we cooperated or not. He spoke carefully, as people speak when the truth is heavy, and they are trying not to drop it.

Nancy watched him. Not bravely for show, not stoically, just attentively, like she was reading him how she always read people, taking the measure of what they could carry.

When he stopped, she lifted her hand.

Her movement was small and deliberate, the hand coming out from under the blanket, pale against the hospital white. She reached toward him and touched his hand with her fingertips first, then settled her palm fully, as if she were anchoring him. As if she were saying, without a word, "I understand what you're doing. I know this is hard for you, too."

The room changed the instant she touched him.

"It's okay," she said.

The room changed the moment she said it. Not because the facts had changed, but because the emotional labor associated with them had shifted. Nancy was doing what she always did: making it easier for someone else to stand in the truth.

The doctor looked surprised by her reaction, caught for a moment without professional footing. He nodded once, quickly, as if acknowledging something he hadn't expected to receive.

Nancy withdrew her hand and leaned back. The work was done.

Before she could go, there were permissions to sign and blanks to fill. The future always arrives with paperwork.

"Take me home," she said.

11

Homeward Bound

Nancy said it so plainly, as one would ask for water. "Take me home."

By then, the room had already shifted into practical mode. The neurologist had stopped talking. The truth had been spoken aloud and locked into place. Hospice wasn't just an idea to consider anymore. It was a delivery window. The bed. The oxygen supply. The quiet machinery that would ensure her comfort and care. The equipment would arrive the next day, and after work, I would drive back to the hospital because once the house was ready to hold her, Nancy could be discharged into it.

I walked out of the hospital carrying paperwork and a strange calm that always arrives when feelings would otherwise knock you over. The parking lot lights made everything look staged, as if everyday life were still happening for other people in neat rectangles. I got into my car and sat for a moment before turning the key, letting the silence settle around me like insulation.

I drove away as if I were carrying something breakable. Not Nancy. Yet. Just the plan.

I drove from the hospital northward toward my own house because I had to, because preparation is what I do when feeling would crack me open. But the word "home" sat in the passenger seat like another person. It had weight. It had history.

And that's when memory arrived, not as nostalgia, not as sentiment, but as recognition.

The word "home" stayed with me on the drive, heavy and complicated, and it pulled me back to the first time Nancy had to rebuild from nothing.

It was 1998, and Nancy knew her marriage was over. She was experiencing the quiet containment of a split, which she had known was coming. And still, she hosted Thanksgiving anyway. She kept things normal. She made sure everyone ate. She made sure the children laughed. She absorbed the fracture quietly, so no one else had to carry it yet. Nancy made sure the kids were fed and laughing at their table, and while everything else stayed normal.

The collapse happened shortly after, like a door being kicked in. Nancy's finances were in ruins when her husband left, with about $30,000 in debt. She had a leased car that was about to expire. She had no prospects. No plan that wasn't improvisation.

When she called me, her tone was the one she had used her whole life when things were bad: controlled. The facts were delivered as if she were giving a report rather than asking for help. She was not begging. She was briefing.

So, I solved what could be solved. I paid off the debt. I bought Nancy a new car so she would not have one more deadline hanging over her. We got a U-Haul. We packed the pieces of her life into boxes that suddenly seemed too small for what they held. The plan was to move her and Chelsea back to New Jersey and rebuild there, quietly and steadily, without speeches.

There was little to bring; Nancy had been cleaned out. While we were parked at a motel overnight, someone broke into the truck. The next morning, we saw the open cargo door. Looking at what little she had, it was all there. Only a truckload of sentimental memories of a lost life, of value only to Nancy.

As we were driving up, the cab was quiet for a long stretch, and Nancy finally said, "Thank you." I told her it was never necessary.

She stared out the window like she was watching her old life recede in the glass. "I just feel…defeated," she said, and the word came out smaller than she meant it to.

I looked at her and said the only thing that mattered, the only true thing, no matter what had been taken.

"Best sister ever."

She smiled, tired, relaxed, and answered without thinking, as if it were a language we had invented long ago.

"Best brother ever."

On moving day, the new car was parked on the street while we finished loading. Nancy was going to drive it. I was going to drive the truck. Everything was finally lined up: paperwork, logistics, a direction forward, when a teenage girl driving down the street got startled by a bee. She jerked the wheel and lost control.

The impact was sharp and sickening, metal-on-metal, then the new car I had just bought for Nancy launched up into a neighbor's yard like it wanted out of the whole story.

For a second, nobody moved. The moment was too absurd to understand. Then Nancy ran, not to the car, but to the girl. She went straight to the driver's window and leaned in. She was calm immediately, as if a switch had flipped in her.

"It's OK," she told her. "You're OK. It will be OK."

She helped the girl breathe. She called her parents. She kept talking in that steady voice until the panic drained out of the child's face and turned into crying. Nancy stayed with her on the stoop like she was sitting with one of her own students, like the accident had not just taken her first hope of rebuilding a new normal.

I called the truck. I dealt with the police. We drove a U-Haul north because the move still had to happen, even if the universe wanted to make a joke first. Later, after the car was repaired, I flew back to get it and drove it up to New Jersey myself, finishing the loop we had started.

Her world changed in more ways than one with a crash. But we rebuilt anyway. We always rebuild. We leaned on each other like we always had, just forward motion and the quiet agreement that neither of us was going to let the other fall alone.

Now she was saying it again, in a different key and with a different kind of urgency. "Take me home."

She hadn't yet talked about it in practical terms. Not the way Mom had been forced to years earlier, when Dad left, and she had to learn to drive, to work, to become a person in the world instead of the wife inside a house. Mom's pivot had been immediate, late, and punishing, and it wasn't theoretical. It was a clipboard, a schedule, and a fear she could not talk herself out of.

Mom signed up for driving lessons because there was no other option. The first time I took her to a parking lot to practice, her hands stayed locked on the wheel as if it might bolt. Her shoulders climbed toward her ears. She stared straight ahead and whispered, "I can't," like she was confessing something shameful. I stood beside the car and talked her through it anyway, pointing at the empty painted lines as if they were a road. She inched forward, stopped too hard, started again, and each restart cost her something.

Then came the job hunt. I watched her put on a brave face and walk into interviews with that careful, shy posture of hers, trying to make herself smaller so she would not bother anyone. I watched her come back out with her eyes too bright, blinking fast, the rejection already written on her face before she said a word. When she finally got hired, she was treated like a person who had missed the only acceptable door. No college degree, no proper credentials, nothing that impressed the people who liked to be impressed. They spoke to her with that polite condescension that is still cruelty, making her feel inferior without ever raising their voices.

At night, she would come home, go quiet, and then break. She would cry as someone cries when they are trying not to be heard, shoulders shaking, face turned away, as if even grief had to be modest. I didn't know how to fix it. I only knew that Dad had left, and now Mom was being forced into the world that scared her, and the world was not gentle with her for showing up late.

I watched what it did to her body. Stress isn't just an emotion. It's a chemical reaction. It settles into joints. It settles into sleep. It settles into the immune system as a cold settles into a building. Mom's rheumatoid arthritis had its own medical origin. Still, I can't separate it emotionally from that rupture that came first. I watched her come home after those early job interviews, shoulders pitched forward like she was trying to make herself smaller, and sit at the kitchen table with her purse still on, hands flexing and rubbing at her fingers as if she could work the fear out of them.

In the years that followed, I watched that same fear turn into something physical, swelling and stiffness and fatigue, until it felt like the marriage leaving had found a second way to stay, and it hastened her decline, made everything harder, and shortened her.

When Nancy's marriage ended, I wasn't only seeing Nancy then. I was seeing the echo of what came before. I was seeing the outline clearly. I was seeing what happens when a woman defines her life around a man's career, only for the man to leave and the woman to pivot late, under stress, with a child watching.

Nancy had left home right after school to get married. She had built her life around a different classic trajectory. She hadn't built the framing of her own separate economic survival because she'd assumed, as many people do, that marriage was the structure itself. While Nancy had driving experience and a foundation, she relied on the same assumptions Mom had when the floor dropped out from under her.

Now that the structure was gone, she needed a new, practical start, not in an inspirational sense but in the literal sense. She needed money, shelter, transportation, and work.

In essence, she was struggling and starting over with nothing.

That word can sound dramatic until you see it up close, until you watch the math of it play out in a real conversation.

One of the first things I did after arriving at Nancy's home in Virginia to discuss her prospects was take her to lunch at a little luncheonette. The kind of place that served food family-style, plates meant to be shared, bowls set down in the middle as if the world was still normal and generous. The place smelled faintly of coffee that had been on the burner too long and something fried that never fully leaves the air. The vinyl seat squeaked when we slid into the booth. Condensation gathered on the water glasses and made slow rings on the table. The wait staff moved with the easy familiarity of people who had seen every kind of day walk through their door. They kept my coffee full without asking. They checked on Nancy a little more than they checked on me, not out of pity, just instinct, the way good servers do when they sense someone is running on less sleep than they admit.

Nancy did not cry. She did not dramatize. She had that resigned calm she wore when life had become a series of problems to be managed. She talked, and I listened, and what she described was not a crisis with a headline. It was a month-to-month grind. Bills arrived before the money did. Money was spent before the next bill came due. Late payments that became fees, and fees became their own kind of tax. She explained how she was juggling deposits, moving one payment just far enough to cover another, always one envelope away from the whole thing collapsing. As she spoke, she kept tearing the edge of a sugar packet, not to eat the sugar, but just worrying it between her fingers until it split cleanly.

Nancy mentioned her teeth the way people mention something they have already tried not to think about. She needed dental work. It wasn't vanity. It was real. But there was no money saved to fix them. Not because she didn't care, but because priorities had become a matter of triage. Rent. Food. Gas. Daycare. The basic humiliations of scarcity make you look at every purchase as a moral decision, and you can feel the judgment in your own hands even when no one else is judging you.

She told me about tutoring, the way she'd pieced together income in Virginia, one student at a time, the checks small and irregular. She said it plainly. You can't survive on that. You can't build a life on tutoring checks. There was no anger in her voice, just the exhausted honesty of someone stating the obvious after trying everything else first.

I was already doing what I always do. Taking the pieces. Sorting them. Looking for the first rung that could hold weight.

Luckily, she still had her teaching license. That was the one rung of a ladder that hadn't broken. I said it out loud, not as a pep talk, but as a fact. We had something. We could build from something.

Nancy nodded, stirring her coffee slowly, listening the way she always listened when she wanted a solution more than comfort. The waitress passed again and topped her cup, and for a second, the scene almost looked ordinary, just a brother and sister talking over lunch, steam rising between us. But the conversation underneath it was about survival.

I suggested she lean on the license. I suggested daycare at first, something she could do quickly, something that would get her on her feet while she rebuilt her résumé and found a stable position. I wasn't trying to steer her away from what she wanted. I was trying to get her to shore up the basics. A foundation. A floor that wouldn't give way.

Nancy didn't argue. She didn't defend. She just let the ideas land, weighing them the way she weighed everything then, not in theory, but against the reality of her life. And as we sat there, the plates between us, my coffee refilled again, I understood something I didn't want to understand. This lunch was another version of our diner scenes, the ones that replayed across our lives whenever one of us needed the other to help turn trouble back into a plan.

Nancy heard me. She didn't reply. But she was still emotionally oriented toward the relational world, visitation, family, and was more focused on buffering others and herself from the practical realities. She was more emotionally grounded than I am, in that she stayed connected to people even when they failed her. I'm more pragmatic. I move toward structure and solutions, sometimes too quickly. I pull away from people when they become untrustworthy. Nancy leaned in.

So, for a while, she leaned on me, and I did what I could to reboot her world. I set out to give her a fresh start. I paid off her debts. I bought her a new car. I handled logistics, paperwork, and all the unromantic mechanics that keep a person from falling through the cracks. The alternative was to watch my sister live inside the same slow collapse I'd watched my mother endure.

Love in our family often looks like a function. It seems like speed. It looks like getting ahead of the next disaster, so the person you're helping doesn't have to sit in the wreckage, feeling ashamed.

My wife and I were focused on building a house for our growing family now that the youngest of our two girls had arrived, so we rented a condo as a temporary shelter, an in-between place meant to feel like progress. It did, in a usual way. We had a plan. We had a future we could point to. The condo was the bridge.

Then Nancy and Chelsea moved in, and the bridge became crowded. Nancy tried to make herself small enough to fit into a space not designed for her life, of course. That sounds like simple behavior. It is not. It is a posture she put on as one puts on a coat they do not like, buttoned high and kept tight.

She moved through the condo as if her body took up too much air. She kept her voice half a notch lower than it needed to be, and she would pause at the edge of a room, waiting for a cue, waiting for permission, waiting for the moment when entering would not feel like interrupting. If she opened the refrigerator, she did it quickly, and she closed it softly, as if the hinge could complain. If Chelsea left toys out, Nancy would scoop them up before anyone saw, stacking them into neat piles like evidence being removed.

At the sink, she washed dishes as if speed could prove character. The water ran hot. Soap and steam. She scrubbed with a kind of urgency that was not about cleanliness; it was about not being noticed, not being the reason someone sighed. If a plate clinked too loudly, she would glance up, eyes flicking to faces, checking for irritation. Then she would smile, reflexive, polite, and say something like, "Sorry, I have it," even when no one had asked.

She folded herself into the routines of the house. She made her coffee small. When my wife said something sharp, Nancy would laugh as if it were funny, or as if being agreeable could keep the air from turning solid. When someone teased her, she would agree with the tease, quick, preemptive, so nobody else had to do it for her. Gratitude is supposed to be cheerful, so she performed cheerfulness as some people perform a job interview, with her back straight and her needs hidden behind her teeth.

And the apologies came out constantly, almost unconsciously. "Sorry," Nancy said as she passed behind you. "Sorry," she said when she reached for something. "Sorry," when Chelsea needed anything. "Sorry," when she existed in the hallway at the same time as someone else. Not overwrought, not self-pitying, just steady, like a metronome ticking in the background of her days.

As small as Nancy tried to make herself, the truth was that the condo wasn't big enough for all the feelings inside it. Doors didn't close cleanly.

Rooms weren't really rooms. Everything was shared: air, sound, routines, tension. Adults keep score without meaning to. They feel disrupted. They interpret silence as judgment, and movement as intrusion.

Our children and cousins love each other as children do, like magic. To them, this was play: games, sleepovers, the small joy of another kid in the room. They enjoyed having Chelsea there. They didn't see "extended guest." They saw "cousin." Kids can turn a cramped space into a kingdom.

But for adults, being together is different. For them, together means the bathroom schedule becomes a negotiation. It means food disappears faster, and someone notices even if no one says it. The living room never entirely belongs to anyone. You can't relax because someone else is always there to witness your relaxation, or your irritation.

Then there was my work. Y2K was coming. I was working in consulting at this point, which meant travel. It meant leaving on Mondays and returning on Fridays with my head still half inside a client site and my body already tired. My weeks were spent at airports, client buildings, and in rental cars. My weekends were supposed to be recovery. Instead, they turned into hand-offs.

I would come home, and the condo would be full, not just of people, but of the weight of people trying to be polite. Everyone was "fine." Everyone was trying not to say the sharp thing they were thinking.

The welcome of our home didn't disappear in a single argument. It thinned. Slowly. By degrees. By the accumulation of minor discomforts and unspoken resentments. Nancy felt it. Of course she did. She was sensitive to atmospheres. She adjusted herself accordingly, growing ever smaller, quieter, more helpful, because that's what she did when she didn't want to be the problem. At the same time, she handled her divorce like she handled everything: silently, with a calm face and an internal storm no one was invited to see.

Nancy's settlement was very low, and my having to support her was now on the table until she could stabilize. Seeking solutions, I constantly reevaluated our options, but they were limited. Nancy wasn't built to battle financially. She leaned on emotion and faith to steady herself, to keep going day to day, while I kept trying to turn her situation into a plan with steps and numbers.

For my father and me, this set off a new dynamic. He was as assertive as I am in business matters, but short on the ante when it came to helping.

I remember one call with him in particular. I was at my kitchen table with a legal pad in front of me, the kind that makes a mess look manageable if you give it columns. I had written down what Nancy's settlement was, what her bills were, what she owed, and what she would need to get through a month without borrowing from the next. The numbers did not argue. They just sat there.

Dad listened, and at first, he spoke the way he usually spoke when he was comfortable. Quick, certain. The same tone he used for sports, for politics, for anything he could take a side on without being asked to carry it.

"Try this," he said. "Have her do that. Ask her lawyers for more."

He said it like it was a play call.

I explained again what the settlement actually was, what it meant in real life, and what it left Nancy with. I could hear myself being careful, keeping my voice even, laying it out in plain terms so it couldn't be misunderstood.

Of course, Dad did what he always did when he heard something he didn't want to hear. He got quiet. This was not a thoughtful kind of quiet, nor was it the quiet of someone absorbing hard news. It was a retreat. The line went thin with pauses. I could almost feel Dad waiting for me to get him out of it, hoping I would take the burden off him by changing the subject or by solving it without his help. The silence stretched long enough that I checked the receiver against my ear, as if the call had dropped.

"You still there?" I said.

"I'm here," he answered, but the words came slowly, as if each one cost him something.

In that lull, I heard something else, faint and close to the mouthpiece. A second presence on the line. A small shift, a breath, and then Liz's voice, not directed at me, but at him, as if she were feeding him lines. She must have been on the other landline extension. Her hand wasn't covering the receiver properly.

"Tell him to have her go back," she said, half-whispered, sharp with certainty. "Tell him to make the lawyer do more. That's what lawyers are for."

Dad cleared his throat, and then he repeated it almost word for word, as if the suggestion had appeared in his mind fully formed.

"Well," he said, "she needs to fight. She needs to push back. She can't just accept it. She should go back to the attorney. She should make them do their job."

It sounded assertive, but it also kept Dad out of the line of fire. He made no offer of money. No offer to cover a bill. All he did was dole out instructions from a distance. He could stay in the conversation as a voice without becoming a hand. And now I could hear where the voice was coming from, the deflection taking shape in real time, Liz tossing him ideas like lifelines so neither of them had to admit what was being asked of them.

I felt the frustration rise in me, sharp and familiar. Dad could be forceful when the subject was winning. When the subject was responsibility, he became quiet and slow, full of pauses, leaving room for someone else to step in.

And that was the new dynamic. Dad's silence became a tool. His suggestions became a way to look involved while staying clear of the cost. It gave him a focal point for deflection, and it left me doing what I had always done, taking the weight that arrived and turning it into something that could be solved.

That night, as I drove back from the hospital, I went over the things that came to mind.

Tomorrow, the hospice bed would be delivered, as would the oxygen and other machinery. After work, I'd drive back to the hospital to discharge Nancy into the home we would make around her, her last home.

But I could still feel the earlier version of home, too: the condo bridge, the cramped rooms, the unspoken friction, Nancy trying to be invisible, me traveling for work and returning on weekends to a house full of people, strained.

Two northbound journeys. Two versions of rescue. In both, Nancy was trying to make it easier for everyone else.

I can still feel the weight of those years strung on a key ring.

Even now, driving, my hand sometimes closes around a jumble of metal and plastic that shouldn't still matter, even if it's the keys to places Nancy was forced to live in. Apartments that were too small, temporary rooms that were never meant to hold a whole life. They ride with me like evidence. Like a journal I never asked to keep.

After the condo, after the first thin sense of "we're not going to die from this," Nancy moved into her own small apartment and tried to make ordinary life out of what had happened. It wasn't glamorous. It was functional. A sparse living room, cheap groceries, the sort of place where you learn quickly what you can live without because you don't have the luxury of pretending.

Nancy's frugal years started there in earnest. This phase of her life was her time of quiet discipline, of making do. Stretching food. Choosing bills. Learning that "maybe later" is a permanent category to sort things into.

Struggling financially certainly changes your priorities, whether you admit it or not.

A while later, Nancy told me about bounced checks. About the debt. It wasn't that she didn't care, but scarcity turns everything into triage. You choose what hurts now and what can hurt later.

Not wanting to see her suffer Mom's fate as I had lived through it, I paid for what I could. I took the pressure off where I could. Having to watch my mother's late-life pivot, I had learned something ugly and useful: Redefining your life late is brutal. It isn't inspirational. It's exhausting. It's fear with a calendar attached. And the body pays for it.

So, with Nancy, I wasn't just helping a sister. I was trying to prevent a repeat. As Nancy was more emotionally grounded than I was, more relational, she kept focusing on visitation schedules, visit coordination, and maintaining a workable story for Chelsea. I was pragmatic. I wanted structure. I wanted to work. I wanted stability. Nancy wanted the people around her to hurt less.

For a while, she leaned on me, and I let her. I didn't mind the weight of it. However, I did mind everyone else's silence.

I can still see one of those late nights in the rented condo we stayed in while waiting for my new house to be built. The place would go quiet after Chelsea was asleep, the kind of quiet that isn't restful, just empty. I would sit out on the deck and look toward the northern New Jersey hills, dark shapes under a darker sky. The air had that night-cool edge that makes you pull your shoulders in. Somewhere below, a car would pass, and the sound would fade the way everything fades when you're trying not to think too hard.

Nancy came out after a phone call. I could tell before she said anything. Her face had that tightened look, the one she wore when she was trying to keep herself from falling into anger. She moved as if she were carrying something heavy, trying to do so neatly. She had been talking with her ex-husband, trying to figure out the next moves, and the conversation had left its residue on her.

She stood in the doorway for a second, as if deciding whether to disturb me, then stepped onto the deck and came to the chair beside mine. She sat down and looked out for a moment, not at the view exactly, but through it.

"How are you doing?" I asked.

She exhaled, small and controlled. "OK, I suppose."

That was Nancy. A few words. Minimal complaint. No demand that I fix it in that instant. But I knew the mechanics of her days then. She was the one who dropped Chelsea off at her former in-laws' for visitations. She was the one picking her up again. She was the one driving back into a life that still didn't feel settled, a life that kept forcing her to rehearse loss in practical errands. It left her blue in a way she didn't quite name, off-balance in a way that had nothing to do with her body.

We sat with it a moment. The night air. The quiet. My mind was already reaching for plans and contingencies, for structure, for how to make the next week less fragile. I wanted stability, the way a drowning person wants a ledge.

Nancy lifted her head a little higher, almost as if she were reminding herself how to stand on the inside.

"I have faith that things will be all right," she said.

It was the most Nancy sentence in the world. Not denial. Not naivete. A choice. A decision to not worry about what she couldn't control, to keep herself from being consumed by the unfairness of it. Her faith sustained her from collapsing into depression, and my presence, I think, gave her a ballast in the dark, something steady to sit beside while she did what she always did.

But that sentence also carried tension for those around her because it raised the long-standing question we kept circling back to. What does it mean to help someone who won't fight as others would? Someone who chooses peace over justice, even when peace costs money.

Then we all moved from the rented condo to my newly constructed home in central New Jersey.

We finally moved when the new house was finished. A new home promised to make everything feel settled. Lacking other options, Nancy and

Chelsea moved in with us, too, into the fourth bedroom. All of us under one roof, brand new walls trying to hold old stress.

It should have been a relief. In a way, it was. There was space. Some doors could be closed. Some routines could be established.

But the increased "space" of the new house didn't eliminate friction. Instead, it just gave it room to echo.

Nancy was working on new routines after the divorce, on visitation, on rebuilding her life inside another person's household. She tried to be invisible again, helpful, quiet, grateful, but now there were more variables. Kids. Food.

While we had more square footage, the place became smaller.

In my family's brand-new home, Chelsea and our girls were kids. They wanted candy, juice, and sweets, as kids do. Nancy's parenting style was more indulgent than ours and didn't align with how we were raising our kids. And when the girls argued, as cousins do, it created tension that wasn't just about children. The tension in joint family dynamics arose as adults interpreted the arguments as evidence. Household values and clashes began to chafe, gathering into rising storm clouds.

And there was money, always, quietly given money.

In those days, I was busy establishing myself in a new house, and I was the primary earner. There were new-house costs that don't show up in the brochure: landscaping, repairs, appliances, the constant drip of "we need" that follows you room to room, and supporting Nancy, directly and indirectly, created pressure. Not because I resented Nancy. Because scarcity, even relative scarcity, makes people feel trapped.

Eventually, the hospitality ended, and whatever was on a person's mind then was said.

Nancy would have to get a job and make her exit.

My wife and I spoke about it briefly and privately. Not as a debate, not as a speech. Just the sober recognition that we couldn't keep living on top of each other and calling it sustainable. There was no villain in it. There was fatigue. There was the ordinary limit that arrives when a household is stretched past what it was built to hold.

So, I asked Nancy if we could talk. It wasn't a formal sit-down. It was the kind of conversation you stage around logistics, because the house is full of ears and you don't want the words to become part of the walls.

She was in the garage, halfway between staying and leaving. The door was open, and cold daylight spilled in, flattening everything. The garage still held too much of her life. Stacked bins, taped boxes, and a few moving items we had pulled from storage after we left the condo. The air had that garage smell: dust, cardboard, and a faint trace of motor oil. Nancy had her keys in her hand and her bag over her shoulder. She was heading out to her former in-laws to pick up Chelsea.

I stepped in beside her and kept my voice low, not because I was whispering, but because the house was close behind us. The only sounds were the soft rattle of keys and the distant hum of something running inside.

"Nant," I said.

She paused with her hand on the car door and looked up at me. She didn't ask what. She didn't need the setup. Her face shifted in the smallest way, like she had already been carrying the same thought and was waiting for someone else to say it first.

"I need you to start thinking about next steps," I said, keeping my tone practical because practicality was the only way I could say it without breaking apart. "Work. A place of your own. A plan."

She held still for a moment, eyes lowered, and I could see her swallow. Then she nodded, small and steady.

"I know," she said softly.

Somewhere in the house, a door clicked. Both of us went quiet for a beat, listening, as if footsteps might follow. Nancy tightened her grip on the keys, then lifted her shoulders, that familiar gesture of bracing.

"OK," she said, and it was both agreement and a way of keeping herself moving. She opened the car door, slid in, and started the engine. The sound filled the garage and covered what we hadn't said. Then she backed out slowly and drove off to pick up Chelsea as if nothing had just shifted, as if she hadn't just been asked to imagine a different life.

Then her face changed, not drastically, but in that small way people change when the shame arrives, trying to keep it contained. She looked down at her hands.

"I shouldn't have come," she said.

"That's not what I'm saying," I answered, too quickly.

But she kept going, because Nancy's instinct was always to take the burden off everyone else by putting it back onto herself.

"I put you in a bad spot," she said. "I put your family in a bad spot."

She said it plainly, without accusation, as if she were logging a fact. Like if she admitted it clearly enough, she could make it right.

I felt awful because the truth was more complicated than that. Nancy did need a job. She did need her own footing. But she also needed time, and time is the one resource people refuse to give when they feel crowded.

So, I kept things functional. I told Nancy I would help. I told her we would make a plan. I did not dress it up as a moral lesson. I did not pretend it was easy. I just tried to get her from that moment to the next one without letting it turn into humiliation.

Afterward, you could see what she did with the information. She became even quieter. Even more helpful. She moved through the house like someone practicing how to leave without leaving a mess, trying to make her exit feel like relief rather than rejection.

So, we moved Nancy again.

Another U-Haul carried Nancy's things away from our house. Another set of keys was handed to her, and a new attempt at a fresh start that wasn't actually fresh, just necessary, began.

I helped her move into a small shared home, one of those arrangements that looks workable on paper and feels precarious the moment you step inside.

It wasn't a normal house with a normal front door. It was the converted back end of someone else's place, two rooms carved out of what had once been private space. To get in, you had to go around back, where the entrance felt like an afterthought, an old staircase rising into darkness. There was no porch light, no welcome, no ordinary sense of arrival, just a bare bulb hanging outside that threw a thin yellow circle onto the steps. At night, it made the place look temporary, even when it wasn't supposed to. The type of rental where you understand, before you've even set a box down, that you're not meant to take up too much space.

We moved fast, because I always do when I'm anxious. I kept loading the U-Haul, lifting, stacking, making decisions about weight and balance, and what could slide and what couldn't. I was in that narrow, familiar mode, solving the problem in front of me so I didn't have to feel the bigger one behind it.

Then the gate latch got me.

It was a stupid, sharp accident, the kind that happens when you're moving too quickly and not looking where the metal edge is. I swung past the gate, and the latch caught my scalp, clean and vicious. There was a moment of nothing, then the sudden warmth, and then my hand came away wet.

Not a trickle. A gush.

Blood ran down my face and into my collar, and I felt that strange, detached clarity that comes with a real injury, how your mind goes quiet and starts sorting the next steps like a checklist. I stepped into the garage and pressed rags against my head, holding pressure, trying to keep the bleeding contained. I could hear the sounds of moving outside, the ordinary noise of boxes and voices and footsteps, and I didn't want to turn the day into another emergency, another scene, another reason for Nant to feel like the problem had followed her into the next place.

I kept the rags on, kept my head down, and slipped past them as if I needed something from the car. I grabbed my keys without announcing myself. I got in, drove to the emergency room, and sat under fluorescent lights while someone stitched my scalp back together. The doctor peeled back what felt like a flap of skin and worked with calm, practiced hands as I stared at the floor and waited for it to be done.

When I came back, I put on a hat.

I walked back into the move like nothing had happened and went right back to loading boxes, lifting furniture, and packing the truck. The day continued. Nancy's life still needed to be moved from one place to another. My job, as usual, was to keep the machinery running.

I didn't tell the kids.

I didn't want them to be scared. I didn't want Nancy to feel guilty. I didn't want to add one more "problem" to a day already full of them. So, I wiped the blood off, hid the wound, kept moving, and later patched myself up.

A metaphor, if you want one: bleeding quietly while you keep everyone else calm.

Nancy settled in. I drove home with the key ring feeling heavier in my pocket.

Teaching, at least, gave her something solid. Nancy loved teaching. She had a compass for it. She could be bossy, strong-willed, certain, sometimes exhausting in the way only a person with a clear internal standard can be. That strength was part of what made her a good teacher. It was also part of what created friction in a shared household. Strong people don't always fit gently into other people's routines.

Meanwhile, I still talked to Dad sometimes. He'd say he sent Nancy something to help her, as if something would ever come as help. Liz would admire what I was doing; she'd say the words, the little compliments that sound supportive, but not much else would follow.

Then I would hear about their trips. To Spain. England. The kind of trips that imply money is not, in fact, impossible. The type of spending that reveals priorities. Lost youth being reclaimed, earned for them, as if the past was a bill that entitled them to pleasure now, without any obligation to pay forward, without any urgency to stabilize the child and granddaughter who were falling.

All the while, Nancy was rebuilding from the bottom up. At the same time, I was carrying the load. Dad was deflecting, mainly. Liz applauded from a distance, then boarded a plane.

Still, Nancy kept her focus where it always went: on Chelsea, not on frictions behind reality, or on making the story survivable for someone else.

Competence returned. Disappointments stayed. Meanwhile, my work kept pulling me farther away, consulting, travel, the road, so that "home" became something I only visited on weekends, carrying exhaustion back into a house that had become, for a time, a shelter for too many lives.

I'd done this kind of preparation before, quietly, in advance, back when keeping Nancy safe required forms instead of medicine.

12

Good Penmanship

My penmanship is horrible. Definitely not one of my core strengths. In a week like this, that becomes a small liability in itself, which is why I texted myself the to-do list instead. Even the notes I'd written on the back of Joe's eulogy, the paper still in my pocket, were already degrading into guesswork. I could make out every other word, and the missing ones mattered.

Before Nancy could be discharged, there was paperwork to attend to. Hospice tasks. Signatures. Calls that had to happen in the proper order. So I drove back to my home to organize it. There were all sorts of forms, lists, and phone numbers. The kind of administrative reality that makes grief feel like a job you can't clock out of. I spread things out as I always do when something feels fragile: I try to make it visible and sortable, and to reduce the chance of missing a critical detail.

In the middle of that, pen on paper, names on screens, I stopped and thought about something that wasn't medical. People. The ones Nancy had loved before her life had narrowed down, the ones she hadn't spoken to in years, not because she didn't care but because she didn't want to be the reason anyone carried worry.

"Can I reach out to some of your old friends?" I asked her later.

Nancy's instinct was immediate. "I don't want people worrying," she said.

"I know," I told her. "But…now it doesn't really matter if they worry anymore."

She sat with that a moment, and then she nodded once, quiet permission, not surrender.

"Okay," she said. "You can."

I didn't do this because I wanted to be away from her, but because I knew what the next twenty-four hours would look like if I didn't get ahead of the details: hospice forms, power of attorney confirmations, the call chain that had to run in the proper order so the bed didn't arrive before there was space to put it, so the discharge didn't stall because one signature was missing or one fax didn't go through.

The house was quiet when I walked in, like a room that knew something heavy was coming and was pretending not to.

I went straight to what we now call the office, with a desk, a printer, and folders that always seemed to multiply. When we moved up from the condo into this house, it served as the fourth bedroom. For a while, it was Nancy's. Her things sat in it the way a person's things sit when she's trying not to take up too much space, folded, stacked, kept neat enough that the room could be "given back" without an argument. Even when she needed help, she had a way of making sure it didn't cost anyone anything.

Afterward, she moved on, after that first year, after life rearranged again, the bed went out, the dresser went out, and the label changed. "Office. "

I set my laptop on the kitchen table and spread its contents out: Nancy's life in documents. Names, dates, addresses. The tidy boxes make a person look manageable when she has been holding herself together with nails and willpower.

I pulled out her tax returns.

I'd done Nancy's taxes for years. One more way of keeping her from sliding sideways. But this time, I wasn't pulling them out to file them. I was pulling them because I didn't want to worry about a funeral home later. That sentence feels wrong to say, even now. Practical and obscene at the same time. But I know myself. I know what happens when I leave something like that for "later." Later becomes a moment when I can't think straight, when grief turns my brain into fog, when the smallest logistic decision feels like a personal betrayal.

The paper asks for facts, and grief refuses them.

So, I registered for an undertaker's services and filled out the form, knowing it was her vitals for the death certificate. I looked up cremation services. I gathered the power of attorney to prove you are authorized to do what you are about to do. I did as much preliminary work as possible early on so it wouldn't catch me by surprise later.

And while her name sat on the screen in official boxes, reducing ordinary life to lines and numbers, I felt the weight of a key ring in my pocket. I still have keys to the places Nancy was forced to live in. It's not on purpose. They are not sentimental artifacts. I just never took the key ring off. There is an apartment key. A house key that stopped being hers. A key to a place that was never meant to hold a whole life. They ride with me like evidence.

I stared at her tax return and thought, *"This is also a marker of survival."* What she earned. What she didn't. How thin the margins were. How much of her adulthood was spent improvising stability while pretending it didn't cost her pride.

I closed the laptop for a moment and sat back, letting the present do what it always does, pull the past forward by the collar.

Because when Nancy said, "Take me home" in that hospital room, she wasn't only asking for the hospice bed, oxygen, and nurse schedule to be coordinated. She was asking for the oldest thing she'd asked for without ever saying it out loud:

A place where she could be without being a burden.

That is what that tiny home outside Trenton had been.

In the early 2000s, when she bought that house, she did so to claim her own space. That was her front door. A key that meant she wasn't borrowing space anymore.

I remember the first time I saw the mortgage papers on the table, the crispness of new keys, how her face lit up and then tightened again, as if she didn't trust joy to stay. When you've had so much taken, you learn not to celebrate too loudly. You handle good news carefully, as if it might crack.

Her Trenton area home made her feel relaxed enough to breathe. But there lay the trap: Once you breathe, you notice how easily breathing can be taken away. Chelsea, always watching, had something stable to lean on when Nancy returned to teaching. But stability doesn't live in a vacuum. It lives in a world of money, distance, and bodies that get tired. I tried to keep helping, but with me constantly traveling for work, my options were limited. After all, the support I provided them with had always been the kind you can do from the side: money, repairs, planning, the unromantic mechanics.

There's a kind of help you can't deliver from a hotel room. That's where Brian came into the picture. I think about him now because in this hospice phase, Chelsea and Brian were the ones in the room with me. Their presence carried a weight. They understood what was happening to Nancy's body and what was happening to the rest of us without needing me to translate it, either.

Brian had met Nancy in Stockton, back when she was still teaching and still trying to pretend the floor beneath her feet wasn't shifting. He entered her life quietly, making no announcements and no demands. He was not a romantic hero. Not a savior. He was something even rarer: a steady witness.

He was a devout Catholic, and Nancy was a person of faith. Their connection sat in that world of prayer and duty, in the shared language of endurance. It was platonic, but intimate in as many ways as two people can be intimate when their bond isn't about romance: It's about showing up.

I can see the objects of their relationship even now: a church parking lot after an evening service, the dim light of a dashboard as someone sits and finishes a difficult call, the soft cadence of familiar words spoken in a kitchen when the day has been too heavy. Faith-filled words. A late-night phone call.

The type of support that costs him something, quietly.

Brian didn't help Nancy from a distance. He helped her daily. Bore the inconveniences for it. Suffered the unglamorous. He was there on random Tuesdays when fatigue hit her like a wall. He was close enough to notice small changes. Close enough to carry things. Close enough to keep Chelsea from feeling like the whole world was collapsing.

He was close when Nancy's body began to revolt, which was a blessing. He was there for the pain. The fatigue. The fog was more than just "tired." The symptoms didn't come with a clean narrative arc. When she finally went to the doctor, fibromyalgia arrived like a sentence, one of those diagnoses people debate when they're not the one living inside it. But I watched what it did: how it narrowed her days, how it made ordinary tasks feel like punishment.

Once again, this was eerily similar to watching Mom's rheumatoid arthritis take hold under stress. Different diseases, different mechanics, but the same cruel truth: The body keeps score. It takes what the mind tries to swallow and turns it into something physical you can't talk your way out of.

Mom's joints paid for her rupture. Nancy's body paid for hers. In both cases, the bill wasn't just for medical care. It was the cost of redefining your life late, under pressure, with too many obligations and too little margin. I could pay off the debts. I could buy a car. I could make logistics happen. I could handle paperwork, plans, and everything that keeps a person from falling through the cracks.

But I could not, from a distance, sit in the room when the fatigue pinned her down. Brian could.

The Trenton area home had been a lifeline.

Brian had been one, too, as had Chelsea.

And I, moving in and out, traveling, working, returning on weekends, fixing what I could, had been something else: present in the ways I knew how to be, absent in the ways I couldn't control. Financially close. Geographically far. A voice on the phone. A set of keys in a pocket.

As I kept sorting through Nancy's tax returns, outside, the night pressed against the windows. Inside, the house waited. Tomorrow, the hospice bed was due to arrive at Chelsea's. After work, I'd drive back to help because Nancy had asked to go home.

I knew deep in my bones that the story we were entering was the one where the only thing that matters is who shows up. Every day, in the hard moments. In the hours that no one photographs.

That's what Brian had done back then. And that's what we were going to do now.

I searched through Nancy's papers, fueled by pure adrenaline, as I always do, pushing feelings away. In this haze, I found the mortgage documents again in a folder labeled with my sloppy handwriting.

"Ewing."

I had forgotten the exact look of the paperwork, the weight of the envelope, the formal language of a house that was tiny. One bedroom. Built in 1940. Only slightly bigger than Mom's house, where Nancy and I had grown up cramped and stacked on top of each other in narrow rooms. The repetition was so blunt it felt like a joke, life circling back, putting her in a small house again, as if small spaces were all our family could ever afford.

But the Trenton home was different because I was determined that it would end differently.

I had been doing well then, as many consultants do. Money comes in fast and goes out fast, and you learn not to get sentimental about it. I didn't want Nancy to be "set" in theory. I wanted her set in a deed. So, I bought the property jointly with her. Not because she couldn't do anything herself, but because time matters when you're trying to rebuild. Because stability buys you breath. Because Chelsea needed a steady place for school, and Nancy needed a front door that didn't feel borrowed.

I carried that mortgage. Over time, I paid it down. It became one more quiet structure under Nancy's life, one more thing that wouldn't wobble if everything else did.

But just then, Nancy's teaching began to wobble because of her then-mysterious ailment.

Even with Brian close by, even with Nancy holding on to the means by which she always held on, the floor, which had already been shifting, started giving way. Her job didn't just end; it frayed. There were a few bad days. A few misunderstandings. A few absences due to illness, not laziness. Then the box appeared. Termination papers. A cardboard container was placed in her hands, making your whole professional life look like a handful of objects.

In the end, Nancy lost her job.

The house thus became at risk. There wasn't a single shocking foreclosure notice, but there was the slow accumulation of bills, the pain from fibromyalgia, and the loss of energy. Events like this are how things collapse for people like Nancy: not in spectacle, but in gravity. The weight adds up. The margin disappears.

The disability forms arrived soon after, bringing with them the strange humiliation of proving you can't do what you used to do. The language of limitation is printed in tidy sections. Fibromyalgia isn't an easy illness to pin down, if that's what it was. It's a fog in the body. It makes everything heavier. It makes the day feel like a hill you have to climb. Watching Nancy move into disability for fibromyalgia felt eerily close to watching Mom's arthritis claim her. Different diagnosis, same cruel result: Stress doesn't just live in your head. It takes up residence.

By then, in 2004, Nancy still did what Nancy always did: She started caring for someone else. Grandma Arline was getting older now. Her own long life had worn her down. There were lunches where the table felt like a quiet chapel. I can picture Nancy feeding Arline with small bites of rice pudding with gentle patience, the sort of tenderness that came naturally to her because she was built for it. Care-giving wasn't an identity Nancy adopted later; it was her default setting.

And the irony of it all hit me again: Nancy, whose own life had been made small by other people's decisions, still found it in herself to make room for someone else. That year, we decided to do one last Christmas together at my home in central New Jersey. Dad and Liz had moved to Georgia by this point, Dad's dream location, his new chapter. They drove up for the holiday as if geography could erase history. Liz brought her birds. That detail alone tells you that Liz got the things she loved, regardless of whether the household could hold them.

The visit added pressure to the holiday, bringing together too many bodies, too many opinions, too much time to talk. Driven by all this, the family conversation grappled for somewhere to land and vent the nervous tension it had been suffused with. Inevitably, it landed in the elephant in the room: Nancy's disability, at least at first. Then it turned to her money. It turned to her "plan," and then, ultimately, the question of who was going to carry what.

So, I asked Dad for help.

It was Christmas Eve. Upstairs, someone was reading to the kids, the soft cadence of a story drifting down the stairs in broken phrases, a voice doing its best to make the night feel safe and ordinary. Downstairs, the house was lit mostly by the tree. Colored bulbs reflected in the glass ornaments, casting small patches of light onto the walls. The air smelled like whatever had been cooked earlier and the sweet, stale edge of wrapping paper and pine.

I was moving through the kitchen, cleaning as I went, trying to reset the room for Christmas morning. Plates in the sink. Counters wiped. A dish towel over my shoulder. I could hear the low murmur of the television from the family room. Dad was down there with Nancy, the two of them in the same space but not really together. Liz had taken herself upstairs to the spare room and left the television on, her kind of presence, nearby but separate.

I saw an opening. Not a phone call. Not a message passed through someone else. A real window where I could speak to him in person, with Nancy in range of my eyes in the kitchen and out of earshot, so she wouldn't have to sit through it as if she were an agenda item.

I walked into the family room and stood near the edge of the tree light. Dad was in a chair. The television kept talking, bright and meaningless.

"Dad," I said, keeping my voice low because the story upstairs was still going, and because I didn't want this conversation to become part of the house. "Can I talk to you a second?"

He muted the television, or lowered the volume, something like that, and looked at me as if I'd interrupted a commercial. I waited until his eyes met mine.

"I need help with Nancy," I said. I didn't dress it up. "Just until she stabilizes. I'm doing what I can, but it's not sustainable."

Dad's face changed slightly, the way it always did when a conversation turned heavy. He did not look at Nancy when he answered. He looked past her, toward the safe objects in the room: the television, the plate on the side table, the remote in his hand, anything that wasn't her face.

His voice stayed practical and small, like he was discussing a leaky faucet, not a life.

"Well," he said, and the word dragged out like a delay, "you know I'm retired."

He paused, not because he was thinking, but because he was hoping I would take the burden back, change the subject, let him off.

"Funds are limited," he added. "Things are tied up."

He stacked the reasons one on top of another, each one placed carefully as if it could block the next request. Retired. Limited. Tied up. He didn't say no outright. He built a wall out of explanations and stood behind it.

Then, without any pause for the hypocrisy of it, he pivoted into solutions that cost him nothing. The same script I had heard before, and would hear again.

"Have her apply here or there," he said. "Ask her lawyer for more."

The words landed like a hand-off, not advice. It was a way to stay clean. A way to be involved without being implicated.

I felt something tighten in me. No surprise. I had lived this pattern. But the timing, on Christmas Eve, with the tree lit and the kids upstairs being read a story, made it sting differently. The house was trying so hard to be tender and intact, and here he was, still practicing the same evasions, still finding the safe objects to look at, still asking me to carry what he wouldn't.

Upstairs, the reader's voice rose and fell, calm and steady. Downstairs, Dad picked the television back up with his eyes, already shifting toward distraction as if the conversation had been concluded by his refusal to engage.

Later, when I went upstairs past the spare room, I could hear Liz's television through the door. When she eventually surfaced, she told me she admired what I was doing. She said it like someone offering praise from a chair they have no intention of leaving. Her eyes stayed on the screen. Her body stayed turned away. She didn't really bother to fit in with us because, by her posture and her silence, she was there only for Dad.

My mind naturally and inevitably went back to Grandpa Alfred's funeral then.

Nancy and I went there with Dad and his brother, a few cousins, and sparse attendance that made the room look sad if you didn't know what Grandpa Alfred had been. Grandma Arline sat with the quiet dignity of someone who had survived decades by swallowing. Nancy comforted her because Nancy always did. A small, low-key service unfolded, no grand speeches. No myth-making.

Then the funeral director asked if anyone wanted to say a few words.

No one moved a muscle or made a sound.

Not a cough. Not a shift in a chair. Stillness. It told me everything I needed to know.

The director waited a beat longer than was comfortable, then cleared his throat and said, "Well...he had good penmanship."

I couldn't help it, I laughed.

It was funny, and it was accurate in the bleak way accuracy can be. A life reduced to the one thing no one could argue with.

It hit me as both absurd and perfect. I leaned toward Nancy and whispered, "I'd better do better. My penmanship stinks." An inside joke, small and bright in a room that didn't have much brightness in it. We carried that line with us for years. A sentence that made us laugh because it was true, and because it was also a warning.

And sitting now in my home with Nancy's paperwork open in front of me, looking up identifiers for a funeral home because I knew what it felt like to be lost in grief and logistics at the same time, I felt that chill settle in. I saw it for what it was: recognition, not fear.

What a person leaves behind, if you're not careful, can be summarized by someone else in a sentence you didn't choose.

That the only antidote to that kind of legacy in our family has always been the same:

Show up.

Pay it forward.

Do better than "better."

I texted Chelsea to confirm the equipment was scheduled for delivery when she or Brian was home. I then finished Nancy's paperwork on the computer, making sure that at least my penmanship wasn't falling short. Out of habit, I grabbed a spare binder to manage it all.

Packaging everything up with a change of clothes and supplies for a few days, I headed back south to Nancy and Chelsea's new home.

13

Home

Chelsea's house in Roebling was new to her, new to Nancy, and new to the phase we were about to enter. A brick row home on a tight street, close to the sidewalk, close to the neighbors, built for working families who lived upright lives in narrow footprints. Inside, it had the kind of layout that looks straightforward on paper, a living room up front, a dining space that funnels you toward the kitchen, and stairs tucked in where they always are in houses like that. About eleven hundred square feet of ordinary life, the type of place that is supposed to hold birthdays and groceries and chores, not oxygen tanks and medication logs.

We tried to take the hospice bed upstairs anyway, because that is what you do at first, you assume the bedroom is where a bed belongs. Two of us on the frame, one person guiding the feet, rotating it inch by inch, calling out the turn like a sofa delivery. The stairway narrowed fast. The angle tightened. The landing did not give. The bed struck the house's geometry and stopped with finality. There was no way to force it without damaging the walls, the bed, or the people holding it.

So, we backed it down, carefully, slower than we carried it up, like returning something fragile to the ground.

And that is how the living room became the room.

Nancy looked at it, then at me.

"Well," she said, "put me in the living room like Grandpap, just don't drop me this time. And I don't even subscribe to the Sunday paper."

I could see her wry smile, even though she couldn't really see me anymore. She still knew exactly how to bust my chops with sarcasm when we both needed it.

It was dark humor, but it was ours, a small pressure valve. And once Nancy said it, I knew exactly where our minds would go when the house went quiet.

As Nancy settled in, we began reminiscing, and I connected her with a few old friends we had grown up with near Mom's house when we were children. Once Nancy allowed me to, I started reaching outward, searching for names that had gone quiet decades ago. Nancy had lost contact with most people long before this. Not because she didn't care, she did, but because she never wanted to be the reason someone carried worry. One particular name came back first: Kathy.

Kathy had grown up near Mom's first house, near that dead-end street when Nancy and I were kids. She and Nancy were best friends in that totally unquestioned way childhood friends are. They were pen pals when life pulled them apart, and somewhere along their journey, the letters stopped, and the years did what years do.

I found her on social media and sent a message that felt like it belonged to another lifetime.

It was Bill.

She responded fast. Later, she told me, "I knew immediately it was you, and I knew immediately something was very wrong."

We got on the phone. I didn't dress things up. I told Kathy that Nancy was terminally ill and that if she wanted to talk, we could set up video calls. Kathy didn't hesitate. She said yes as if the question had never existed.

In the days that followed, I started arranging calls, little rectangles of light on a screen, old names and old faces reentering the room. Nancy couldn't see or hear well anymore, not the way she used to, but something still reached her. You could tell from how her mouth softened, how her hand tightened around mine, and how the room felt briefly less clinical and more like life.

Kathy did one better than calls. She flew out to see her.

She told me later that it had been her husband who pushed her. He said she would regret it if she didn't go. He said the money didn't matter. What mattered was showing up. Kathy listened. She booked the flight. She didn't make a production of it. She just arrived.

Brian and I picked her up and took her to a nearby small hotel. The house was already crowded, the living room compressed by the hospice bed, the dining table, the equipment, the rhythm of people rotating through a space that no longer belonged to normal life. We didn't want her to feel like one more body in the way. We wanted her visit to have room.

When she came to the house, she came like someone stepping onto sacred ground, moving carefully, voice low, eyes taking in the scene before she allowed herself to react to it. She sat in the living room with us first, hands folded in her lap, listening as we explained what had changed, what the hours looked like, when the nurse would come, and how Nancy was doing that day. The hospice nurse arrived while Kathy was there, and Kathy watched quietly and respectfully, letting the professional do their work without trying to insert herself.

Then we brought her to Nancy.

Kathy sat down at the side of the bed and did not flinch. She didn't lean away from the tubes or the quiet machinery. She leaned in. She took Nancy's hand and held it as if it had always been her hand to hold. She climbed onto the edge of the bed the way close friends do when there is no longer any need for formality. No panic. Just presence.

She started talking, and it wasn't exactly a conversation. It was a gathering. She talked to her the way people speak when they are trying to fit decades into minutes. The old neighborhood. The dead-end street. The dumb kid stories. The funny things were small. Who married whom? Who moved where? Names that hadn't been said in years reentered the room like they still had a right to be there.

Nancy couldn't always track the words, but her face changed as Kathy spoke. Her mouth softened. When her eyes opened, they tried to find the source of the voice. Her hand tightened around mine and then around Kathy's, as if her body understood before her mind could. For stretches of time, the room felt less like a hospice and more like the past, like childhood, like sunlight on a front lawn, like a house before it became a place where people came to say goodbye.

At one point, Kathy was back in the living room talking with Chelsea, and Nancy turned her head slightly toward me and whispered, her voice thin but clear.

"Take her to dinner," she said. "She's our guest."

Even then, even there, Nancy was still arranging care, still making room.

That night, Brian and I took Kathy out to Nancy's favorite pizzeria. The place smelled like baked dough and garlic, and the heat from the ovens fogged the front windows. Kathy ate, but slowly. She kept circling back to Nancy, to the shock of seeing her like that, to the relief of being able to sit beside her anyway. She said again, quieter now, that she was glad her husband had insisted. She would have carried the regret if she hadn't come.

The next day, when it was time for Kathy to go, she returned to Nancy's bedside and sat with her one last time. Her voice softened. The stories slowed. And then there was a pause, long enough that you could feel Kathy searching for words and accepting, at the same time, that no words were correct.

"Goodbye, my old and dearest friend," she said finally. "Until we meet again."

She leaned in, hugged Nancy as gently as she could, and kissed her on the head.

I drove Kathy back to her hotel for her flight the next day in near silence. The silence wasn't empty. It was full of what you can't say without breaking open. In the car, she turned to me and hugged me hard, like she didn't know what else to do with the grief she'd just carried back into the present.

"I'm so sorry, Billy," she said.

People who knew me from my youth called me Billy. Hearing it just then, out of that old world, hit differently. It made the whole arc feel exposed: the carefree days, the years, and now this.

I went back to the house and sat with Nancy again. She was quieter after Kathy left, like the goodbye had landed where goodbyes landed. After a while, she squeezed my hand.

"Thank you," she said. For the moment. For letting one last piece of her life return to her in person.

There would be more calls after that, more cousins, more friends, faces on screens, voices trying to reach her. But Kathy's visit had been a goodbye you could feel in the room. Nancy held it, and for a moment, so did I.

Chelsea had bought the house in Roebling not long before Nancy and I met at the diner. It was purchased with the proceeds of the trust I set up, and I was relieved she finally had a place that could be home for herself, for Nancy, for whatever came next. I had wanted that stability for her for a long time.

Roebling sat south of where I lived. For the first few weeks, I would stop by after work, stay long enough to get the job done, then drive home. We began orchestrating the hand-offs early, based on Chelsea's schedule, Brian's availability, and my drives, because the real requirement was simple: Nancy could not be left alone.

The house was old, as Roebling itself is. It came from a time when the town ran on shifts and whistles, when men walked to work, when families learned to live inside narrow footprints and call it normal. The rooms were not small exactly, but they were purposeful. Hallways ran tight. Corners turned quickly. The stairs rose in a long, thin run, as if the house expected people to travel light and keep moving.

Modern needs feel big in a place like that. Not because the house is wrong, but because the house was built for a different kind of life. A sofa, a dining table, a crib, and a Christmas tree all fit inside. A hospital bed is a different category of furniture. It arrives with metal rails and a remote, the promise that someone will lie in it while everyone else keeps functioning around it.

Once the bed was in the living room, the logic of it settled in almost immediately. The front room had the best light. It had air. It had the easiest access to the kitchen and the bathroom. It had enough space for someone to sit close, for someone to pass through, for the small practical movements of care to happen without feeling like we were constantly bumping into each other. The living room did not isolate Nancy. It did the opposite. It kept her in the stream of the house.

She could hear the ordinary sounds of everyday life. Footsteps. Cabinets. Water running. The murmur of a conversation that was not being staged for her benefit. She was not upstairs behind a closed door where dying becomes private and lonely. She was where life still passed by, where someone could reach her without climbing stairs, where she could still be part of the home's center of gravity.

At first, the bed being downstairs was simply what the house demanded. Then it became what we wanted. Nancy said so with her tone, even before she said it with words. We all agreed, quietly and with relief. The bed in the living room was not a compromise. It was the right answer.

Against one wall, a drape covered a bookshelf of binders. On the other side, the dining table was pushed up against the wall, creating a narrow path from the living room to the kitchen. Nancy's head was toward the kitchen. Her feet were toward the front door and the stairs.

She was where she belonged, at the center of the home. Home isn't a feeling in hospice. It's a layout. It's where the work must happen.

The routine started slowly. Hospice nurses came in and out with prescriptions, advice, and check-ins. It became clear early that they would not be doing daily hands-on care. We would. Day to day. Hour to hour. And we had to work out the coverage so Nancy would never be alone.

We exchanged our cell numbers with the hospice coordinator, and they gave us an off-hours call-in number, since we realized the nurses didn't respond around the clock as hospital nurses do. It was shifted coverage, a rotating crew, and the house was now the ward. Medicines and supplies came through them, bought through their system, delivered like we were stocking a small unit. They told us to get gowns with back openings for easier changes. They spoke carefully about pain medications. There were no prescribed opioids yet, only if we got closer or if she truly needed them. "She doesn't seem to need it now," they said, like "now" was something you could trust. That was the moment it clicked: Hospice wasn't a person who would arrive to do the work. It was a framework. The work was ours.

Even getting to the house was a challenge. The street was tight: the row homes had space out front for one car, and after that, you were hunting. Most of us parked in a small lot at the end of the street and walked back in. It wasn't far, but it was never empty-handed. Bags. Food. Supplies. A pillow you forgot you needed until you were already there. On nights when you arrived tired after work, the walk felt longer than it was. Not a deterrent. Just another small tax paid in steps. We managed. We always seemed to manage.

One afternoon, Chelsea went downstairs and began opening the moving boxes containing the decorations. The basement still had that in-between look, half-storage, half-life, with cardboard stacked like a reminder that nothing about this year had been settled the usual way. She came back up with strands of lights and a bundle of ornaments, arms full, her hair falling forward as she climbed.

"We're doing it," she said, and there wasn't much room to argue with the tone.

We moved the tables to make space. Chairs scraped the floor. The living room shifted and reshaped itself around the hospice bed, around the dining table pushed aside, around the equipment that had become furniture. Then the tree came up, the base first, and we wrestled it into position at the foot of Nancy's bed. When it finally stood upright, it looked both right and strange, like a holiday placed into a room that had become a vigil.

Chelsea plugged in the lights, and they flickered on, soft and low. Nancy's face changed when she saw them. Her eyesight had been fading, but the lights were close enough, gentle enough, that she could still catch them. They twinkled at the foot of the bed where she could see them without turning her head.

Chelsea started hanging ornaments the way people do when they need something to be normal. She pulled out the ones marked with dates and names, the little record of holidays past. "First Christmas" ornaments for her and her husband. "First Christmas" for the year she was born. Pieces of evidence that time had moved forward and held them, at least for a while. Each ornament went up carefully, as if the tree could be a timeline and not just a decoration.

Somewhere in the middle of it, Chelsea started singing under her breath, then louder, letting the words carry her.

"It's beginning to look a lot like Christmas," she sang, half serious and half daring the universe to disagree.

I looked at Nancy under the tree, the bed, and the lights, and the whole arrangement, and my mouth did what it always does when I don't know how to hold the moment without breaking it.

"If Santa visits and sees you under the tree, Nancy," I said, "you're going to give him a start. Better have a plate of cookies ready for him."

Nancy smiled, small but real. The room loosened for a second. It wasn't relief we felt, not exactly. Just a breath.

We pulled Christmas forward. Nancy loved it. The tree stood at the foot of her bed. Lights twinkled low where she could see them even as her vision faded. And the church group agreed to come by and sing carols, as if the house needed, at least once, to be filled with something other than the sounds of machines and footsteps. Stockings went up. For a while, the room looked like life.

Nancy wanted oxygen nearby. It wouldn't cure anything, but it eased her. We made sure it was always close enough that she didn't have to ask twice. The green canister sat beside the bed in silent reassurance, something physical she could see and believe in. We paid extra for it and later had to return it separately, full, like an item checked out from a life that was ending. But while it was there, it gave her comfort, and that made the hassle worth it.

Nancy and I recalled the time when we would visit our mother's parents. Mom grew up in a small coal-mining town, and her home doubled as a funeral parlor; her uncle, an undertaker, used the living room for viewings. We remembered how strange it was visiting and having meals next to an open coffin. When our Grandpap Shem died, he, too, was at our side as we waited for the funeral the next day, an open coffin next to the dining room table.

Death and dying were routine for us in unusual ways by now, close enough to comment on, familiar enough to laugh at. Nancy was in the dining room, too, now. My thoughts shifted to our Grandpap Shem's viewing so many years ago. The funeral was held at his house, arranged by his brother, Uncle Norman.

Uncle Norman had lost an eye young, and in a coal town, that was the same as losing a future. During the Great Depression, you didn't get any sympathy from anyone. You got reassigned. When the mines closed, and the work dried up, he did what the family always did: He pivoted and carried his share. The town had limited options, so he became a mortician. It wasn't glamorous. It was necessary. And the family treated it the same way they treated everything hard: close together, practical, and laughing when they could.

"You remember Uncle Norman?" I asked Nancy.

"Yeah," she said. "When Uncle Norman babysat us, what were we, ten? That one time?" She looked at me. "He took his glass eye out and put it in a glass of water and said, 'Don't move. I'm keeping my eye on you!' and then left the room."

"Yeah." I laughed. "I was petrified and couldn't move a muscle."

Nancy smiled. "And then I teased you and said, 'Billy, there are dead bodies in the basement.'" She said it as though she could still see my face from back then, like she was still ten and still enjoying it.

"Mom came to pick us up after, and Norman told her we were the best-behaved kids he'd ever seen," she reminded me. "He said we didn't say or move a single muscle."

"Yes," I said, "and when Grandpap Shem passed, just before the service, Mom and Aunt Joan called me over."

The joke had been plausible because Mom and Aunt Joan hadn't been strangers to bodies. They had both worked as part-time mortician assistants alongside family, helping Uncle Norman and another family member in the funeral business.

Mom once said, "It's just like dressing a mannequin."

Nancy and I had looked at her when she said it, years before, because it was such a strange sentence to land in such an ordinary kitchen. But she'd meant it literally, not cruelly. When they first relocated to Brooklyn, the family needed money, and the mines back home had closed. So, she and Aunt Joan took the work part-time because work was work, and someone had to do it.

That familiarity didn't prevent disagreement, but it meant there was no fear in the room, only logistics and opinion.

They recruited me for the wake. They didn't do so by making a formal request or even providing me with any explanation. It was just assumed that

I would help. I was capable. I had already proven that. This ask was simply the next step.

They argued over his glasses. Not whether he should have them. He always wore them. Everyone agreed on that. The argument was whether they looked right on him now: Should they be lower on the nose as they always sat, familiar and imperfect, or higher on the nose to something he never was? Mom wanted them fixed higher. Aunt Joan said that people would recognize him more quickly if he looked like himself.

I stood there listening, waiting for the decision to land, while Grandpap Shem lay in front of us like a task that still somehow felt like a person.

Then Mom looked at me and said, "Lift him."

There was no softness in her tone. No apology. Because the work requires directness; bodies don't respond to gentle language. So, I put my arms under Grandpap and lifted him.

He was heavier than I expected and somehow, not heavy at all. A strange contradiction, weight without life. His shoulders rolled slightly as I raised him, and his head wanted to drift backward in that loose way that makes you realize you are holding something that will not help you.

"Higher," Aunt Joan said.

I lifted again. The coffin lining bunched under Grandpap Shem. The suit shifted. I could feel my own breath change, turning short, controlled, because if you let your mind attach, you lose your hands.

Mom grabbed the Sunday papers, funnies and all, and shoved them under him, tucking them as one would tuck a towel under a mannequin to make it sit right. She adjusted, then adjusted again, flattening the stack as if it were bedding.

"There," she said.

It raised him, propped him into a better angle, made him sit higher in the coffin so he was more visible, more presentable. It was so practical it was almost absurd, and that absurdity was the only thing that kept the room from collapsing under what it really was.

After they settled him, the glasses debate resumed for half a minute, then ended with Aunt Joan deciding that with glasses, he would spend eternity. Everyone at the wake pretended that the decision was obvious all along.

At the funeral, at age eighteen, I was one of the youngest pallbearers.

I wore dress shoes. The ground was wet. It rained that day, steady enough to make everything look darker than it was. The grass gave way underfoot in that soft, unavoidable way, and we moved as a unit because that's what you do when you're carrying the weight of someone people loved.

As we walked the coffin toward the grave, my footing slipped. Not dramatically. Just enough.

The coffin shifted. I was near his head. And I heard it: A dull thump inside the box, of his head settling again. Unmistakable.

What I remember isn't the sound as much as what rose instantly in my mind afterward: his crooked glasses, and the loose funny papers placed with him like a small mercy. The details came uninvited and stayed.

I didn't say anything then. I didn't say anything out loud afterward. You don't announce something like that. Instead, you carry it in silence, like one more private task in a family that always had tasks.

But when I told Nancy later, she laughed. She always laughed when she remembered in relief rather than in cruelty. If anything, her laughter was recognition.

For Nancy and our family, death was always in the living room, close enough to eat beside, familiar enough to laugh at, and patient enough to wait for its turn.

Not because it was funny in the usual way. Because it was ridiculous in the only way our world could be, Sunday papers used like shims, a debate over glasses, a coffin shifting in the rain. A life reduced to logistics, then patched back together with the funny papers.

Even now, when I visit, I still think about it: Sorry, Grandpap Shem.

So, behind the scenes, I worked with Chelsea to transfer authority where it belonged: power of attorney, bank access, and Social Security logistics so that nothing would break later. Nancy wanted that handled. Chelsea needed it. We did it quietly, ahead of time, the way Nancy preferred.

I started by talking with Chelsea and reviewing Nancy's arrangements with her. I asked what Nancy would want for the funeral, what Chelsea could manage, and what would be easier later if we did it now. I told Chelsea to choose the urn. We picked one and described it to Nancy.

Nancy, still herself, offered her own solution. She suggested just digging a hole in Mom's grave. I joked that I didn't think Mom would appreciate it, and we laughed because, even then, even here, the family language stayed intact. I told her I'd take care of it.

Chelsea's husband didn't trust the town water. The pipes were old, as was the house, and Roebling had its own history, and he didn't want Nancy to drink from it. So, there was bottled water everywhere, cases stacked where you could fit them, plastic crinkling underfoot, the quiet evidence of a household trying to control what it still could. We drank a lot. It became one more thing to monitor. I bought a water cooler to help with management, make it easier and cleaner, and create one less daily friction point. You learn fast that hospice isn't only about medications. It's about the small supplies that keep the house running.

The seating inside the house was limited, and sometimes I needed to step out anyway to get some air, regain my composure, and let the pressure drain from my face before I went back in. I would sit on the back porch for a few minutes, listening to the house breathe through its newness and its strain, the quiet behind the quiet.

Not long after they moved in, I noticed there was no grill out back. It was such a normal thing to have and to be missing. A detail that made the house feel unfinished, as if the life that was supposed to happen there had been interrupted before it started.

After Joe's passing a few months earlier, I had stopped watching the Jets play; I had no desire to see another game. Something in me had closed. But I still had my old tailgate grill, which I'd fire up for a game, and I brought it to Chelsea and Chelsea's husband. It was just one more way of making the house functional, one more small transfer: If life was going to keep going here, it should have the basic tools. And giving it away felt like admitting I wasn't going back to who I'd been before.

In the first few meals I had at home with Nancy, we normally shared our food. We sat at the table and talked as Nancy lay in the hospice bed adjacent to it. At first, Nancy was both actively talking and listening without missing a beat. Then gradually, she mainly listened.

The house became filled with equipment and small tasks. And I kept one other life running at the same time, like a second stove left on low. As her illness progressed, her appetite slowed, and she ate smaller portions. Then only sips. Then nothing. But she could still see the Christmas lights twinkle, and that gave her comfort.

14

Work

"You are a teacher, and you need to focus on your job. You don't get that many days, and you need to save them for later," Nancy said to her before sending Chelsea off for work.

Chelsea and I knew immediately what "later" meant.

Nancy wanted normalcy, and she valued routine. She told Chelsea to keep working, too. She didn't want the house to stop running as it ordinarily would just because of her. Chelsea and I both worked in some way to keep our minds and to bring a sense of normalcy to the room. Year-end was approaching, and as the holidays drew near, I kept working. As time went by, Chelsea's house grew crowded with visitors and hospice nurses. Through the throng, Chelsea, Brian, and I moved around Nancy in the room. It was full of action and the labor of many goings-on. The room was full of bodies crossing, hands busy, small tasks stacking into the next ask. I didn't work because it mattered more than Nancy. I worked because stopping would have made me feel fear all at once.

I needed it for two reasons. One was a distraction, something structured to hold onto between care routines, such as when Chelsea, Brian, and I traded shifts. The other was continuity. Nancy took comfort in routine. Seeing me work steadied the room. It reassured her that things were still functioning, that someone was still in charge.

So, the routine settled even more. The subsequent days were filled with calls. Emails. Meetings that began and ended on schedule. Calendars that kept filling themselves in as if nothing nearby had changed. I started taking my calls from the driveway, from the guest room, sometimes from the car with the engine off and a notebook on my lap. I muted myself often. Listened more than I spoke, contributing only when needed, and logging off when I could.

Taking a call, ending a meeting early, sitting with Nancy to measure out medicine, logging it in the binder, then resuming the calls for the next meeting were now routine. One could work the timing of meetings well to ensure that all things for Nancy, work, and care logistics were done like clockwork.

A call. An early logoff. A spoon of medicine. A note in the binder. Back on mute. I learned to manage the timing between meetings so that Nancy's work and my work stayed aligned.

In those first days, it wasn't the work itself that threatened to collapse. It was the calendar, the sheer number of people who could put something on it, as if time were infinite and I were still the same person I'd been a week earlier.

My admin was the only one who understood it the way I needed her to. She didn't ask for the story. Or the details. She just took action. She watched my calendar like a guard dog. She cleared what could be removed. She shortened what couldn't. She pushed meetings out, then pushed them again, and when someone tried to slide something back in, she stepped between us, as if her job wasn't scheduling but protection.

She called me once and said, "I told them no."

"Who?" I asked.

"Everybody," she said, and I could hear the satisfaction in her voice. "You have hospice. They can wait."

I didn't tell her how much I needed that or how much I appreciated it. I didn't have to. The silence between us did the work.

Not everyone took the hint, though. My boss struggled the most with my being out. I understood the pressure he was under as the year came to a close. I understood what it did to him, how it narrowed his world until the only thing he could see was a deliverable and a deadline.

It happened on a call that should have been routine.

A grid of faces, most of them half-lit by laptop glow. Someone's background was a corporate logo, and someone else's was a kitchen. My camera was off. I was sitting in a quiet corner of the house with a notebook on my knee, the door not quite closed, listening for movement downstairs, listening for the next need.

He ran through the agenda quickly, clipped and efficient, like people get when they are trying to keep a lid on the week. A few status updates, a few action items. Then he circled back to me, the missing square.

"So," he said, and the word carried that practiced lightness, the tone people use when they want to say something sharp without owning that it is sharp. "I suppose we have to support you."

He smiled as he said it, as if he expected a polite laugh, as if it were an aside, as if he had handed me something small and harmless. The sentence did not land well.

It felt like a verdict. Like a reminder that the help I needed was an inconvenience my boss was generously tolerating. Like the cost of my absence had been tallied, and this was him letting me know the number.

For a beat, nobody moved. No one spoke. You could feel the silence spread across the call, like how cold moves across glass. I didn't react. I kept my face still, eyes on the screen. I let the moment sit there without rescuing my boss from it. My hands stayed on the notebook. My breathing stayed even.

I didn't have the energy to teach my boss how to be human.

In the space that followed, something shifted. The boss's smile faltered, just slightly, as if he heard his own words at the same time we did. He looked down at his notes, then back up, waiting. Testing the room. Waiting to see if anyone would laugh, or correct him, or pretend it was fine.

No one did.

The call continued, but the air was different after that. My boss kept talking, but with less confidence, like a man who had stepped onto a floor and felt it give a little underfoot.

Later, I heard his boss corrected him on this. Not gently. From what I was told, it was a stern reprimand. It was a short correction: something like, "This is what we do; this is what people are for; do not make this harder."

Everyone reacts differently when under strain. Some people are excellent at business and terrible at humanity. I didn't blame him. I just filed it away. I noticed who made the circle tighter and who, like my boss, made it smaller.

Privately, after work and caring for Nancy, I'd go for a walk and cry. I'd sigh, inhale the brisk fall air deeply, then hold my breath, slowing my emotions. Thus, I would open the door again with composure, ready for the next ask.

Thanksgiving was nearing. We talked quietly about plans, about having one nice last meal together as a family. Nancy liked the idea of it. Another marker. Another familiar ritual is still intact.

The mornings developed their own rhythms. Brian would bring McDonald's Big Breakfast and sit with Nancy, carefully cutting the food into small pieces she could manage. She barely ate, just a few bites, but she enjoyed the routine of it. The sharing. Sitting together over something ordinary.

While Brian was feeding her one morning, I overheard Nancy say something quietly. She told him that when she was gone, he should move closer to his daughter and grandchild. There was a pause, long enough to feel him register it, to know he had heard. Brian didn't respond to the words themselves. He didn't acknowledge them. Instead, he looked back at her plate and asked gently if she wanted another bite. The moment ended there, not denied, not argued, but deferred. It was his way of staying present without letting the future enter the room.

I started taking my conference calls at Nancy's bedside. I negotiated contracts while carefully and methodically giving her fluids and medication. She liked listening in, found comfort in the cadence of work talk and the familiar confidence it exuded. Sometimes I'd explain what I was doing afterward, or we'd briefly talk about it, the conversation serving as a distraction and proof that the world outside the room was still functioning.

In hospice, the hours don't belong to you. They belong to the next need. We began tracking fluids and output more deliberately, as the hospice requested. Numbers went into the log quietly. No commentary. Just accuracy. Duty expressed through order.

One afternoon, the house was so busy that there was a constant traffic of people trying to be helpful without getting in the way. Someone had come by to visit, one of the friends who stood near the doorway with their hands folded as if the room were a church. Chelsea moved between the kitchen and the living room with a cup and a pill bottle. Brian was standing close by, steady as ever, doing his soft-shift work, straightening a blanket edge, checking the water, watching Nancy's face for discomfort.

I had a call I couldn't dodge. I took it from the side of the living room, angled just far enough away that I could still see Nancy, but not so close that every word felt like it was being spoken into her bed. Laptop open, notes in hand, and headset on. My voice lowered out of instinct, like lowering your voice could make the world less rude.

On the screen, there were the usual faces, speaking in the usual cadence about contracts. Timelines. A negotiation that wanted to sprawl, people talking around the point, as if they had the luxury of time. I didn't.

Nancy lay there with her eyes half-closed, listening without looking like she was listening. That was one of her gifts, even sick, the ability to sit still and take everything in. The room smelled faintly of whatever medicine we'd just managed, and the Christmas lights were still on, soft behind her, giving the whole scene a strange holiday calm that didn't match the facts.

The voice on the other end started hedging, trying to soften a commitment, inching around something that needed a yes or a no.

I heard myself shift.

My tone changed, as it does when I stop accommodating and start executing. My sentences became shorter, clipped. My words became cleaner, no extra warmth in any of them. This was the firm voice I used when safeguarding time, protecting scope, and holding the line.

"No," I said, calm but final. "That doesn't work. Here's what we're doing."

I could feel Chelsea glance over at me from the kitchen doorway. Not annoyed, not asking me to stop, just registering that the other world had entered the room again.

Nancy registered it, too.

Her eyes opened a little more. Not wide, just enough to catch me in her peripheral vision. Her mouth tightened into the smallest grin, the one that says she recognizes a version of me she's seen a thousand times, the one that used to show up at family dinners when someone tried to run a con or bend the rules.

I kept talking, steady and professional, setting terms and boundaries like a man reading from a clipboard.

Then I felt it, the shift in the air beside the bed.

Nancy turned her head slightly toward the visitors, toward Chelsea and Brian, the person standing awkwardly near the doorway. Her movement was slow, deliberate, a queen turning to address the court. She lifted her hand from the blanket with effort, as if even that small gesture had to be approved by her body.

Her index finger extended in a pointed, unmistakable line. As she aimed it at me, her eyes brightened. She looked at Chelsea and Brian, then back at me, and her face filled with that familiar mixture of pride and amusement, like she was watching the family's designated problem-solver do his one useful trick.

"That's my brother!" she said, loud enough that everyone in the room could hear it. Not a whisper. Certainly not in hospice voice. She said it as a statement, mostly as a claim hers to make.

Chelsea smiled, the sort of smile that hurts a little because it's real. Brian's mouth lifted, too, small and tender, like he understood exactly what Nancy was doing, how she was taking one of the last remaining moments of ordinary life and turning it into a tribute.

The visitor laughed softly, relieved to be allowed to laugh.

On my screen, someone kept talking, unaware that in the room with the dying woman, a different transaction had just taken place, one that had nothing to do with contracts. I stayed on the call, still firm, still negotiating, but my throat tightened anyway. Because Nancy had little control left, she couldn't manage the timeline, or the medicine, or how her own body was narrowing. But she could still do this.

She could still see me clearly. She could still name me and point her finger at the one thing she knew would hold.

"That's my brother!" she had said, and now, she smiled at me with pride.

There was another call around this time, one that should have been routine, which is precisely why it wasn't. My boss had a new obsession with cameras at the time. He thought people weren't paying attention if he couldn't see them. He worried they were making faces, rolling their eyes, checking out. So he started treating the camera like a loyalty oath.

That morning, I dialed in the way I always did, already on mute and already listening. My camera was off at first because the room I was in wasn't the one I wanted displayed. My boss scanned the screen. I could feel him doing it in the pause before he spoke. He didn't call my name, but he didn't need to. There was only one blank square.

"We need cameras on," he said. "If your camera is off, turn it on. We need everyone present."

He meant it as a small public correction, intending to make a point. In his mind, a camera was proof. Of respect. Attention.

I looked over at Nancy. She was in bed beside me, and I was in the middle of my caretaking duties, moving slowly, even as my hands wanted to rush. I held a medication cup in one hand, a spoon in the other, caught in the careful rhythm of getting her to take what she needed. The work required quiet focus, but the call was still running, and I was already multitasking in a way that felt absurd.

So I turned the camera on.

The little light clicked. My face appeared on his screen. The background stayed out of view as best I could manage, but I could still feel the exposure, the thinness of privacy in that moment. I kept my expression neutral and my voice professional, answering questions as needed and nodding at the right points. In contrast, my hand kept moving just off-frame, doing the real work, the kind you do because the body in the bed has to be cared for, whether a petty boss believes you're paying attention or not, without narrating any of it.

Even without that, someone noticed soon enough. Of course they did.

"Bill," a voice said, cautious, like they were approaching a strange animal. "What... are you doing?"

For a second, I considered offering him the polite version of what I was doing. The soft version would reassure the video callers that everything was normal.

But nothing was normal in my life anymore, so why bother?

"My sister is in hospice," I explained, keeping my voice level because I couldn't afford to shake. "I'm giving her her meds. So, if you can please get to your point, I don't want to keep her waiting."

Silence.

I muted myself immediately after I said that, because Nancy heard it and she laughed; one quick burst, surprised and delighted. Thus, the call accidentally served its only functional purpose: giving her something absurd to enjoy.

I looked at her to find that she was grinning, eyes half-lidded, the laugh still in her throat.

"You tell them," she whispered to me.

And I had. I kept working the spoon. The room smelled faintly of medicine and the sweet artificial fruit of whatever we'd managed to get down. On-screen, tiny faces stared from small boxes, rearranging their moral priorities in real time.

After that, nobody mentioned cameras again. At least not to me.

I closed my laptop for the day and focused exclusively on the room now.

Chelsea had bought a memory book. One of the guided ones with prompts, meant to be filled out while you still can. Favorite holiday. Best day. First job. The kind of questions that sound harmless until you realize they are quietly asking you to inventory your life while you still have the chance.

We were doing fine. We were even laughing. Nancy answered with that calm diligence she had, as if the book were a student and she was helping it along. Chelsea sat close, a pen in hand, writing as Nancy spoke. I could hear the smile in Chelsea's voice when she read the prompts aloud. Then we reached "biggest regret."

Nancy changed then in small, noticeable ways. Her eyes dropped to the page. Her voice lowered. Chelsea held the pen as it mattered. She said, very carefully, as one would confess a grave sin, that when she was seven, she saw a shiny button at Woolworth's and took it. Just took it and slipped it into her pocket. The room went still for a second, startled by how seriously she carried it. How long had she carried it? A small bright thing with a lifetime of weight attached. I told her I would make it right. I would find the same button and return it.

Then I admitted the problem. I did not know how to find a Woolworth's anymore. That cracked it. Everyone laughed, even Nancy, the seriousness loosening at the corners of her eyes. Chelsea's pen scratched faster across the page, trying to capture it, grinning as she wrote.

I said, "If that's the worst thing you've ever done, then I'm in trouble. I'm going to need help on the other side."

They were still smiling, the kind of smile you get when the room has been permitted to be light for a moment, and I felt the opening. It wasn't planned. It was instinct, the way I reach for a story when I can't stand the seriousness being the only thing in the air.

"You want to hear mine?" I said.

Nancy's eyes were on me. Chelsea leaned in slightly, as if she already knew whatever was coming was going to be trouble.

"When I was about twelve," I said, "I had a chemistry set. The kind with a little Bunsen burner. I was not supposed to use it in the kitchen."

I paused there because that line always gets a reaction. It is the universal preface to disaster.

"But I did," I said.

I could see the scene as I spoke it. The kitchen table under the overhead light, white Formica with those 1970s patterns, the kind that tried to make plain surfaces look cheerful. My careful, excited hands were setting up my experiment as if I were a real scientist, not a kid playing with fire in his mother's house. The burner lit. The blue flame steadied for a second, almost beautiful.

And then the wobble. The burner was tipping, slow and fast at the same time. The sudden lick of flame touched where it should not touch. The sound, a soft *pop*, and the smell, sharp and chemical, as the laminate blistered and curled. A dark scar spreading in a shape that could not be called an accident if you were the mother walking in.

"I panicked," I said. "So I did what any responsible twelve-year-old does. I tried to cover it up."

Nancy laughed first. Chelsea followed, the laughter coming out like a release.

"I blamed it on a candle," I said. "An overturned candle. Like we had candles on the kitchen table just casually burning down the house."

That got them again. I could hear how hungry we all were for something that wasn't grief.

"Mom was furious," I said. "Not just regular mad. The kind where she didn't even have to raise her voice. She just looked at me like, Really. This is who I'm raising."

I let the moment sit there, their smiles still in place, the room warmer than it had been a minute earlier.

"So put in a good word," I said. "My rap sheet is long. When my time comes, I'm going to need a good word."

Chelsea laughed. Brian laughed. Chelsea's husband laughed too, the sound filling the room in a way that felt like oxygen. Nancy could not see Chelsea's face from where she was, but she heard the laughter and knew she had gotten what she wanted. A moment of honesty, written down. A moment that did not ask anyone to perform grief. Chelsea looked up from the book and gave me that small, absolute kindness.

"Sure thing," Nancy said.

Humor eased the room. It let the truth sit there without crushing anyone.

My girls came to visit during this time for support. Their childhood bond remains strong, even now that they are in their twenties. It was the first time they really saw Chelsea being comforted by others rather than having to manage everything herself. They also saw me differently, not just as a father, but as a brother. The shift didn't need to be discussed. It registered on its own.

Work gave others a way to interact with me without saying the wrong thing. They could ask about timelines and deliverables rather than about feelings. It spared everyone the effort of language when language wasn't up to the task.

Sometimes absurdity showed up in the form of an email, like a reminder about an administrative deadline. It might land as a cheerful note about an upcoming initiative, too. Someone asking if I could "circle back" before the end of the day, as if the end of the day were a real boundary in a house where time had turned elastic.

I would answer what needed answering and kept my responses short and accurate. No emotional leakage. It wasn't that I was cold. It was that I was conserving. Every extra sentence was fuel I might need later when the night turned hard.

As weeks passed and Nancy faded, I started working less. The routine had done its job. It had steadied her just as it had steadied me. Eventually, there was no need for scaffolding anymore.

At night, I stayed in Nancy's old bedroom upstairs, directly above her. Nothing had been moved from the last time she'd gone to the hospital. Crackers still sat where she had kept them, nibbling at them when nausea from the LMD made eating too difficult. Upstairs, the room held the version of her that still belonged to the world. The small things she'd collected and kept for years were still there, arranged as she liked them, because the room had been hers long before it became mine.

There was a shelf with Grandma Arline's knick-knacks on it, and Grandma Arline had bequeathed little objects to Nancy that didn't matter to anyone until the person who loved them was gone. And there was the barometer I'd given her years earlier. I'd bought it when I worked at Epstein's Department Store, with my first paycheck, proud in a way only a kid can be proud, proud that I could buy something that wasn't required, proud that I could give my sister something that felt like a real gift instead of a borrowed one.

Seeing it there now, still intact, kept, did something to me. It was proof of continuity. Proof that Nancy carried me forward in her own quiet way, the same way I was holding her now.

The rope was there, too, installed fairly recently. It was just a piece of practical engineering to be used when Nancy needed to pull herself up from bed. It ran from the bedpost toward the window at the foot of the bed, a crude line that said everything: the body failing, the mind still trying, the stubborn will to do one more thing without asking for help.

I kept a change of clothes up there for weeks. I laundered Nancy's soiled gowns. At first, the stains were just from spilled food and slushies, bright colors, sticky sugars, evidence of what she could still take in. I washed them without thinking, because thinking made it worse.

Brian took most of the day shifts. He was an Eucharistic minister, devout in a way that wasn't performative. Each day before he came, he made sure prayers were spoken. He would show up with prayers for all of us. We led his shift as if it were a liturgy, quiet, deliberate. Nancy would clasp her hands. The day would be steady. It wasn't about fixing anything. It was about holding the day in place.

He enjoyed feeding Nancy. He did it with patience and attention, as if it were a sacred task rather than a messy, challenging one. When my day was spent, when Chelsea and her husband were tired, when I was shifting from conference call to bedside, Brian would step in to whatever else needed doing without asking.

Brian would bring her smoothies from a place called Wawa, and she loved them, smooth and cold, something she could accept without effort. We ate our barbecue, and she had her smoothie, and for a brief moment, the house held a version of itself that looked like a family again.

The harder I worked, the more I could hold things together. The more I held things together, the less anyone could see what it was costing.

Projecting stability itself has a hidden cost.

15

Mortgaging the Future

The email from the funeral home arrived while I was working on a contract. Having previously completed the paperwork, the bill was coming due.

"Financing available and deferred payment plans for all packages." In another window, I was reviewing financing for new services at work. Now this.

I had the money for this, but Nancy wouldn't want to spend too much. We talked through what mattered and what didn't. Our mother never used credit. I avoided it. The plans we made would be simple, frugal, as Nancy had lived. Financing was for big things like homes. Everything else, if you could manage it, was cash.

But by then, I'd already learned I couldn't do transparent support. I was forced to split finances, one clean personal card, because any visible spending on Nancy invited a conversation I couldn't afford to have. So, the card I used that night wasn't ours. It was mine.

I paid the funeral expenses with my personal credit card on one screen while I filed my corporate expense reports with my corporate card in the other window. When one is so busy signing, reviewing, doing, and completing, the numbness of repetition helps defer the pain. Multitasking care for Nancy and a career also meant quietly preparing paperwork. In between care and conference calls, I planned for the after, as Nancy expected I'd also do, though it was left unsaid.

I wasn't trying to be grim; I was trying to spare my future self the harder decisions while being shattered.

The funeral financing arrived that night, quietly, matter-of-factly, with the expectation that a responsible adult would respond. But there was a clock on it. The funeral director needed the service lined up before the holidays.

He was short-handed, he explained. He needed names, dates, vitals, permissions, everything that lets staff move. And because Nancy had no life insurance, he needed payment up front.

He didn't say "later" or even, "We'll settle after."

I remember staring at the screen and feeling the oddness of it: money moving through a wire or a card swipe while Nancy's breath moved through her lungs. Two systems running at once. One kept a body alive for now, the other prepared for what would come after.

I wasn't paying because I'd given up. I was paying because I'd learned what happens when you don't. When someone dies, the family turns into a small committee of shocked people who cannot find the correct documents, cannot remember basic numbers, and cannot think past the next hour. They look at you because you are standing. So you stay standing. You become the person who can still read the question and fill in the blank without shaking.

And if it sounds cold to do that while she was still alive, it wasn't cold. It was love expressed in the only language I knew how to speak under pressure: Do the hard thing now so the people you love won't have to do it later while they're falling apart.

So, after one conference call, just before I was to give Nancy her medicine, I paid for Nancy's funeral. That sentence is wrong in the same manner that specific proper sentences are wrong. It's too clean, too practical, like you're describing a hotel reservation instead of the end of a person's life. But it happened anyway because the world demanded it.

To do it, I opened my laptop and pulled up the tax returns I'd saved, which I'd gone through before. Nancy's returns were always there on my computer, like a private record of her survival. They weren't interested in how wealthy people structure their finances. They were modest. Tight. A life held together with tape and good intentions.

Still, I saw again, in surprise, as I had every time I had seen it: Every year, right there in the return, there was that same line.

Donations.

Tithes.

Even when she was struggling, even when the margin was thin, and she had to choose between what most people would call necessities, Nancy kept donating, giving to others.

As a person of faith, Nancy gave anyway, regardless of whether she could afford to. It drove my wife crazy.

I was doing Nancy's taxes in my office. The return was open on my screen with multiple windows layered across it: the tax software on top, scanned PDFs and account pages underneath, boxes and lines waiting to be filled in. Receipts were spread beside the keyboard, and one of my binders for her year's activity sat open on the desk, tabs sticking out like bookmarks to a life reduced to categories.

One charity receipt was on top of the pile, plain and obvious, close enough to the screen that it looked like it belonged there.

My wife came to the doorway and stepped in without saying much. She moved behind me and leaned slightly over my shoulder. I could feel her reading without turning around. Her eyes dropped to the receipt on the desk, then went back to the monitor, and she stopped in that way people stop when they've found the one detail that changes their mood.

"What's that?" she asked.

I knew what she meant. She wasn't asking about the whole return. She was asking about that receipt.

"Nancy's donations," I said.

My wife's face tightened. She looked again at the paper, then at the line on the screen it tied to, as if she needed to see the habit in both places. She pointed once, a short gesture toward the receipt and the number, the way you indicate something that shouldn't be there.

"Why is she doing that?" she said. "She can't afford it."

Then she said the part that landed hardest, because of how flat it was, how practical, how certain.

"That's your money," she said. "That's our money."

I felt the familiar mix rise in me: sadness first, then annoyance. Not because the math was wrong. The math was obvious. But because I was back in that position again, trying to hold Nancy's dignity on one side and my marriage on the other, with no real support outside my own effort. My wife saw it as something out of place, something to be corrected. Nancy saw it as practice, a way of staying steady and human even when her life was tight.

"It's what she does," I said. I kept my voice calm, not because I felt calm, but because I didn't want the conversation to turn into another fight that lived in the house.

My wife shook her head and walked away. The office went quiet again, the tax software still open, the binder still splayed on the desk, the charity receipt sitting there like it had no idea what it had just triggered.

But that was Nancy for you.

The tithes never elicited a lecture from Nancy. She never defended it. She didn't even announce it. It simply appeared on the forms, year after year, like a signature she refused to change. If you asked her, she'd probably shrug and say something small, something that sounded like practicality, not holiness. Yet I knew that doing this wasn't small to her. It was a way of saying: My life isn't only what happens to me. I still get to decide who I am inside it.

That's the part people miss when they call it irresponsible. They hear "donation" and think "waste." They picture a jar on a counter, a plate passed down a row, a religious cliché that can be skipped without consequence. Nancy heard something else. She heard obligation, gratitude, steadiness, an exchange with God that wasn't based on whether her circumstances were fair.

So yes, it sometimes annoyed me, because I saw the ledger. I saw the furnace problems, the thin grocery weeks, and the way life punished her for not having margin. But the irritation was also fear. Because if she stopped being Nancy, if she stopped doing the few things that made her feel intact, then what was left? A woman reduced to injury and loss. A woman who would start to believe the judgments coming at her from every angle.

I think, too, that I was put off because her giving exposed something uncomfortable in me: how quickly I could become transactional under pressure. How easily could I start measuring love in dollars, repairs, hours, and favors? Nancy was quietly refusing that.

She wasn't careless. She wasn't stupid. She was faithful in a way that didn't ask permission from her circumstances. The giving wasn't performative; it was almost stubborn. She believed that what you do when you have little is the most accurate measure of what you think. And if she stopped, she would feel like she was becoming someone she didn't recognize.

I stared at that line item more than once, feeling two things at once: Respect and frustration.

Respect, because her integrity was laid bare. Frustration because I was the person who had to widen the margin when her integrity narrowed it.

That double feeling, admiration and irritation living in the same chest, was the emotional signature of those years.

It was also the beginning of a more resounding crack that didn't start with Nancy at all.

Once Nancy lost her job, and I bought her house, the side grumblings began. The accusation didn't arrive as a single sentence. It arrived as suspicion, usually in increments. A tone. A glance when Nancy's name came up. A comment about "options." A suggestion that "a lot of people work through pain." It was always framed as realism, never cruelty. That's how it gets traction: No one wants to be seen as sentimental when "realism" is on the table.

Since Nancy's chronic illness didn't come with a cast or a scar that made her pain visible, it became easy to turn it into a character flaw. Fatigue became laziness. Needing rest became "not trying." The days she stayed in bed became proof, somehow, that she could stay in bed and work. Logic didn't matter. What mattered was the story people chose because it kept their hands clean.

Once that story took hold, the household math changed. Every time I helped Nancy, it wasn't seen as assisting Nancy. It sounded as if it had been taken from someone else. Not because there wasn't enough money, but because there wasn't enough emotional permission.

That's what I didn't understand at first: The argument was never purely about finances. It was about control. It was about who gets to be seen as "deserving." It was about keeping the family narrative tidy, aligning our obligations with the approved list, and confining our generosity to the acceptable targets.

When you're in that kind of environment, you begin to negotiate not only with reality, but with how it's perceived. You begin to predict reactions. You begin to preempt fights. You begin doing the thing you never wanted to do, and you start hiding the ways you love people.

I can still see the faces around me. The looks meant the conversations wouldn't be just conversations. It was going to be a verdict. The stress of supporting Nancy—financially, logistically, quietly—had been building for years, but by that point, it had shifted from help to something else. It was now, I saw with a hollowness in my stomach, being reframed as a burden.

At first, this was just an annoyance. Standard friction occurs when one party becomes responsible for a problem created elsewhere. But annoyance doesn't stay small. It grows teeth. It becomes an explanation for everything.

Then, openly, questions about whether Nancy was faking her illness were raised. I, too, had questions, as did Nancy. For a long time, doctors weren't able to diagnose her illness. They suspected fibromyalgia, chronic pain, the fatigue that emptied her days, which became suspect in the way diseases become suspect when they don't come with obvious visuals. No cast. No bandages. No clean scan that satisfies the skeptic. Nancy's suffering was real, but it wasn't theatrical. It was the kind that makes you look "fine" on the outside while your body is doing something private and punishing on the inside.

The phrase floated in from other angles: from Liz when I would call her, initially from within my own home, as side comments, supposedly "just being honest." But when it started to rise and boil over, the framing shifted from Nancy as family to obligation.

Nancy wasn't just my sister anymore. In that narrative, she was a drain, and once a person gets recast as a drain, everything about her becomes evidence.

Her tithing became evidence of this, as did her quiet, uncomplaining nature. Even her dignity, the way she didn't beg, how she didn't cry on demand, became proof that she must be fine.

It was a kind of betrayal that didn't involve shouting. It involved certainty, the chilling kind.

The argument at the counter is never fully resolved because arguments like that never are. They settle into policy. You can feel the ground of the marriage shift as the unspoken rule becomes: This topic is dangerous.

The next layer, the layer people use when they want to make coercion look like morality, came soon after. It came up in ordinary moments, when a tuition envelope arrived, when a car needed work, when the house needed something expensive and unglamorous. One night, my wife said it straight across the kitchen table.

"You need to focus less on supporting her," she said. "You need that money for other things, and stop paying for her choices."

"Our kids need to go to college," she continued. "We have bills. We have plans. We can't keep doing this."

I listened. I nodded in the right places. I kept my face calm, because I understood the argument even as it landed like a threat. But inside, my body reacted before my mind finished sorting it. My jaw tightened. My shoulders went stiff, as if I had been braced for impact and still got hit.

What I felt wasn't confusion. It was the moral trap of it. Being asked to choose one set of family over the other, to declare priorities in a way that turned love into a hierarchy. And the frustration was sharpened by the simple fact that I had the means. This wasn't a zero-sum emergency. I wasn't choosing between tuition and rent. I could support both. So the demand wasn't really about math. It was about permission. About whose needs counted, and who got to decide what kind of man I was allowed to be.

I didn't argue the words. I just felt the verdict underneath them: If I helped Nancy, I was taking from my own family. As if family money was a pie, and any slice handed to Nancy was stolen from someone else. As if the years I'd worked—the travel, the strain, the building of a life—existed only to serve one approved set of needs.

It is hard to explain the force of that argument because it sounds reasonable to people on the outside: Nancy is old enough to fend for herself.

But that's what made it powerful: It was an argument without compassion, one that ignored my ability to earn a living and simultaneously support myself, my family, and Nancy.

It didn't matter that I earned enough to do all this. It didn't matter that we weren't starving. It didn't matter that my support for Nancy wasn't a hobby, but a form of triage. Once the story becomes "money is wasted," then pressures rise, and decisions are questioned.

So, I learned to handle Nancy's support in private. There would be no more debate with others.

From then on, if I had to help Nancy, I did it in ways that created fewer ripples. If I had to pay for something, I paid for it and moved on. I learned, painfully, that in specific environments, transparency isn't a virtue; it's fuel. It gives the argument something to bite into.

So, I withdrew. From others, but not from Nancy. From the conversations about Nancy. My life began to split in a way I didn't name at the time. From then on, I inhabited two roles. One was the individual and bifurcated Nancy, to protect her and me from the questions. The alternate role was the private role: brother, rescuer, the person who kept another life from collapsing.

The split ultimately led to something else. Private meetings. At first, this felt temporary, a practical workaround. Meet somewhere neutral. Handle something quickly. Don't make it a "visit" that becomes a referendum. A parking lot. A diner booth. The quiet corner of a store.

Once the pattern began, it turned into its own kind of exile. Nancy became progressively less welcome in my home the longer her continued support was offered, not because I didn't love her, but because the household story had shifted. She had become a stressor, an argument, a symbol.

Hence, love was forced underground. And that was the true fault line of those years: not money, exactly, but how money changed relationships. The way support made social visits feel like a burden, or how you could walk into a room and feel your generosity hanging in the air like a smell, noticed by everyone and discussed by no one.

Even when you earn plenty, you can still feel that guilt, the sense that helping one person is, somehow, misdirected and foolish. The irrational feeling that your own life is being mortgaged not only to keep your sister afloat, but to keep peace overall.

That phrase, "mortgaging the future," sounds dramatic, but it's exactly what it felt like. Not because the money itself would ruin me. Because the emotional debt was compounding.

To me, it was a debt I was willing to take on to correct years of wrongs. Our lives deserve more than a fine balance sheet and good management. To not harm and give with an open palm. Doing more good in this world than consuming. If that was how I'd be judged, then so be it. Our world was full of judges' opinions but little help, mercy, or compassion.

As I helped Nancy, I thought of the legacy of one such judge, who loomed large in the past and kept showing up, uninvited.

Grandpa Alfred.

Even years later, even after his death, he could still cut.

I remember visiting him just before he passed, and somehow Liz came up: her appearance, her habits, the things Grandpa Alfred loved to savage. Liz had been born with a lazy eye, and any vulnerability someone had, for Grandpa Alfred, he weaponized with his vitriol.

"Bob disappointed us," he said, meaning my father. "How could he marry that woman? And that eye! That's your mother stabbing beyond the grave at that eye!"

Even on his deathbed, he couldn't resist his own impulses. He had a talent for cruelty that was almost athletic. And what made it worse was that his lines were often funny despite being vicious. He could make you laugh, then make you feel dirty for laughing.

There's an irony here that took me a long time to see. My father spent his early life trying to earn Grandpa Alfred's approval, in the way he carried himself, the way he entered a room, and the way he acted as if he had to prove he belonged there. Then, as he aged, he stopped seeking Grandpa Alfred altogether. Not in a healed way. In a severe way.

At some point, Dad no longer wanted anything from Grandpa Alfred except distance. He was no longer trying to be the good son. He wasn't trying to argue, either. He stopped listening. And that, more than any act of rebellion, was what truly offended Grandpa Alfred. It wasn't the choice of Liz that disappointed him most. It was the fact that Dad no longer cared what Grandpa Alfred thought about any of it.

For a man like Grandpa Alfred, being ignored is worse than being opposed. Opposition still means you're in the game. Being ignored means you've walked off the field.

Over time, their relationship dwindled into something close to nil: holiday appearances with polite surfaces, conversations that didn't go deep enough to cut, the long, quiet months in between where nothing was repaired because no one was trying to fix it. Dad had learned to survive by leaving emotionally before he left physically.

Then Grandpa Alfred died, and Dad did something I didn't expect at the time but understand now: He abandoned Arline entirely. No further contact at all, as Dad's world narrowed to just him and Liz, growing increasingly isolated.

When I questioned this decision, he said, offering me, with indifference, a sentence that sounded like nothing more than an excuse: Arline had been "brainwashed by him," he said. As if Arline's endurance, the years of staying, absorbing, managing, being the container for Grandpa Alfred's anger, made her complicit. As if the fact that she lived with Grandpa Alfred meant she had chosen him over the boys and therefore didn't deserve loyalty back.

Dad washed his hands of her. And in doing that, he gained a kind of freedom I'm not sure he deserved: freedom from the obligation to face what Grandma Arline had done for him and his brother when they were children. Freedom from the discomfort of being seen clearly by the one person who could say, "I was there. I know what you lived through, and I know what you became."

Thus, it fell to Nancy to keep that connection alive.

Nancy, who never had the luxury of cleanly cutting people off, would visit Arline. She would sit with her, bring her something small, ask the gentle questions that make an older person feel remembered. Nancy did it with the same instinct she had in every other part of life: If someone is vulnerable, you don't leave them alone with it.

There's a scene I carry with me that doesn't have any drama to it, which is why it stays. We are in a small place, not beautiful, just functional, where you can hear a refrigerator cycle on and off. Grandma Arline is older now, the sharp edges of life rounded down by time. She offers food, as it is the most reliable language she still has. She isn't educated as Grandpa Alfred demanded. She is educated in care. She knows what warms a person up. She knows what fills a stomach. She knows what makes people feel safe in a room.

Nancy watches her with an expression that is half affection, half sorrow. Because Nancy understands the cost of being the woman who subordinated their life and needs in a house full of men, only to be left to fend for herself alone when those covenants are over. Nancy understands what it means to keep things running while someone else gets to be "the head" and take credit for the order.

I remember thinking at that moment, "*This is the cycle we keep inheriting.*" Men stepping away. Women staying. Women feed the world while the world decides whether they are worthy of being loved back.

These ideas bring me back to the questions about Nancy's tithe donation line item and the quiet decisions I made to keep Nancy afloat. Because none of them were new. The language changed, the decade changed, the money moved through different channels, but the moral question was the same:

When someone becomes inconvenient, do you keep showing up for them?

Dad answered that question in many ways by showing up for Liz and retreating from everyone else. And if Grandpa Alfred was angry about anything in the end, it was the realization that Dad had learned Grandpa Alfred's true lesson: You can choose where your loyalty goes, and no one can make you put it in places that feel like work.

Nancy learned a different lesson from this: Loyalty is what you do when it feels like work.

I carried that line with me for a long time, because it was so perfectly him: unable to stop stabbing, unable to stop scoring, unable to let anything be simply human.

Those years when Dad was making excuses, and Liz was destroying cars, my sister was being labeled a fraud in my own kitchen. So, in those moments, Grandpa Alfred's voice felt less like history and more like a seed that had grown into a family trait, as did the way people justified neglect by turning the person in need into a problem.

When I think back on that period, I don't believe in scenes like how I do with hospice. I guess in transactions and tight conversations, there is a steady narrowing of what can be said aloud.

I think of Nancy's tax return glowing on my screen late at night. I think of the donation line item. I think of being asked about why I should help, and of my wife and Liz saying she could do more for herself. At that same moment, I think of Dad's deflection of help, looping like a broken recording—he, in turn, rather than helping Nancy, indulgently buys Liz a new Mustang, then Liz recklessly drives it right into a ditch. The thoughts: absurd and obscene. And I think of my key ring getting heavier with the invisible weight of running two lives at once.

Once my life split into two, there emerged the part I wanted to say out loud in those years but didn't: I wasn't only spending money. I was spending emotional credit. Every quiet payment bought a temporary calm on one side and a deeper suspicion on the other. Every private meeting brought my sister a little dignity and cost me a little openness in my own house. The balance sheet couldn't show it, but my body felt it.

Maybe that is why I kept doing things "in advance." Because advance work is how you control damage, it's how you reduce the number of moments where someone you love must beg for basic decency. It's how you make sure the person who is already tired doesn't have to fight for one more thing.

If Dad gained his freedom by walking away from Grandpa Alfred, from Grandma Arline, from obligations that felt like old debts, I gained something else by staying: a kind of identity I didn't ask for, the one who shows up when other people don't. That identity came with a cost, too. It made my life smaller in some ways. But it also made my love legible.

In the end, with Nancy, legible love mattered more than comfort.

Privately, I was becoming the person who handled everything in advance, because in my experience, "later" is when the worst things happen and you're least equipped to handle them.

Which is why, years later, when Nancy asked to go home, and I returned to organize burial paperwork while she was still alive, it didn't feel like new behavior.

It felt like the final version of an old one.

A brother paying in advance for what he knows is coming, because he has learned, repeatedly, that if he doesn't, no one else will.

When the house became leverage, relationships went underground.

Once care goes underground, it changes form. It starts to look like parking lots, envelopes, and keys you keep even after the doors are gone.

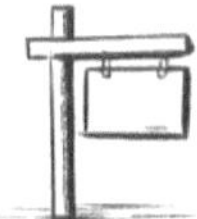

16

For Sale

"It's okay," she said. Her voice was calm, almost gentle, as if she were talking down a skittish animal. "You've done more for me than anyone. I'll figure something out. I have to trust in God."

Nancy reached her hand out and touched my wrist. Her hand was warm. So thin and yet so steady. She comforted me while I was telling her I was pulling away the one thing I'd built to protect her.

I had parked outside Chelsea's house and sat for a beat with the engine off, hands still on the wheel, as if the car were a small shelter I hadn't yet earned the right to leave.

A few doors down, a FOR SALE sign leaned into the townhome window. It shouldn't have meant anything. It did.

The sign caught my eye with its white post, clean lettering, and the promise of "new beginnings" for someone who hasn't yet learned what endings cost. It wasn't even straight. It sat crooked, half-slumped, as if the house itself had given up the effort of appearing normal. Wet fall leaves were stuck to the inside of the glass pane behind it, dark, pressed flat, like they'd tried to get in and then died there. You can't tell by looking which houses were loved and which houses survived. You don't know which ones held laughter and which ones held shame. A house is a house until you've lost one.

I got out, shut the door quietly, and started walking up the path to Chelsea's front steps.

The cold air hit my lungs, and a wave of deflation rolled through me, quiet, involuntary, like my body admitting what my mind was still trying to manage. I took a deep breath and rebuilt my face into something Nancy could live inside for a few more minutes.

In the few seconds between the curb and the door, my mind reached for a related memory and pulled it forward by the collar.

A house for sale. A forced sale. A different sign, a different year, the same taste of something being taken.

That was a decade ago, when the tiny Trenton house stopped providing the stability and respite it was supposed to, and the pressure to sell the property began to build as Chelsea graduated from college and started working.

The timing mattered to my wife, practically: Chelsea was no longer a child who needed the house as an anchor for school. The original reason for the purchase of the house, Chelsea's stability, had, in her mind, expired. In that framing, the house had done its job.

We were in the kitchen when it finally became a direct conversation, ordinary setting, ordinary lighting, and weekday fatigue. No raised voices. No theatrics. Just like how long-running issues get handled in households: a few sentences at a time, repeated until they become policy.

"Chelsea's graduated," my wife said, looking at a piece of mail as if the mail itself proved the point. "She's working. That was the whole reason we did this."

I didn't argue with the facts. Chelsea had grown. She did have her own path. Meanwhile, my daughters were moving toward college age, and the next set of obligations was no longer theoretical. Tuition wasn't a concept. It was a calendar.

"I can carry both," I told her, because I could. The math wasn't the problem.

My wife nodded once, as she'd already accounted for that answer. "It's not only money," she said. "It's how long this goes on. It's the principle of it. We can't keep doing this forever."

That's what the argument was, stripped down: not whether Nancy deserved help, but whether the help had an end date or not. Whether there was a point at which helping turns into a permanent arrangement you didn't agree to. Chelsea's graduation was the marker being used as the end date. A line is drawn because lines are easier than nuance.

I tried to keep things in the practical lane, the one where I could operate without losing my footing.

"So, what are you saying?" I asked, even though I knew.

"I'm saying it's time," she said. "Nancy needs to figure out what's next."

There wasn't much more to say after that, not without the conversation becoming something else: accusations, motives, old resentments. I didn't want that. I didn't want a scene. I wanted the subject to be contained.

So, I did what I did when I was trying not to detonate my own life: I turned it into execution.

I remember calling Nancy. I didn't do it in person. That would have made it a scene. I did it as I did all hard things when I was trying to keep everything from tipping over: a phone call, a measured voice, a sentence delivered like paperwork.

"Nant," I said, and even saying her nickname felt like stepping onto thin ice. "I'm being made to sell."

I let the sentence sit long enough to mean what it meant, without adding commentary that would turn it into a plea or a fight.

I explained the timing as cleanly as I could: Chelsea was working now; the rationale people had accepted before was no longer being accepted; the pressure had become constant. I didn't frame it as cruelty. I framed it as reality, because reality was the only language that wouldn't embarrass her and wouldn't inflame my home.

Nancy absorbed it, as she always did: quietly, immediately orienting toward what needed to happen next.

"I understand," she said.

Then, like she was trying to make it easier for me to say the rest, she started talking about options, places she could look, people she could ask, and ways she could make it work. Restrained. Not pleading. Just compliance shaped like planning.

I broke the news to her as gently as I could, and she understood and made plans as best she could. It was time I told her, and she needed to move on, because I couldn't keep supporting the home like I had been, at least not openly, and not with peace inside my own house.

What it felt like to me, though, was betrayal. A cold kind where people look you in the eye and tell you that you're being unreasonable for caring about the thing you promised would keep someone safe.

I remember the sale contract, listing the home and having Nancy clear out. I was careful not to use anything that hard, but, in the end, she had to go elsewhere, and she knew that deep down.

I remember how paperwork can make a human story read like a technical correction. I remember how it felt to sign something I didn't want to sign because the pressure had become constant, and I was tired of living in a household where every act of care for my sister turned into a debate.

After the call, I emailed her the listing, photos, price, and the clinical language of "charming" and "cozy," as if a house's only meaning were what strangers could imagine within it. My finger hovered over the send button for a second longer than it should have. Then, I hit send.

And when the email flew away, I felt physically sick. Not metaphorically. My stomach tightened, my throat went hot, and I had to sit down at my desk like I'd been punched.

That was the real receipt: nausea. Guilt that didn't need words.

There's a moment in forced, hard choices, which to me was to preserve peace, not because you agree, but because you can't hold the line anymore without losing everything else you're trying to protect. It's not surrender so much as fatigue.

Once the decision was made, the next phase arrived: the brutal logistics sequence no one talks about because it's too humiliating to say out loud.

Nancy needed notice. I had to give it to her. Even writing that sentence makes my stomach tighten. I had paid for that house. I had bought it for her because I wanted her to have stability. I had fixed its furnace. I had paid the mortgage. I had defended the idea of surety for years. And now I was the one telling her she had to leave.

The situation wasn't simple. It never is. Nancy didn't want to make trouble. She didn't want to be the reason my household erupted. She understood pressure, maybe better than anyone. So, she didn't fight the way a person would if she were thinking only of herself. She absorbed it. She tried to comply. She tried to find a quick solution so no one could say she was "refusing."

But the housing market doesn't care about a person's dignity. It cares about timing. It cares about credit. It cares about how landlords look at disability and quietly decides you're a risk.

Hence, Nancy struggled to find housing. While she looked, the tiny Trenton area house emptied in stages. Rooms that had held a life became bare and echoing. The emptiness didn't feel clean; it felt like loss. And while she searched, while she tried to figure out where she could go and how she could afford it, something happened that I didn't know at the time.

She stayed at any place she could find so as not to burden me with the fact that she was homeless. But she also squatted. I didn't learn what that word was until hospice, years later, when the veil had dropped, and we were finally saying true things without pretending they were polite. When Nancy told me, she did so in a matter-of-fact manner. She wasn't confessing the way a guilty person confesses. She said it like a person describing a fact she had endured: She had nowhere to go yet, so she stayed. Quietly. Hoping it would be resolved before anyone had to name it.

As I sat near her, I asked her for her forgiveness, and we supported each other as best we could. In the end, she said that my support was more than she ever hoped for, and things turned out fine. The irony was hitting me as she lay dying.

I didn't know. I was working. I was traveling. I was dealing with the sale, the repairs, and the household pressure, and I thought the timeline was cleaner than it actually was.

It wasn't.

Selling Nancy's unoccupied house then became a different kind of problem in and of itself. Not emotional, but physical. The heat failed when no one was there to notice. The pipes froze. Problems like that multiply in silence.

Then, the house flooded. I was on the road when the temperature dropped hard, one of those sudden freezes that makes the world feel brittle. I remember thinking, absurdly, as I sat in some anonymous hotel room, that I hoped the place would hold. I remember actually praying it would, as if that would keep copper from splitting.

No such luck.

When I walked inside and saw the water damage where there shouldn't even have been water, smelled the wet drywall, and felt the sick realization that everything I was trying to manage was always one failure away from becoming a bigger catastrophe, it all hit me at once.

Water was pouring into the basement, as a secret pours out once discovered: fast, unapologetic. I stepped onto the stairs and felt the air change: colder, damp, wrong. The sound wasn't a drip. It was a steady rush.

The shutoff valve was underwater. That's the part that sticks with me: The thing designed to stop the damage was submerged in the damage.

I fixed it. That's the method I use in my role: repair, pay, keep going. I got the pipes fixed, repaired the damage, and brought the house back to sellable condition. I kept the process moving because if you stop, the whole thing collapses, leaving you with a half-finished disaster and everyone blaming you.

I called the plumber and said the only sentence I had left. "Of course," I said, like it was a joke, like it wasn't. Then the furnace went, too, because why the hell not? Once a house starts failing, it does so in a chorus.

I called Nancy, and she stopped by to help. We pumped water out. We dragged soaked debris out. We cut away what couldn't be saved. And when the basement water got pushed into the backyard, it froze into a ridiculous, shining sheet, a backyard ice skating rink no one asked for, created by necessity and bad timing.

Nancy helped where she could. She came back to the house from her new quarters to help keep an eye on the place. This was just one of the small acts she performed as if to say, "I'm not just receiving. I'm still contributing." Her pride needed that.

I was low in that period, low in a way I didn't show much, because showing it would have made a scene I couldn't manage. I felt sick about the sale. Sick about having to give her notice. Eventually, the family circle narrowed to exclude my sister, both because of distance and because of anxieties about support.

Nancy, being Nancy, kept trying to comfort me. She told me she was okay. This was one of the cruelest things about her goodness: She would reassure the person who rescued her, even while standing in the wreckage of what had been taken from her.

When the house finally sold, I set aside the proceeds and kept them in a separate bank account. I did so deliberately. Not because I needed the money, but because I needed proof that the sale was unnecessary and assurance that, if emergency funds were needed later, they would be available. I kept it separate and let it sit there as a private ledger: evidence that the pain had been endured.

In the same period, my method of supporting Nancy changed, too. I started giving her cash whenever I could meet her, handing it to her quietly in a parking lot.

Eventually, Nancy found a more permanent place than her hastily arranged temporary stays had been. A one-bedroom. It was small enough that things had to be negotiated inside it. Chelsea took the room. Nancy took the rest in a curious mimicry of how Nancy, Mom, and I had lived in that second tiny home after Dad left. If you haven't lived that way, you don't understand what it costs—the constant adjustment, the sense that privacy is a luxury—just like how you can never fully stretch out because the space won't allow it.

But the important thing was that she was housed. She was not on the street. She had a door she could lock.

Chelsea was working by then, carrying more than a young woman should have to take. Brian was there, thank God, close enough to help in ways I couldn't, steady in the daily. And my household boundary hardened.

Meanwhile, my work started requiring me to travel more. So, I did. I dove into work, for it was where the rules were clear, and competence was rewarded rather than questioned. Work was also the engine that kept me doing what I was doing: the checks, the repairs, the cash in envelopes.

Inside that apparent "solution," there was still a long tail of sadness because the real loss of the forced sale wasn't only the house. It was the message it gave. That Nancy's well-being could be voted on. That my care for her was negotiable. That love had to be hidden to survive.

As I reached Chelsea's steps now, years later, outside the house where Nancy would spend her last weeks, I glanced again at the For Sale sign down the street and felt the old grief flare up in a new form.

A house for sale is supposed to mean possibility. But for us, it had meant exile. I knocked, then let myself in, and the present swallowed the memory again, the sound of the door, the smell of the house, the familiar weight of what was coming.

When family becomes unsafe, you start looking for belonging in older places: names, photographs, stories that don't exclude but hark back to a more pleasant interaction like Grandpap and Grandmam's world through reunion.

There was one more small exile I didn't understand at the time. When Nancy had to move, she couldn't fit all her things in her new home. That's what downsizing means when you're already living small: You throw away pieces of yourself. Some binders had to go.

She handed me one of them as if it were nothing, like it wasn't a part of her.

"I can't fit this anymore," she said. "You keep it. It's a family tree; Uncle Shem and I worked on it. It's Grandpap Shem and Grandmam Cathryn's side."

I told her that I'd keep it safe, with the other binders that held her life as my life has always held things: in paper, in tabs, in proof.

I didn't know then how soon that binder would find its way back onto a table, how, in the middle of hospice, it would show up by mistake like a message, and how Nancy would look at it and say one word that turned the room.

17

The Reunion

When I walked into Chelsea's house, the first thing that hit me was the smell, fresh hamburgers and hot dogs, just made on the deck, drifting in from the tailgate grill outside. I had files under one arm, as I always do, paperwork, folders, the kind of things that make you feel less helpless because at least you can hold them. Nancy had handed me some of it in the hospital. Other pieces I'd collected on my own: the practical artifacts of an ending that required proof.

In my shuffle, car to driveway, driveway to porch, porch to foyer, I set the stack down on the dining table, and something slid free.

When I glanced down, I saw that it was a binder. I picked it up, and it was thicker than the rest. Heavier. It was the type of binder that looked like a school project until you opened it and realized it was a life project. The spine was worn from being carried, opened, and carried again. There were tabs, loose pages, and notes in margins. Old photocopies of documents that had traveled through a few hands before ours.

I had brought it with me by mistake, but I didn't mind that I had it now. After all, it was the family tree binder Nancy and Uncle Shem, my mother's brother, created before he passed.

I lifted it from the pile. "Look what showed up in my stack."

Nancy's eyes followed it. Her face shifted in that small, instant way that told me I'd hit something true. "That," she said. "That reunion."

Brian stopped chewing. He wiped his fingers on a napkin as if he needed a reason to use his hands, then leaned close enough that Nancy could catch him without straining. "She talks about it all the time," he said quietly. "How much it meant to her."

Brian was eating, one hand on a burger, the other resting on his knee like he'd paused mid-bite without realizing it. The smell that had met me at the door was still hanging around the room, and it pulled a thread through time.

Because the reunion had smelled like this, too, burgers on a grill under a pavilion, paper plates, the warm grease-and-smoke of a cookout, the type of food that says: We're here, we're together, we're feeding each other.

The binder sat on the table like an accusation and a gift, all at once. An object from an earlier era of our lives, back when "family" still meant something you could chase. Back when the past felt like a puzzle you could solve instead of a weight you carried.

I stared at it for a second, and the room changed.

The binder was one of the means Nancy and I tried to keep our dead present in our lives. Our mother, especially. We missed her as one would miss a compass, less for the memories and more for the direction you lose when she's gone. Mom had been the connective tissue in this. The storyteller. The one who knew who belonged to whom and why it mattered.

When she died, the line went quiet. Nancy and I would talk about it sometimes, just two siblings talking plainly in those moments when the phone goes quiet, when the subject drifts toward the truth. We missed Mom as a presence, but not just emotionally. Practically. We missed her as the keeper of names.

Nancy had started this family tree years earlier with Uncle Shem. They didn't have the money to travel. They didn't have the money to hire anyone.

They did it the old way: notes, photocopies, scraps, a stubborn willingness to keep digging.

They started with what they had. Then life made the project into a luxury. Nancy had bills, after all. Her body had limits. Chelsea had needs, too. A family tree is beautiful, but it doesn't keep the heat on.

The binder became one more thing she loved that she had to sit on a shelf. That is, until my life, unexpectedly, gave me time.

For eight years, I commuted weekly from New Jersey to various client locations across the country. It sounds glamorous if you say it fast. It wasn't. It was a grind: airports, delays, rental cars, the constant sense of living in two places while fully belonging to neither.

If you're stuck in enough terminals, you either go numb or you find something to build. And because idleness has never been easy for me, I needed a project that could turn waiting into progress.

One week, I found myself staring at another delay and remembering the binder. Nancy and Uncle Shem's handwriting. Mom's stories. The silence that had replaced her.

Hence, I subscribed to Ancestry. It started as just something to do at the Denver Airport, a way to occupy hours that would otherwise evaporate. But then, over time, the project actually stuck. Like how a puzzle catches when you find the edge pieces, and suddenly the whole thing feels solvable.

Building this didn't fix the past, of course. It gave it borders, so it stopped spilling into everything.

Nancy and Uncle Shem had started with what they had. I had what they didn't: time.

Late at night at hotel desks, under harsh airport lighting, with my laptop open beside a plastic cup of coffee, I expanded their work. I traced lines forward and backward. I followed branches until they forked. I filled in the gaps.

At first, it was just Mom's side that I worked on, for that was the side Nancy and I loved talking about. Mom's line felt warmer, given everything. It felt like belonging. There were Welsh roots there, and even in documents, you could sense a cadence, a stubbornness that wasn't cruel. Humor. Humanity.

And yes, there were a few famous names tucked into that line, like very distant cousins such as Queen Elizabeth II, Prince Charles, Al Gore, Jessica

Simpson, and Richard Nixon, which made Nancy laugh, as she always laughed at irony: Of course, Mom's side has famous folks. Nancy and I joked that Mom would have liked to know that Grandpa Alfred now had reason to approve.

It wasn't the fame that mattered. It was proof of continuity. Evidence that we belonged to something larger than the narrow slice we could see.

After a while, inevitably, I went over to Dad's side, too. That's when the project's tone started to change. Dad's background didn't feel like a puzzle to be solved in the same way. It felt like a wound that kept re-opening as you traced it backward. The further I went, the more I saw the same themes repeating: poverty, institutions, broken homes, people moved like inventory.

One detail hit me hard because it made everything else make sense: We had an ancestor who had apparently been arrested and transported to Australia. That is a sentence that sounds like trivia until you understand what it is, removal made official. Displacement turned into family history. After that, there were workhouses. Separations. Children who were treated as burdens to be managed. Each of these revelations hit hard in its own way. Still, I kept going.

Because in the middle of it, something interesting, that I hadn't entirely expected, started happening: The project brought Nancy and me closer together. We started talking more because of the tree, a subject we could delve into without bringing up Nancy's illness. It gave us a shared mission to keep pursuing. It let us keep Mom in the room with us without turning every conversation into a mourning session.

Whenever I discovered something new, I would call Nancy and tell her what I'd found. She would laugh or gasp or go quiet in that way she went quiet when something mattered. She wasn't doing the heavy research anymore, but she was present in the project with her insights, reactions, and questions. The tree became a shared space between us, extending its branches over the gap in the middle to connect us once more.

It also gave me an idea: If Mom had been the connective tissue between us and our stories, maybe we could rebuild some of it with other people, and Nancy, too. With that in mind, I started reaching out to the people I'd discovered on various branches of our family tree by email, phone, and text messages. I reached out to cousins we'd never met and entire branches that had drifted away from us long ago.

Sometimes I didn't hear anything back. Other times, all I would receive would be polite distance. But sometimes I got a voice on the other end saying, "Yes, your mother's name was…"

In April 2019, before COVID, a reunion took shape. Not a formal thing. Something grounded in a place that meant something to us: a small grove-style amusement park in Pennsylvania. The type of place that still smelled like fried dough and pine trees and summer. A place that held a specific sort of family happiness: ordinary, domestic, unrecorded.

For Nancy, it was a thrill. Not because she was chasing novelty but because she yearned for belonging. Because she had lived through years when family was narrowed and fractured, becoming conditional. The idea that actual blood relatives might show up simply because we were connected was intoxicating.

She lit up the way she did whenever something expanded her world. Meanwhile, our daughters got to see family lines that had been missing. As more relatives popped up, they stopped being just names on a page but faces and voices. They got to see that family wasn't the only people who could hurt you. It could also be the people who arrived with curiosity and warmth.

That day, under the pavilion, you could feel it: happiness with family. Not movie happiness, something quieter and real. People laughing. Kids wandering in and out of the shade. Adults comparing memories over paper plates, passing food down the table, calling out names across the benches. Beyond the pavilion, you could hear the park living its life. The distant rattle of a ride. A tinny song is looping somewhere. The smell of fried dough drifted in, then pine, sunscreen, and charcoal.

Nancy was happy.

You could see it in her smile, how it stayed put instead of flashing and disappearing. It widened slowly, like it had room, and it softened her whole face. And you could hear her. Nancy had a laugh you could pick out in a crowd, a bright, unguarded sound that carried, the kind that made other people turn their heads and start smiling, too, even before they knew what was funny.

Relatives we hadn't seen in years came up to her, and she did not hesitate. She hugged them the way you hug someone you've missed, not the careful half-hug of obligation. Arms around shoulders. Cheek to cheek. A squeeze that lingered an extra second, as if she were confirming they were real. Hands kept finding hands. A palm on an arm. Fingers interlacing for a moment. That simple warmth of contact that says, "You're not alone, you're in the circle."

I watched her take it in with something like disbelief. She looked from face to face as if she were taking inventory of a fortune she didn't fully trust would last. Every so often, she would pause, smile again, and you could see her trying not to cry, not out of sadness, but out of being overwhelmed by something she had been starved of. Then, gradually, she settled into it. Her shoulders dropped. Her breathing slowed. She let the moment hold her.

And it was there, beneath that pavilion roof, with paper plates and the background noise of an amusement park, that the word arrived.

Not "reunion."

Not "family."

The other word.

The one that turns a day into a marker for the before-and-after. Hence, she waited until we were alone for a moment. She didn't want to make a scene. She never did. She didn't want to steal the day from everyone else.

Then she looked at me, steadily, and she said, simply:

"I have cancer."

The day was still bright, and the pavilion was still whole. Everything was ordinary, pretty even until it wasn't. That sentence? It didn't belong in that place. It felt like someone had dropped a large stone in the middle of a picnic, crushing everything beneath it with a *thunk*.

For a second, I couldn't hear the amusement park anymore. I could see the pavilion roof, the paper plates, Nancy's face. I could hear her voice, calm in a way that said she was bracing you. But the ground shifted.

Again.

"I'm sure it's nothing," she said, offering hope wrapped in understatement, a way to keep the pavilion standing.

But even then, something in me did what it always does: It moved from "why" to "how." How were we going to handle this? How bad was it?

How soon?

Years later, in hospice, the artifacts I was handling would change from binders to bank statements. Still, the purpose of my hands would stay the same: to make protection enforceable, to make decency real, to keep my sister safe in the language our family most reliably honored.

And then it would be time to order things one final time.

18

Trust

"**B**illy," Nancy said, laughing as we ordered her urn, "just make sure it has my name on it somewhere."

She picked one she liked, a pretty blue one with butterflies. It was a modest thing from Costco. Even then, her frugality and humor were intact.

When she said this, I couldn't help but remember when it was time to inter Dad and Liz, there were two identical urns before me on a table, all that was left of them for all the chaos my Dad and Liz had given us. I handled ordering Dad's urn with the same business pragmatism he would have appreciated.

When Liz died, I repeated Dad's funeral options exactly, right down to the same blue urn, hymns, and funeral options, only changing his name to hers. Nancy was always amused by my sarcastic irony, which creatively settled it all, reconciling it without speeches. It wasn't missed, evidently, by the funeral director, either. She picked up on it and aligned with my needs and humor. Nancy loved it.

The director looked at the two identical urns, then at me, and said in a deadpan beat, "Round and round she goes…"

I asked, "Who is who?"

She flipped them gently, making sure one hand remained on the urn's lid to prevent any spillage, and pointed. She winked, smiled, and said, "Names are on the bottom."

Later, I remembered this, and when we were ordering Nancy's urn, I told her, "Name's on the bottom, Nant."

She laughed and nodded, smiling.

Late at night in hospice, between medicine doses, I opened Nancy's laptop, and I reviewed her finances once more, to keep my mind busy, in the manner I'd reviewed a thousand other things in my life. I kept calm as I worked, going through everything methodically, because there were tasks to be done and because my hands needed something to hold.

Chelsea had gone to bed. The house had that quiet that only comes when the day's caregiving has ended. Still, the night's vigilance has not begun. A dim lamp burned in the corner like a small agreement against darkness. I could hear the machine in Nancy's room doing its steady work. Somewhere upstairs, the floor creaked as if the house itself were remembering to stay awake.

Nancy slept, if what she did at that stage could be called sleep. She drifted in and out of it, carried by medication and exhaustion and a body that was pulling inward.

On my screen were deposits and dates, the tidy language of bank statements. I spotted it then. A trust deposit.

There it was, buried among numerous ordinary transactions, that one line that would look like nothing if you didn't know what it represented, what it took to create. I stared at it longer than I expected to. Here was proof, on a late-night screen in a hospice house, that I had once tried to build a stable foundation the only way I knew how:

By making it legally unavoidable.

I clicked until I found the source, the payor line, the trace that told the truth. The deposit matched a check cut from the trust I had created for Liz as the estate payout for Nancy. The dividend I hoped to use for Nancy's salvation after I kept my promise to Dad, after Liz was cared for.

My mind slipped back in time as I stared at this thing, scurrying away from the lamp and the quiet house and flitting to the day the promise became paper to the days when we knew that Dad was dying.

His heart was failing at the time, slowly but persistently, like a door that no longer closes properly. He and Liz were living outside Atlanta by then, the place he had wanted to go, where he would get to enact his dream of a clean retirement and start a fresh version of life that didn't include the mess he had left behind.

We rarely visited. Not because we didn't care, but because the gravity of our lives pulled us elsewhere, and also because visiting Dad and Liz always carried its own cost. It meant navigating Liz's temperament, her sharpness, her ability to sour a room in under a minute. It meant choosing which parts of yourself you were willing to leave at the door.

Dad's decline changed the equation. When I saw him again, after the diagnosis, I could tell that he was scared. In his fear, he did something that surprised me: He reached for competence. He reached for me.

He knew, without saying it plainly, that Liz wouldn't be able to manage what was coming. He knew she could spend whatever was in reach. He wanted a solution, not a fight. Something he could believe in as the lights went out.

So, I built one.

I set up the trust carefully, with structure, with protection built in. I used the skills Dad had once insisted I learn. The ones wrapped up in my accounting degree, the business major he mandated over my engineering desires, to create something he never created on his own: a mechanism that forced him to do right by Nancy.

The trust carried two meanings at once, at least for me: the legal one as an instrument that could hold money in place until it was supposed to move, and the other one as the quieter contract Dad and I made without poetry, stating that he would let go, and I would handle what he'd left unfinished.

Nancy was part of those conversations, not in the weeds of paperwork, but in the emotional reality of the situation. When the trust was established, she asked me something that wasn't criticism so much as a quiet attempt to keep me from hurting myself.

"Are you sure you want to go through all this?"

Her voice carried that familiar blend of love and worry: Nancy, seeing the load I had, offering me an exit.

I told her the truth.

"We need to set things right," I said. "Otherwise, Liz will spend as she always does. She'll turn money into chaos. I'll care for her, and what's left, then you'll be set."

Nancy didn't argue. She rarely did when she knew the decision had already been made. She went quiet in that way she did when something landed in her chest, and she didn't want to show it too openly.

The trust wasn't about sentimentality. It was about functionality. It honored my commitment to keep Liz safe, managed the money, and ensured that Nancy would inherit only after Liz's care needs were met. Then Dad died, and everything accelerated.

People think death is one event. It's not. It's paperwork, calls, timing, flights, decisions stacked on decisions. We had limited time. We had planes to catch. We had obligations waiting at home.

Dad was cremated.

We were in the funeral home parking lot afterward, luggage at our side. The urn wasn't hot, exactly, but it had that recent warmth that makes your mind insist on what it means.

The funeral director said, calmly, that she'd give it a few minutes. There was nothing theatrical about it, just a practical person managing some practical detail so we could travel.

Across the street was the church where the memorial would be held. On the other side, close enough to walk if you had to, was the bank.

My lawyer met me in the church lobby before the service, with a folder in hand. Not because it was a good time, but because it was the only time we could do this, for the reality of the world is that a signature doesn't care whether your father's ashes have gone cold yet or if they're still warm.

Unfeeling, I signed where the tabs told me to and initialed where the lines told me to. The trust paperwork was clean and brisk in the manner the law can be when it isn't pretending to be human. We set the account. We made it real. The machinery that would care for Liz and later protect Nancy was thus locked in while people were still arriving with casserole dishes and condolences.

That's what Dad had entrusted to me. Speed and follow-through without any fuss or delay.

After Dad died, we held his memorial and then, later, we held Liz's service at the church she attended, the one Dad had started going to with her. The sanctuary was familiar to the church people in a way it was not to me. They knew the rhythms, the coffee setup, who would bring what, who would stand where. They had known Dad and Liz together, week after week, the same couple in the same pew. It showed in the way they greeted us, like they were hosting the closing chapter of a story they had watched unfold from the inside.

Afterward, we had a memorial service at that local church. Coffee was served afterward, as churches always do, as if caffeine could keep grief from taking over the room.

I spoke. I gave Dad something honest, heartfelt, a clean goodbye, nothing cruel or complicated, because death is not the moment to settle old accounts. Nancy and I moved through it as we always had, a team, exchanging glances, doing the quiet work of keeping ourselves composed.

After the service, while people milled around and talked in that odd post-service tone, half somber and half social, I thanked some of the local women who had tried to be kind to Liz. They spoke of Dad with an easy warmth. You could tell they had liked him. One of them, Southern, smiling, said, "Your daddy was nice, but…that Liz…she's a challenge," and then she did the thing Southerners do when they're trying to be polite while still telling the truth.

"Bless her heart."

Then another woman, Northern, transplanted, plainly uninterested in the local softness, leaned in close enough that her voice didn't have to travel.

"Oh, honey," she said. "Cut the crap. She was a bitch."

Nancy and I looked at each other just then and couldn't help but smile. Not because we enjoyed cruelty, but because it was relief and confirmation that we weren't imagining the problem, we weren't "too sensitive." Liz could be difficult in ways that drove away help, and then she felt abandoned when it disappeared.

After Dad died, I did what I said I would do.

As I promised, I took care of Liz. At first, I tried to support her from a distance with phone calls, arrangements, and requests to the few local contacts I could still reach. I treated it like any other complicated situation: build a system, set expectations, contain chaos.

But chaos has a way of leaking. Often, I would get a call from someone local, usually a church volunteer who had offered to stop by and help with groceries or a ride.

"She was…rough," the woman would say, and you could hear the embarrassment in it, like she didn't want to gossip about a widow.

"What happened?" I'd ask, already knowing.

There was always a pause first. Then the details would follow.

Liz would comment on people's bodies and clothes as if she couldn't help herself. It didn't matter that nobody had asked. She would remark on someone's hair, weight, skin, shoes…Really, anything that was visible was fair game. If someone tried to redirect her, she'd snap back at them, talk over them, correct them, insult them, and then act as if they were the problem for having feelings about it.

Once, I arranged for a cleaning person to help, someone reliable who had done this kind of work before. The woman was there, working, trying to finish the job, and when she said she needed to leave on time, Liz laughed and said, "What, you think you can just leave? I ought to chain you to the wall."

It was delivered as if it were a "joke." It landed like a threat. The woman finished what she could, gathered her things, and didn't come back. That became the pattern quickly enough. People arrived with good intentions, and within a visit or two, they were gone, burned out, offended, or just plain done. The church volunteers rotated: one would try, then disappear; another would take a turn, then quietly stop answering the phone when I called. Help didn't end with a sensational confrontation. It ended with silence. Fewer returned calls. Fewer names that were willing to try.

Liz wore people down not because taking care of her was impossible, but because she could turn care into conflict in under a minute, make a simple errand feel like an argument, make a kind offer feel like an insult, make a volunteer feel like a target.

Then, Liz had a stroke. It wasn't the kind of stroke that immediately killed her. It was the kind that rewired her in smaller, stranger ways first. At the beginning, it looked like ordinary confusion, misplaced words, and little stalls in the middle of sentences, until I realized what it was: She was losing nouns.

She could still talk around things. Verbs and adjectives survived. Her tone did too, as did the impulse to cut. But when she reached for the object or the label, her mouth would stop, and her face would tighten with frustration, as if the word were sitting just outside her reach.

"Hand me the…the…You know, the thing," Liz would say, chopping the air with her fingers.

This was the new pattern. Liz would start a sentence, going, "That… that…" and then hit the blank. The sentence would collapse in on itself before it could become a weapon. She could still radiate contempt, but she couldn't land it with language the way she used to. The edge was still there; the blade had gone dull.

Then, because Liz always needed somewhere to put the irritation, she would try to pivot into what she'd always done: assign blame, name the target, score the point.

When Nancy heard this, she didn't miss the irony of it.

"It sounds bad, but when I try to talk to her, it's like I am on the $20,000 Pyramid game show, guessing the words," I would tell Nancy.

"That's a God nod," she said in response, half joke, half theology, because of course the first mercy wasn't comfort or healing. It was a restraint, and Liz could no longer offend anyone.

Another thing that the stroke meant was that Liz could no longer drive. That, more than anything, forced a decision on us.

I moved her to assisted living.

Having made that decision, I walked into her house, and there I fully understood the gravity of the situation.

The mess inside was not just a mess. It was squalor. There was dog feces, garbage, and a stench that told you standards had been slipping for a long time. This had become the type of place that makes you realize a person's inner chaos eventually becomes visible in their environment.

I cleaned what I could and hired help where I had to. Over time, it became clear that Liz wasn't only "difficult." As doctors' visits followed, I came to understand that dementia had gotten its hands on her. At first, it manifested itself as just repetition, asking the same question three times in ten minutes, irritating but easy enough to dismiss. Then she started forgetting she'd just eaten, calling me to report some "emergency," only to drift off into an entirely different topic mid-sentence. Over time, these annoyances moved into the wholly different territory of genuine disruption.

The first time I saw her wandering the apartment half-dressed, I told myself it was a one-off. Heat. Confusion. A bad day. But it happened again. The boundaries that used to keep a person private and contained—clothes, bathrooms, and modesty—began to give way. I arrived once and found her in the middle of the room with a pot on the floor, using it as if it were the most logical thing in the world. She didn't look embarrassed. She looked practical. As if the room had become the bathroom and no one had informed her otherwise.

Then came the accusations.

Liz started calling me by my Dad's name regularly. Then she became convinced that the neighbor had stolen her dentures. She said this with absolute certainty, the kind that doesn't ask questions. It wasn't "I can't find them." It was "He took them." I searched drawers, purses, the sink, the trash, under cushions, places you would never put teeth on purpose, but where a mind might set them down for "just a second" and then erase the act. Sometimes we found them. Sometimes we didn't. The certainty never changed.

At the facility, the target shifted to staff. Liz's laundry was "stolen." Her things were "missing." A shirt she couldn't locate became evidence. A sock became a grievance. The story always had a villain because it's easier than admitting your own mind is slipping away.

I visited her. I managed her. I fielded complaints, calls from staff and from Liz, even from people who had tried to help and were now tired. I learned to ask the same questions every time, calmly, like a checklist: When did you last see it? What color? Where were you standing? Who was with you? And then I'd do what I'd been doing my whole life, go looking, quietly correcting reality without making her feel exposed.

That was the pattern: small misjudgments at first, then a life that couldn't hold a coherent day.

Five years.

That's how long I carried her through calls, visits, updates, and interventions, trying to keep her stable and cared for, both for her sake and for the sake of everyone around her.

Once, on an outing, she came back with a new sweater and the bright, pleased look of someone who'd managed a normal errand. Later, when she wasn't in the room, I noticed a security tag still attached, one of those hard plastic ones you're not supposed to walk out with. There wasn't a receipt, nor was there a bag. Just the sweater, as if it had simply appeared.

I didn't confront her. There was no point in it. Dementia doesn't respond to being corrected as a teenager does. It doesn't blush. It doesn't learn.

I found the head of the unit instead and asked for a private minute. I handed her cash, enough to cover what the sweater would have cost, and said, quietly, that I wanted it handled properly. There was no report. No embarrassment for anyone. No phone call that would turn into a story, the way stories spread in facilities. The staff member looked at me with that expression people get when they recognize a family's method: not denial, just quiet repair.

That was how it went after that: I stopped trying to restore Liz and focused on preventing damage. As her cognitive decline progressed, Liz's world kept shrinking. First, it was a private room, her own bedroom, her own space, her own door to close. Then, as her needs increased and her memory thinned, she was moved into smaller and smaller units with greater and greater supervision, fewer choices, and less room for a person to pretend they were still independent. Eventually, her space was reduced to what she could safely occupy: a shared area and a room just large enough for her bed.

At some point, she stopped consistently recognizing people. Names fell away from her mind. Faces became unfamiliar. Even offers of help stopped landing as help because you have to remember who someone is before you can receive what they're giving.

And then the body joined the mind in letting go. Liz lost the ability to swallow. Food became a risk. Water became a thing to be negotiated; she would refuse it. The facility started talking about interventions, about keeping calories going, about tubes, about forcing a body to continue a process it no longer seemed able to perform.

I learned the hospice options then, this being my introduction to it, which prepared me for what was to come in some small way. I reviewed the process and then signed the hospice order. Not because I was giving up, but because I wasn't going to turn her last chapter into a fight with gravity. I wasn't going to force-feed a woman whose mind was already gone from the room.

She passed peacefully, in her sleep. Afterward, I cremated her, too, with the same style urn as Dad, same service format, and I reran the funeral to close that chapter efficiently and honorably and, yes, with names on the bottom.

With that, the chapter closed. Sitting here, now, in Chelsea's house years later, between medicine doses, staring at that trust deposit glowing on a screen, I could feel the line connecting it all. Dad had trusted me, and I had honored that trust. The instrument of that trust moved money the way we'd designed it to move, with care first, then inheritance as an act of decency made enforceable.

The trust, I figured, would ensure that Nancy, my sister, my co-narrator, the person who carried goodness through every version of this family, would not be left unprotected if I could help it, or so I thought. For me, that was what the trust had been: an attempt to force decency into a family history that often avoided it.

Now, in hospice, as Nancy drifted in and out downstairs in the living room below me and I upstairs in her old bed, I felt the aching irony of it.

We had made her "safe" on paper. But paper didn't stop time. Not when her body became the battlefield.

19

Treatments

Chelsea's place had a few steps up to the front door, and the glass showed that it was the hospice nurse who came, wearing a mask. Thanksgiving prep was already underway somewhere in the kitchen: frying sausage for stuffing, butter, onion, the beginnings of side dishes, and tradition.

Masks had become a force of habit. Since the pandemic, there was residual fear, too. Yet, with Nancy, there was no fear, only grace in death's acceptance.

For a second, it struck me as funny, not funny like a joke, but funny like how your brain catches on to an out-of-place detail when everything else has become too heavy to hold directly. Nancy wasn't contagious, yet Nancy was dying. The mask felt like muscle memory, like a remnant of years when danger had been invisible and everywhere.

Maybe it was a habit. Perhaps it was policy. Maybe it was just the nurse's own way of moving through houses now, carrying the old world forward, even when the new world had changed its meaning entirely.

She greeted me quietly, checked her supplies, and moved toward the familiar routines: listen, assess, adjust. The calm competence of someone who knows how to be inside other people's endings without collapsing into them.

I watched her for a moment and felt that strange collision of timelines. The mask wasn't only a hospice. It was the pandemic, when distance became love's new definition, when "protecting someone" often meant staying away from them.

Nancy's years of treatment for her cancer coincided with managing the onset of Liz's dementia during the pandemic, and she had been living in that contradiction. The hospice nurse wearing a mask made me recall a picture Brian sent me of Nancy when she rang the bell at the hospital. The treatments are complete, and she is wearing a mask.

I couldn't visit her the way I wanted to. I could call, though, which is what I did. Not just when something was wrong, but as a practice, like checking a vital sign, like keeping a line of connection open so Nancy wouldn't feel abandoned. Every time I called, I did the same thing: I tried to make her laugh.

That was my role with Nancy, because humor was the rope we used to climb through hard rooms. Because if I could get her to smile, if I could hear even a thin little laugh at the end of a sentence, it meant she was still herself. It meant illness hadn't taken her voice entirely.

She would answer weakly sometimes, her voice breathy, doing the work of conversation while her body did the work of suffering. Her tone would be soft, as if her voice had shrunk to conserve energy. She didn't want to worry me. She didn't want to turn the call into a report of misery.

Nancy rarely ever complained. She didn't narrate her pain. Instead, she always edited it for other people's comfort. That wasn't denial. It was character. Nancy had always carried pain quietly. She could name what was happening; she wasn't pretending it wasn't happening, but she refused to perform it.

So, she'd talk, and in return, I'd tell stories.

I'd push toward something that sounded like everyday life, even while her days were being governed by fatigue, nausea, and the clock.

Then came the surgery. The double mastectomy that we all hoped would work. Even writing those words makes my chest tighten, because it's the kind of treatment that sounds clinical until you remember what it really is: a body altered most intimately, out of vanity or preference, but for pure survival's sake.

After that surgery, Nancy was in the kind of pain that would have flattened most people. She was bedridden in that small apartment where recovery felt like confinement. She could not move much. She had to accept help in ways that ran directly counter to her pride.

Then came chemotherapy, and the nausea this brought on wasn't just "feeling ill." It was a full-body revolt. Food became impossible. Smells became threats. Sleep became fragmented and thin. A day became something you endured hour by hour.

The mercy, sometimes, was as small as a sleeve of crackers on the nightstand, plain enough to tolerate, practical enough to keep her from going empty.

I would ask Nancy about her appetite, as it was challenging with chemotherapy. She responded with a humor beat, always looking for the bright side. Very Grandpa Shem, I thought.

"Well, chemo suits me as I've always wanted to drop a few pounds and fit into my favorite outfit. Now I can," Nancy said on our calls.

I'd keep going, because I could hear her breathing change when she started to laugh.

"Oh, don't make me laugh too much," she said once. "It hurts when I do."

So, I reached for a story. Grandpa Shem's mustard plaster, his confidence in it, and his certainty that the cure was equal parts mustard and personality.

"You should try putting a mustard plaster on 'yar elbow,'" I said in Grandpap Shem's Welsh accent.

Nancy laughed. She tried to stop herself, but couldn't. Then she groaned, half scolding me and half grateful.

The radiation followed next, and she tried, she really did. In her quiet, determined way, she showed up because she believed showing up mattered. But radiation did what it could. It burned her skin horribly. It turned her body into a map of pain. It made endurance start to look less like courage and more like cruelty.

At some point, when she could no longer tolerate it, she stopped. Still, she didn't complain. Never once.

She'd mention her pain as a fact sometimes, something that just existed, and do so almost casually. Then, she'd pivot to something else. She was always ready for stories. Always ready to ask about my life, my work, my girls, as if her own body weren't in the middle of an assault.

Sometimes, after we hung up, I would sit there staring at the phone, feeling rage rise in me with nowhere to go.

Don't rage at her, rage at the unfairness, I'd tell myself. *Rage at the fact that she's been cheated of ease for so long, cheated of the comfort of a marriage, then by poverty, then by illness, and now even the attempt to cure her demands an amount of suffering that feels obscene.*

That parallel period is hard to explain to people who haven't lived inside layered responsibility. Hard things overlap. They stack. They fight for oxygen. Most days, I felt like I was walking a hallway with doors on both sides, one opening into dementia logistics, the other into cancer, and there was no room in the corridor to sit down.

During COVID, our calls became the norm of our days. It was how I checked on both Liz and Nancy. It was how I stayed in the same life without being in the same room.

Remote support thus became the defining feature of our relationship for a time. Nancy would be coming off treatment or bracing for the next one, and the hospital rules kept shifting like the weather. There were always many asks. Distance requirements thanks to COVID. Who could sit where? Who could come in at all? The world narrowed to screens and updates and the sound of each other's voices, trying to stand in for presence.

Sometimes I'd call in the morning. Sometimes it was late, after a workday that had already drained me. I would sit in my car with the engine off, or at my desk with a spreadsheet open like a decoy, and I would keep my voice steady because steadiness mattered to Nancy more than reassurance ever did.

"How are you?" I'd ask.

"I'm fine," she'd say, because "fine" was her shield. Then she would do what she always did. She would pivot away from her own pain like she was protecting me from it.

"What's going on with Liz?" she'd ask.

That was Nancy, even when she was sick, turning the call into something she could manage. She gave it a topic. She gave me a problem to solve. She let Liz's chaos distract her from her own treatments.

So, I'd tell her stories, small and factual at first, because that was the only way to say it without letting it become a flood.

"The facility called again," I'd say. "Liz thinks someone stole something from her."

"What did she lose this time?" Nancy would ask. Not amused exactly, just tracking, already building the pattern in her head.

"She can't find her teeth," I'd say. "She's sure the neighbor took them. She's convinced the staff is hiding her laundry. She's angry at anyone who tries to help."

Nancy would make a sound, half sigh, and half recognition.

"She's losing nouns," Nancy said once. It wasn't a guess. It was a diagnosis spoken from a sister who had spent a lifetime reading people through their cracks. "That's why she's less sharp."

"Yeah," I said. "The edges are softer. The chaos is still there."

Nancy paused, then let the irony do what it always did for her. It told the truth without a speech.

"So, she can't call people names anymore," she said.

Dark, but factual. In our family, that counted as mercy.

Those calls became a strange braid. I talked to Nancy through Liz's decline, and Nancy tried to talk me through hers without naming it directly. I told her what the week required: calls, arrangements, decisions stacked on decisions. I treated it like everything else under strain. Build a system. Set expectations. Contain chaos.

But chaos has a way of leaking, as I said before.

"Are you still spending money on her?" Nancy would ask sometimes. Her tone wasn't accusatory, just had that measuring edge it did when it came to Liz.

"Yes," I'd say. "Because I promised Dad I would."

A quiet beat would follow. Nancy let the sentence hang long enough to show she heard the weight in it.

"Is it worth it?" she'd ask. By this, she didn't mean "Is Liz worth it?" Nancy never talked like that. She meant the structure. The promise. The cost.

I'd answer the same way every time.

"I need to reconcile what Dad couldn't," I told her. "I need to make things right."

"For me," she said softly, because she understood the second half of the sentence before I said it.

"For you," I said. "When Liz is gone, what's left should go where it should have gone all along."

Nancy didn't respond with theatrics. She went quiet in that way; she went quiet when something mattered, and she didn't want to break it by talking too much.

After we hung up, I'd sit there with the phone still warm in my hand. My life was split cleanly down the middle. Liz's dementia on one side. Nancy's treatments, on the other hand. COVID is pressing down on everything in between. I watched the trust balance the way you watch fuel in a long storm.

Not obsessively, but carefully.

Because money wasn't love in our family, it was how you made protection enforceable.

Besides, if remote support had become the relationship, this was the closeness I could offer Nancy in that season. Calls. Stories. The quiet work of making sure that when the time came, she would not be left unprotected.

Nancy understood it. She never guilted me for not visiting. She never asked for more than I could give. She knew I was stretched thin. She knew the constraints were real. And in some strange way, our calls became even more intimate because they were so pared down, voice to voice, story to story, laughter as proof of life.

Then, eventually, the words came, almost impossible after years of suffering: Cured. Remission.

However, the doctors phrased it, the effect was the same: We felt as though a door had cracked open toward a future Nancy had stopped fully trusting.

Relief is not simple in families like ours. Relief comes with a shadow. It doesn't erase the desert you crossed to get there. It doesn't give back the years you lost. It doesn't restore the innocence of believing your body is your own.

And yet…

It meant she could breathe without constant dread in her throat. It meant Chelsea could imagine a life that didn't revolve around appointments. It meant I could let myself believe, even just slightly, that all the work had been for something.

Around this same time, Chelsea got engaged.

That season felt like a brief return to ordinary human joys: planning, dresses, invitations, photos. Nancy loved it. She wanted the wedding to be beautiful. She wanted Chelsea to have what she had long tried to protect.

When the wedding came, Nancy was ready for it, as she always was when something mattered.

It was at a local Lutheran church, a small gathering by wedding standards, maybe a hundred people, relatives and friends, and the handful of familiar faces who had stayed consistent across the years. The sanctuary had that church quiet before the music started, the soft shuffling, the rustle of programs, people turning to look down the aisle, and then pretending they hadn't. Chelsea looked luminous in her dress, calm in a way that only happens when you've done the work ahead of time and can finally let the day carry you. She moved with the contained excitement brides have as they try to take in everything without letting it spill.

Nancy had a beautiful dress of her own, chosen with care. She looked radiant, too, but in a way that never tried to compete with Chelsea. She carried herself with a deliberate modesty, the mother-of-the-bride instinct to frame the picture rather than step into it. Her happiness showed anyway. It was on her face, in the way she kept smiling at people as they approached, in the way she held her shoulders as if pride could be posture.

Chelsea and Nancy had planned the wedding well. They had done the work ahead of time, which kept a day from becoming a scramble. The seating, the timing, the small hand-offs, who was responsible for what, and when. The parts that look effortless are only that way because someone thought about them early. Nancy liked that kind of planning. It made the day feel safe.

For a while, it really was.

At the reception, there was supposed to be a cocktail hour outside. Then the rain came, not a drizzle, but a steady, soaking pour that turned the plan into improvisation. People huddled under overhangs and darted between doors. Hair got damp. The shoes got wet. Someone laughed loud enough to reset the mood, and then others joined in, because what else do you do? It became one of those weddings where the weather became a story everyone shared. "Rain is good luck," people kept telling Chelsea, and the phrase started to sound less like a superstition and more like a communal decision to make the day work.

I remember watching Nancy move through the room with a steadiness that felt deliberate. She wasn't pretending she hadn't suffered. She was choosing not to make suffering the day's center. She greeted people first, smiling and present. She would touch someone's arm, lean in, and say someone's name like it mattered that they showed up.

Her face had a light in it I hadn't seen in a long time. This was not the "everything is fine" light. It was genuine satisfaction. Fulfillment. The look of someone who has carried worry for years and is allowed, for one day, to set it down because the thing she feared might never happen had happened.

Chelsea was married. Chelsea was safe. The life Nancy had been trying to protect was finally turning upward. There were extended relatives there, too, some of them people who had been distant for years. Nancy noticed them. Nancy always noticed who was willing to cross a gap. She didn't turn it into a reckoning. She didn't make anyone pay for the years. She let them arrive without interrogation. She let the day keep its shape.

That struck me. Nancy could have used the room as a courtroom. She had enough evidence. She had enough pain. If she wanted to punish her ex-husband socially, she could have. If she wanted to make him a spectacle, she could have. The day offered a clean opening for it.

She didn't take it. Instead, she chose a different kind of control: peace. More concretely, she chose a practical kind of peace, meant to protect Chelsea's photos. To keep the guests relaxed and say, "This is her day, not my case."

I watched Nancy smile through a conversation, then turn and look at Chelsea for a half second, just long enough to confirm what she needed to confirm that she was okay. That people were happy and the day had landed.

Later, when I think about it, that wedding reads like her last happiest moment before Nancy's cancer started metastasizing. Not because she didn't have other good moments after—she did—but because that day had something rare in it: clean satisfaction. A proud, calm sense that she had gotten Chelsea to the other side of a hard story.

For me, it was the last time I saw Nancy look like she could exhale and mean it. Again. After the wedding, there was a home. Nancy's home, specifically, a place she could settle into, a place that looked like an ending to the long struggle rather than another temporary shelter. I remember thinking it with a cautious kind of hope:

She was finally safe. For a brief stretch, the stretch that always feels like a gift in hindsight, that hope held.

The year that followed was, in many ways, our lowest-stress year in a long time. Not because life was perfect. Because the biggest threats had quieted down, Liz was gone. The trust had been distributed. Nancy was in remission. Chelsea was married and building her life. The constant alarms had muted.

Then the holidays came when we weren't invited anywhere.

Not Nancy. Not me.

The family's invitations had narrowed again at this time, as if love were something you earned by being convenient. As if your illness, history, and reality made you too complicated to include at a table.

By then, I was trying to de-escalate wherever I could. I had started doing more things alone to avoid adding pressure to group functions and being one more source of tension in a room already full of it. I didn't announce it. I didn't argue. I just stepped back. Over time, the rituals adjusted without me. The invitations thinned, without any big confrontation. On this occasion, no effort was made to include me in holiday celebrations.

Hence, I cooked my own holiday meal alone. I didn't make a big show of it. I didn't stage a protest. I handled it. I bought what I needed, cooked what I could, ate what I ate, and tried to pretend that it didn't matter.

It didn't matter how quietly I went about this, though, because Nancy heard anyway, and instead of letting me be alone, she drove up to sit with me.

Even though her appetite was off, she said that food had become complicated for her. Even though she was tired, she came anyway.

We sat together. We ate what we could. We talked. We laughed because that was us. It wasn't a perfect dinner, but it was ours. When she left, when we stood at the door and the day was over, I said what I always said to her, the line that had become our shorthand for everything we'd survived.

"Thanks, Nancy, for spending the day with me."

Nancy looked at me, steady, and answered without hesitation, returning it like a mirror.

"Of course, you are my brother."

With that, she got in her car and drove home, and our small party was over.

Tomorrow would be another day. There would be other holidays. In other ordinary moments, we still believed we had time for more, after all. Yet by the time our next Thanksgiving came, we were already counting time differently.

IV
The Night

20

Thanksgiving

The house smelled like warm food, familiar and grounding. It smelled the way Thanksgiving is supposed to smell, settling into the walls and telling you where you are before you fully arrive. It reminded me of past holidays when Nancy loved to host, moving easily between rooms, keeping time and people in check without ever appearing hurried.

Even now, with the hospice bed in the living room and the table pulled close beside it, the house felt purposeful. Thanksgiving had arrived, and Nancy had made sure it knew where to go.

As the weeks progressed and visitors came and went, the circle narrowed again as Thanksgiving approached. Calls slowed. Visits became fewer. The holiday brought family back into focus with its smaller, quieter, more intimate ways.

By now, Nancy couldn't eat anything, but she could still orchestrate things. She directed from the bed like a conductor managing an orchestra, her voice steady, even if the volume was lower than usual, her timing intact.

Who needed what? Where did things go? When would the food be brought out? When should things be slowed down?

Chelsea, her husband, my girls, and I gathered around the table beside her bed. Plates were passed carefully. Conversations were kept light by mutual, unspoken agreement. Someone told a story that had already been told. Nancy smiled at the right places.

Nancy watched it all. Later in the morning, a small group from the church choir, five people Nancy knew well, stopped by. They spoke to her softly, smiling in that careful way people do when they want to bring comfort without asking anything in return. They talked about the music they had sung recently and about the season shifting toward Christmas.

Nancy listened, then named a few songs she liked. Not Christmas yet, she said, but close enough to feel it coming. One of them wrote down the titles. It felt less like a conversation than an instruction. She was already arranging things in her mind, as if a binder existed there, too, with pages neatly turned, nothing forgotten. We exchanged glances and smiled. She was still sharp, still herself.

At different moments, Brian, Chelsea, or I asked if she needed anything. My daughters lifted the room simply by being there.

"I'm good," Nancy said. "Really."

She meant it, not as reassurance, but as truth.

Conversation found familiar grooves. Brian talked about the Eagles and the Thanksgiving football game, and I stayed with him there, keeping my cadence easy, just how holiday conversations are supposed to sound. Plates moved about. Drinks were refilled. Someone laughed louder than expected, then covered the sound with a hand.

This wasn't a distraction so much as permission to let the day feel ordinary for a little while. Nancy followed it all from the bed, tracking voices and laughter, stepping in only when timing needed adjusting. When the story ran long, she redirected. When someone drifted too close to sadness, she steered us back. Even from where she lay, she kept the room moving.

At some point, one of my girls reached for the gravy, and the ladle clinked against the boat, a slight, bright sound in a room that had learned to listen to other kinds of sounds. Nancy's eyes flicked toward it automatically, all the while tracking and managing whose motions caught Chelsea's eye.

"You know what this feels like?" Chelsea said, smiling as if she'd just found a mystery door in the conversation. "Like that Thanksgiving with Santa."

Nancy's mouth curved up into a smile before she even spoke. She didn't have to ask which one. There weren't many that earned a title. My girls looked from Chelsea to Nancy. Old enough now in their late twenties to understand the rhythm of family stories, even when they couldn't remember the origin.

"I don't remember it," one said, half-apologetically, like she was supposed to.

"You were too young," I told her. "You don't get credit for that year."

Nancy made a slight sound, something between a laugh and agreement. Chelsea leaned closer to the bed, like how you do when you're about to pull a thread that belongs to everyone. The girls' mom had bought a full Santa suit: real red velvet, white trim, the whole thing. At home, I'd put it on for the girls, and we'd pretend we were going to catch Santa on camera. With a hidden camera and a waist-high view, the footage was like evidence. The girls loved Santa sneaking in, eating cookies, and putting presents under the tree.

Nancy had been the one who said, "Bring it." She understood what kids needed: a clean piece of magic to hold onto when adults were complicated.

That year, we did what we often did when Nancy, Dad, Liz, and my family were scattered across different states. We combined holidays, collapsing them into one trip, one set of meals, one round of travel, because none of us had the time or energy for separate runs. One year, that meant meeting in the middle and treating it like a hybrid holiday, a little bit of everything compressed into a few days so everyone could get back to their lives. I remember sneaking the suit into the garage as if it were contraband. Dad and Liz were there. The kids were there. Everything looked normal if you didn't know where to look.

"And Liz brought the bird," Chelsea said, and Nancy's eyes closed for a beat as if she could see it.

Liz had a cockatiel, Alfie, and she used to let it out to fly around like it was a party trick, then forget about it. That day, she let the bird out and wandered off, as Liz did, attention always drawn to something else.

Nancy's cats did not wander off.

Chelsea laughed softly. "You and Mom saw it at the same time," she said, looking at Nancy. "Like you were synchronized."

Nancy's smile sharpened. That look she had when she'd fixed something without announcing she'd fixed it. The cat pounced suddenly, and the bird fluttered. The nature show thus began. Liz stayed oblivious to it, but Nancy moved quietly, quickly, and competently, chasing the cat and retrieving the bird as if it were nothing. It was like a small fire put out before it became a big one.

"And Liz didn't even notice," I said. "Not even a little."

"She probably thought the bird had re-caged itself," Chelsea said, and for a second the girls laughed, too surprised at themselves, then relieved when Nancy's face stayed light.

Later, Nancy was cooking, and Liz was in the den watching television, staring fixedly at it as the turkey fire started. Suddenly, flames erupted in the oven. People went running. Voices rose. Chaos was just at arm's length. Liz was sitting three feet away, as if it were a different universe.

Nancy's eyes opened wider at that, the way they always did when the ridiculous part of the memory arrived: Santa.

After we ate, I snuck downstairs to change, and put on the suit, the boots, the beard, all that fake warmth. The plan was simple: come in, do the joy, vanish. Except I'd misplaced the tacky glue for the white eyebrows.

Dad decided to help for a change then.

"He found glue," I said, and Nancy made a slight sound that was laughter already bubbling up, because she knew where this story was going.

The thing was, Dad used superglue. He tacked the white eyebrows right over my black ones like he was installing something permanent. Santa delivered the magic. The kids were thrilled. I slipped downstairs afterward to change back, only to discover I couldn't. The eyebrows were fused onto me. When I finally ripped them off, my real eyebrows came off with the fake ones.

Nancy's laugh cascaded out clean then. A real, genuine laugh. The girls covered their mouths with napkins, laughing, too, and they all shook their heads like they couldn't believe any of us had survived childhood.

Chelsea said, "And then I said it. I was so excited. 'I loved Santa!'"

She paused, waiting for the key line. Nancy's eyes were bright.

Chelsea delivered it perfectly, like she'd been saving it. "But Mom… What happened to Uncle Bill's eyebrows?"

The table broke out in laughter, no one able to contain themselves. Even in that room, even beside the hospice bed, laughter rolled through us, brief, alive, and uncontrollable. Nancy watched it all, still ensuring everyone got fed, keeping the room human.

Watching her that day, I thought of that same Thanksgiving in 1998, those many years ago, when she held things together then, the same as she was holding things together now.

Sitting beside her hospice bed, watching her orchestrate one last Thanksgiving, I understood that this wasn't new. Nancy, as the host and matriarch of the holiday, did it her way, as in the old days. She held things together now when they mattered most, knowing the cost would come later, and trusting that someone else would help carry it when it did.

Later, as the day settled, humor found its way back into the room. Hallmark movies played in the background, with predictable plots and inter-changeable names. Someone joked about how every story sounded the same. Laughter came easily, unexpectedly, and stayed longer than it should have.

As evening came, people began to leave. Care routines resumed. The house quieted. Thanksgiving ended the way it began, held together by inten-tion. The day after Thanksgiving, Nancy was busy, as was I, and I returned later in the evening. She was already asleep. I held her hand before heading up to her bedroom for the night and began our routine.

"Best sister ever," I said softly.

There was no reply this time. I held Nancy's hand, squeezed, and she squeezed back weakly.

21

The Vigil

The days narrowed.

Care became a series of repeated motions of turning, dosing, checking, and waiting. Hospice visited to adjust medications and confirm what we already knew. The real work happened in between.

By then, we had built our own system inside the system to keep things organized. A grid, routines, dosages, prescriptions, and inventory, because nothing about the work was casual anymore. It wasn't "give medicine when needed." It was exact times, exact amounts, what had been delivered, what was running low, what was still sealed, and what was opened. We were, at times, more ready than the hospice nurse, because we lived in the room, and she didn't.

Hospice needed to be organized, and for Nancy, even in hospice, that instinct remained. Next to her bed, behind a drape, was a wall of binders.

My daughters noticed them during their visit.

"Are those binders?" one of them asked Chelsea.

Chelsea pulled the curtain back and smiled. "That's Nancy."

Laughter rose, and one of them said, "Does she have an in-case-of-death binder as Dad does?"

Chelsea nodded and showed her. We all laughed. Nancy would have appreciated that. True to form, there was also a care binder filled with medication schedules, dosages, and notes. Brian recorded the catheter bag's output. We logged everything in carefully.

There was a point when the binder stopped being documentation and became a life raft. When you're exhausted, you don't trust your memory. You trust the grid.

We had a second page, too, full of questions. Things that felt too small to call hospice for, and too big to guess at: What does this kind of breathing mean? How dark is too dark? How long can she go without taking anything by mouth? If she's sleeping, should we wake her for a dose, or protect her sleep? We kept the list folded inside the binder so it didn't look like panic. It looked like planning.

Hospice offered a minister as part of the whole service; we politely declined. Not because we were rejecting the offered comfort, but more because we didn't need it, because the room already had its own kind of faith. Nancy and Chelsea's church friends came by nearly every day. Brian prayed every day. When Nancy had enough lucidity, she would clasp her hands, sometimes fully, sometimes only halfway, and the room would still itself for a few minutes.

Medicines and supplies went through the hospice nurses, and we bought some things out of pocket alongside what they provided—gowns with the back cut for ease, extra wipes, extra pads, extra gloves—anything that made the room more manageable. We learned to keep certain things in one place and never move them: the basket of syringes, the bag of new pads, the little stack of clean washcloths. The slightest inconvenience at noon is nothing. At 2:00 a.m., it feels like sabotage.

Gloves always had to be worn when applying fentanyl. We all feared using it because we had heard stories of sudden overdoses. We followed the instructions exactly. We learned the timing of things. How long before discomfort returned? How small changes mattered. How to read breathing and watch the patterns that were forming, shifting, and dissolving.

Meanwhile, Nancy kept fading. When she was awake, she still asked about people:

How was Chelsea doing?

How were my girls?

Sometimes she asked what day it was.

More than once, she asked when Christmas was.

I answered. There was no reason not to.

That she was asking those questions convinced us she was fighting to stay grounded in time and to pace herself so she could share one last holiday.

As Nancy's lucidity waned, the simple act of getting anything into her became work.

Hospice left a larger oral syringe for us. It looked like a tool you would use on a child, oversized and blunt, marked with little lines that suddenly mattered. The problem was not the syringe. The problem was Nancy. Nowadays, she was asleep more than awake, and when her eyes opened, they often did not land on anything for long. Her mouth stayed slightly open. Her tongue sat back as if it had forgotten what swallowing was for.

The first few times, I tried the obvious way. I spoke her name. I tilted the syringe to her lips and waited. Nothing. She would not rouse in these moments, at least not enough to cooperate, and I could not force it. It had to be offered, accepted, and taken in. Anything else felt like an assault.

That's when I noticed what still worked.

Even when her mind was far away, there was one small signal that her body still answered. If I brushed the corner of her mouth, if I traced a fingertip lightly along her upper lip, there would be a reflex. A tiny movement. A lick. Like the body remembering a basic instruction even as everything else began to shut down.

So, I started using that.

I would sit close to her bed, my shoulder angled toward her head so I could see her mouth and her breathing at the same time. I would carefully draw up the dose, checking the line twice. Then I would touch her lips, softly, once, then again. This was neither playful nor cute. It was just a gentle cue, prompting her tongue to move, which it would, and her mouth would be moistened for a second.

That was my window.

As soon as the reflex came, I would slide the syringe under her tongue, just far enough that the medication would sit where it could be absorbed. I would press the plunger slowly, a fraction at a time. Pause. Watch her face. Watch for the flinch that meant I was too fast or too much. Then another fraction. Another pause. The work had its own kind of rhythm, not unlike dosing an infant, except the stakes were unbearable.

As the days passed, Nancy seemed less thirsty, or maybe thirst was still there, and she could not tell us. The volume we could give her, therefore, shrank. The offers stayed the same. Every time we turned her, every time we checked her, I offered again. Small mercy, repeated. No speeches. Just presence and the next task.

Chelsea found her own method. When Nancy's lips dried out, she stopped trying to convince her to drink and started tending to the discomfort itself. She would take a sponge, dip it in water, squeeze it so it was damp but not dripping, and press it gently along Nancy's lips. Not flooding. Just dampening. A slow pass along the edges, then another. The simple relief of moisture when swallowing had become a problem.

When Nancy was awake enough to answer, she told us plainly that swallowing hurt. Not fussing. Not complaining. Just a fact. Food hurt too. Even a sip took effort, and you could see it in her throat, in the manner in which she braced before the swallow, like someone preparing for pain.

The smoothies became less frequent, too. Early on, I could still get one down with time. I would sit with the cup and a flexible straw, holding it at a careful angle. One slow sip. Then a pause. Then another. I counted small wins. A few ounces. A few more. Each successful swallow felt like a minor miracle, the kind you do not celebrate out loud because you do not want to jinx it.

Some weeks in, the work changed. It stopped being "she can do this if we go slowly" and became "her body is negotiating the terms." The pauses got longer. The sips got smaller. She would turn her head slightly away, not in refusal, but in exhaustion. The straw would touch her lip, and she would not respond. The body was closing doors.

I started watching the catheter bag more than I wanted to at the time. At first, the output looked normal, clear enough that I could pretend it meant stability. Brian would empty it, measure it, and I would log it and tell myself the numbers still added up to time.

Then I saw that the color had changed. It had grown darker, more concentrated, as if Nancy's body were narrowing to essentials and letting everything else go. Brian would hold the bag up toward the light and stare too long, trying to read it like a forecast. The nurse did not need to explain what it meant. The bag was explaining itself.

I wrote the numbers down anyway, then I went back to the syringe, back to her lips, back to the small reflex that still opened the door for a second. Brian measured the drop in volume and looked at me. I recorded it without comment because we both knew what the changes in measurement meant.

Hospice visits were too far in between for the questions that came at night. So, I started researching on my phone as the hours stretched on and the screen light dimmed. I searched the web for signs of the end of life. I watched YouTube videos about breathing patterns and "what to expect," letting strangers name the things we were living through. Sometimes I paused a video because Nancy would make a sound, and I needed the sound itself more than the explanation.

Calls with childhood friends turned into texts. There had been early phone calls, people trying to say a proper goodbye to Nancy, who still had enough energy to hear it. Then she slept more. Talking costs her too much energy. I carried out the updates. Short, factual, merciful. She's resting. Quiet day. I'm here. Love.

The nights were quieter. I took the overnight shifts when I could. The house sounded different after midnight. Pipes clicked. Appliances hummed. The silence wasn't empty; it was watchful.

One particular evening was one of those nights. A whole night, from start to finish, when the house felt like it was holding its breath with us. Chelsea and her husband went to bed. Brian had completed his day shift and left us with a final check-in, calm and steady, as if handing off a baton. The living room dimmed to a few small pools of light: a lamp, the kitchen's glow, the faint outline of the Christmas tree lights. She could still see them from where she lay. She couldn't eat. She couldn't get up. But she could still see the lights twinkling, and it gave her comfort.

I sat by her side. Another chair had been placed near her head so that I could see her whole face, not just the rise and fall of her chest. We sometimes sat that way in pairs, one at her head, one at her side, because the angles matter. You can miss a grimace if you're looking only at the blanket. You can forget a swallow if you're looking only at the mouth.

First check: the log. The times. The last dose. The next window. Supplies placed where they belonged so we wouldn't hunt for them in the dark: oral syringes, gloves, gauze, wipes, the little bottles, the sheet that translated "as needed" into numbers. I lined things up in the same manner I line up tools before a job: not because I enjoyed ordering, but because order is how I keep panic from becoming useless.

I also checked the "inventory" page: what we had left and what we might run out of before the next nurse visit. That page had started as a neat list and turned into a living thing: numbers crossed out and rewritten, a circle around "call tomorrow," a note that said "deliveries," another that said, "ask about breathing." We kept it because we didn't want to be surprised at 2:00 a.m. by something stupid: an empty bottle, a missing syringe, a question we forgot to ask while the nurse was still in the room.

I didn't wake her. I watched. I listened, measuring time by breath. A pipe settled somewhere in the walls, and my body reacted as if it were an alarm. That's what fear does: It tunes you too high. Every slight noise is registered as a threat. Every extended, quiet stretch registers as a threat, too, because quiet can mean peace or absence.

Around 11:00 p.m., I got up and moved Nancy's head. Her mouth was slightly open. I watched her chest rise and fall. I counted. I waited for the next breath. It came, slower than another. I touched her wrist for a pulse and hated myself for doing it, as if my fingers could change the count.

I checked her feet under the blanket. They were cooler than they had been earlier. Her skin looked pale in the lamplight. I didn't go hunting to mottle. I didn't want the image. But my mind went there anyway, and then I was back on my phone with the screen dimmed, searching for words I never wanted to learn.

I sat next to Nancy as one would sit next to a newborn. Living quiet-ly, waiting for any small sound or movement signaling a need. Just after midnight, I would turn Nancy's body, enacting the careful choreography of moving someone who can't help you anymore. The sheet tightened under Nancy's back, the pillow slid into place, a hand on her shoulder, a hand on her hip, the pause afterward while you listen to the sound that tells you you've hurt them. I watched her face as I shifted her. I waited for a wince. What I got was a soft exhale, almost like relief. I wrote down the time and marked it as you would anything that worked: turned, settled, no distress.

Then I waited a full minute with my hand on her shoulder, as if my palm could translate what her face wouldn't show. A crease between her eyebrows softened. Her breathing found its rhythm again. That was the best outcome at the time.

In the quiet after the turn, I did the other small checks that never made it into conversation the next day. I smoothed the sheet so there wouldn't be any wrinkles that could become sore. I adjusted the blanket so it wasn't pulling at her feet. I moved the call button closer, even though she couldn't use it anymore, because leaving it out of touch felt like admitting something I wasn't ready to accept. I checked her hands, cool, a little waxy in the lamplight, and then I stopped, because the line between checking and rehearsing grief is thin.

I sat back down and tried to keep my mind in the room. If I looked too hard for signs, I'd find them. If I didn't look at all, I'd blame myself later. I kept it practical. I did what I needed to do, then returned to stillness.

At one point, I went into the bathroom and caught my reflection in the mirror, eyes bloodshot, jaw clenched, hands still smelling faintly of sanitizer. I ran cold water over my wrists to feel the temperature, to remind my body it still belonged to this world. I drank from the tap even though I didn't want it, because the irony of my being thirsty while Nancy could barely swallow felt unbearable. Then I went back out and sat down again, as if nothing had happened.

Sometime after midnight, I used the sponge again, tracing water along her lips. It looked almost intimate, like something you'd do for a child. She didn't react. Then her tongue moved once, a small reflex, and I took the opening, one measured sip by syringe, slow, careful, more ritual than hydration.

The temptation, in the middle of a vigil, is to fill the silence. To narrate your love. To make meaning out loud. But what she needed most was not language. It was being present. So, I kept it simple. "I'm here," I told her, hoping she could hear. "You're not alone."

Around 1:00 a.m., I stepped away to reset myself. Sitting for hours is its own kind of exhaustion; your eyes blur, your mind slips, and you start to wonder if you'll miss something vital because you blink too long.

I stepped outside for a short walk in the cold. December was coming. The street was still. The type of still you only get late at night in a neighborhood full of people who have no idea what's happening behind one set of windows.

After my walk, I sat on the back deck instead. I chose to sit on my old tailgate chairs. The ones that folded up. The grill was out there, too; the tailgate grill Joe and I had used for games and trips. Since Joe's passing, I couldn't bring myself to care about football anymore, couldn't renew tickets, couldn't pretend the season mattered. The grill had become a relic. Now it was just... there, holding the memory of a life that still believed in the next year.

I checked my phone out of habit, going through whatever texts and emails I had received, then put it down. I put one earbud in, keeping the music low, just enough to keep my brain from drifting into that dangerous half sleep where you wake in panic because you don't know how long you were gone.

Back inside, I did another check and handled the log again. Checked the bag again. Used the sponge once more, running it along Nancy's lips, careful not to push too much. Fluids by syringe, offered more than delivered. You keep offering because offering is what you do.

At 2:00 a.m., I emptied the catheter bag until it read cleanly. The plastic felt warm against my gloved hands, its volume lower. The color was darker, too. I held it up toward the lamp, as if light could make it less accurate. I wrote the number in the binder, then wrote it again in my head, as if memorizing it would help. It didn't. It only sharpened what we already knew.

Sometime after 2:00 a.m., Nancy made a sound, a faint shift in her voice that meant discomfort. Her face tightened for a second, then relaxed. That's when the grid matters. You confirm the window. You measure the dose.

And then you choose in the dark: Give more now or wait and risk Nancy suffering because you're afraid of being the one who "did too much."

I chose comfort. I drew up the amount, delivered it slowly, and waited for it to soften. There was a slight release around Nancy's mouth, the easing in her forehead.

It came. Small. Enough. I wrote the time down immediately. Not because the notebook needed it, but because I did. Because writing it down made it real, and real meant we could do it again when the next wave came.

Near 3:00 a.m., my phone lit up with messages from old friends. Earlier, there had been calls, long goodbyes, voices trying to be brave. Now there were only texts because Nancy slept more, and because we were guarding the energy that remained. I sent short updates. "She's resting." "Quiet night." "I'm here."

Around 3:30 a.m., her breathing changed enough that I sat up and stopped pretending I was calm. A longer pause, then two breaths closer together. Then a stretch that felt too long. I found myself counting again, as one does when trying not to panic. I stared at her mouth, waiting for the subsequent rise. It came… then didn't follow the planned outcome I wanted or the research I'd prepared.

This moment was the hard choice the night kept offering: Call hospice now and risk waking a whole machine for something that might be "normal," or keep doing what we'd already been doing and risk missing the moment the line gets crossed. I stood in the hallway, my phone open and the after-hours number ready. I listened to the house. I listened to my own breathing. Then I called.

The voice on the other end was calm, practiced. The woman didn't sound rushed, but she didn't sound comforting either, as her response was a relay from another duty nurse on the other line. I described what I was hearing, what we'd given, and the timing. She asked a few questions that made me realize how much hospice is, in fact, triage by phone. She didn't give me certainty, no one could, but she gave me something usable: what to watch for, when to call back, what "comfort" meant at that hour. When I hung up, I wrote the guidance down in the binder as if it were scripture.

Near 4:00 a.m., something like grace arrived, brief and unearned. Nancy's hand gave the faintest squeeze in mine. Not strong, but I could still feel it, and that was all that mattered. I leaned in closely. "I'm here," I said again. Her eyes remained closed. She didn't speak. But that squeeze was enough to remind me her body still knew mine, or that love sometimes survives even when language is gone.

A little after that, her face softened in a way I hadn't seen all night. As if whatever was tugging at her had loosened its grip for a minute. I sat there and let myself feel it without trying to interpret it. A minute of not-doing. A minute of just being with her.

The night began to thin. Dawn constantly changes the sound of a house. A distant car. A shift in the refrigerator hum. The world is starting up again, indifferent.

By 6:00 a.m., I could feel my own limits hitting. The sky outside the windows had shifted from black to charcoal, and the Christmas lights looked softer against it. I did one more full check, wrote down the times, and lined up what the morning would need.

Chelsea came down early, and I handed her the binder open to the last page. No theatrics, just a finger pointing at the times, the doses, the note about breathing, and the number for after-hours. She read it the way she read everything in those weeks: fast, competent, and already moving.

"I'm going to lie down for a couple of hours," I told her.

"Go," she said. "I've got her."

Then I went upstairs to wash up, change, and lie down, but I didn't really sleep. Even in bed, I could feel the vigil below me like a magnet.

Before leaving her room, I leaned in.

"Best sister ever," I said.

There was no reply.

Just silence.

22

The Strong Heart

The day-shift nurse checked the hospice logs we kept from the previous day and night, the prescriptions, and ordered refills, then checked on Nancy. She checked Nancy's vitals and then listened to her heart. Her name was Sandy. There were others over the weeks, but she was the one there that day.

She arrived with the calm efficiency, hospice people learn to wear: soft voice, practiced smile, a tote bag that looked light but somehow contained an entire system. She wiped her hands, greeted Chelsea, greeted Brian, greeted me, and stepped into the living room like it was any other room in any other house. Like it wasn't the center of our world.

She asked where we kept the binder, not "do you have one," but where, as if she already knew what sort of people we were. By then, Nancy was mainly bedridden. Her muscles had stiffened. She groaned loudly when we moved her, even with opioids. Brian and I were careful, rolling and lifting the way we had been taught. Nancy ate and drank less. Eventually, not at all. We coaxed medications. We watched. We waited.

Sandy flipped through the pages with a finger that didn't tremble. She scanned times, doses, and notes. She nodded once, then again. She paused on a page and asked a clarifying question, something small, something technical, as if this were a chart in a hospital, not handwriting at a dining table beside a Christmas tree.

That was the strange comfort of her presence: She treated our work as legitimate. She didn't talk down to us. She didn't compliment us in a way that made us sound like amateurs playing nurse. She used what we'd built as if our binder were part of her practice too.

She checked the medications we had out, counted what was left, confirmed what had been refilled, and what still needed to be ordered. When she spoke, she used words like "coverage," "window," "comfort," and "support," and I could hear the limits inside them. The hospice model didn't live in the house. We did. She visited. We stayed.

I asked the question quietly, meant only for Sandy; I didn't want Chelsea to hear it.

"How much longer?" I whispered.

Even whispering it felt like a betrayal, like asking for an answer might summon one. Sandy didn't lower her voice.

"Her heart is very strong," she said, louder than I wanted, sure that Nancy could hear. "Most patients in hospice have a lot wrong with them. Nancy's heart is healthy. Her passing will take a while."

The words were meant as reassurance. They landed as something else entirely because a strong heart prolongs the dying process.

Not that I said that out loud. I nodded, thanked the nurse, and let the moment pass without correction. Inside me, though, something recoiled.

"Strong."

"Healthy."

These were words we spent our whole lives chasing. Words you want to hear at checkups. Words that mean your body is durable enough to do the living part. In this room, those words meant endurance without purpose. They meant waiting. They meant a longer stretch of time where Nancy's body would keep going even as everything that made "going" recognizable fell away.

Nancy's eyes were closed. Her breathing was steady. Her body was still doing what it had always done: enduring. Sandy kept moving. She adjusted the blanket, listened again, checked Nancy's skin, asked about bowel movements, urine output, and how the nights were going. We answered like a team. Facts, numbers, trends. The manner in which you report the day's forecast to someone is a way of deciding whether to send an umbrella.

I watched her stethoscope move, how she slid it under the collar of Nancy's gown without jostling her too much, how she pressed it against Nancy's chest as if that pressure could interpret the whole situation. The rubber tubing was black. The chest piece was cold, even in the warmth of the room.

Sandy smiled faintly when she heard what she wanted to hear. "Still strong," she said, again, like it was a compliment.

My jaw tightened; I could feel it, and I couldn't stop it. Sitting down on the chair beside Nancy, holding her hand, the phrase returned with weight. *Strong, healthy heart.* As if those were uncomplicated virtues. As if they didn't imply more time spent waiting for something that could not be reversed.

My mind did what it always does when a sentence carries consequence: It started running models. If her heart is strong, what fails first? What changes? What does "a while" mean? Days? Weeks? I tried to keep the thought from landing anywhere specific, because specificity would make the room smaller.

When the decision came to perform the spinal tap, I agreed, picturing a gentler fade, graceful, more effortless, not anticipating that what was still healthy in her could lengthen the suffering. Agreed too quickly, maybe. The doctors explained the procedure, the risks, and the limited benefit. I heard enough to decide.

I told myself it was for comfort, that it might buy her clarity, that it would spare Chelsea the prolonged confusion; all those things were true.

What I didn't say aloud was that I was afraid of time stretching without purpose. With that came the old guilt that always shows up when I'm responsible for a lever I can't fully understand. I thought of my father in the ICU years earlier, how the duty nurse told me he was on "life support," how

I flew to Atlanta and Nancy met me there, how I had the DNR in my bag, and still my father was on machines because Liz wouldn't accept it.

I woke Dad not to say goodbye as much as to gain clarity, to have his resolve spoken aloud. Waking him was intrusive, but necessary for the DNR because his request hadn't been discussed with Liz, and he needed to say it for Liz, the doctors, and me.

That was the paradox of these moments: The most precise answers always cost the most to obtain. I had wanted that for her, believing that Nancy deserved to know why she felt sick while doctors insisted that she was cured. She would also like to leave on her own terms, to say goodbye and close the chapters. I had wanted that for Chelsea. I had wanted that for myself, too, if I'm honest, because I didn't want the last clear image of my sister to be confusion.

Now, doubt crept in quietly about the cost of making this decision, and whether waking Nancy had been an act of kindness or cruelty. Sandy's sentence made the doubt heavier. If Nancy's heart was strong, then what had I purchased with that spinal tap? Not extra time, not in any meaningful way. Possibly just extra awareness inside a body that would still have to travel the whole distance.

I stared at Nancy's face and tried not to project meaning onto it. Her mouth was slightly open. Her breathing was even. There were no complaints, no permission, no reprimand. Just her body doing what it had always done: hold.

Brian noticed my struggle before I said anything; he had been quiet most of the evening, sitting back, watching.

Brian had a way of noticing without intruding. It wasn't just Catholic gentleness but attentiveness as a form of respect. He could tell when I was turning inward, the way my shoulders set, how my eyes stopped moving. He could read the moment I slipped into calculation and guilt. When I didn't speak, he waited longer than felt natural, as if listening for something that hadn't been said yet.

While Nancy slept, Brian and I kept our watch as we always did. Two chairs pulled close. The binder is open to the last page. The little basket of syringes and gloves is within reach. In the past, we had filled the hours with quiet talk, half to stay awake and half to keep the room from turning into a tunnel. Brian would offer something small about his day or a story from church, and I would answer with a low voice, keeping one hand near Nancy's, keeping my eyes on her breathing as if conversation could be another kind of monitoring.

That night, I gave him little in return. I checked the log twice when I did not need to. I adjusted the corner of the blanket and then adjusted it again. I lingered longer than usual before writing down a time. When Brian asked a simple question, I took a beat too long to answer, and when I did, the words came out flat, like they had to travel farther than they should. My movements were careful in a way that was not just careful. Slower. Delayed. The pauses between tasks were heavier than the tasks themselves. Brian noticed, like he always noticed. He did not press. He just stayed quietly with me for a moment and kept his eyes on Nancy, as if he could hold the room steady until I found my way back into it.

Then he stood and said, almost to himself, "Hey, Bill, I almost forgot to show you something."

He reached for his phone. I could see him hesitate, like he was checking an old instruction against the moment in front of him.

He didn't look at Chelsea at first. He didn't ask permission. He didn't make it ceremonial. He kept it simple so that something sacred wouldn't become performance. The video began to play. Nancy's face filled the screen, looking alert, then clear, staring straight ahead as if she knew exactly who would be watching and when.

Her voice came through the small phone speaker and filled the room in a way her body couldn't anymore. It was the strangest reversal: this tiny device suddenly carrying more presence than the bed.

"God knew what he was doing when he gave me a brother like you," she said. "I love you, Billy."

The words hit me in a place Sandy's reassurance couldn't reach. My first reaction wasn't relief. It was a sharp internal flinch because love doesn't erase consequences. Love doesn't prove you made the right call. Love shows up and says, "You are seen."

Nancy, always the planner, found a way to assure me. She knew I could make the hard calls, but when decisions were questioned or doubted, she had always found a way to lift me. I felt my throat tighten. I looked away, then forced myself back to the screen, because looking away felt like refusing what Nancy had given.

In the video, she wasn't dying yet. She was just Nancy, plain, direct, no extra words. She wasn't soothing me. She wasn't making speeches. She was doing what she always did when something mattered: saying the true thing cleanly.

The words didn't erase doubt, but they did steady it somewhat. That was what Brian had understood, I realized. Not that I needed to be talked out of guilt, but that I needed a counterweight for it.

Later, after the room quieted again, I sat beside Nancy and listened to her breathing. I held her hand and felt the warmth that was still there.

Strong heart, I thought. *Strong heart.*

I leaned in and said the line as I always did.

"Best sister ever," I whispered.

Once again, there was no reply.

Each night, exhausted, I fell into a deep sleep in Nancy's old bed. I found comfort being above her, knowing she was directly below. I was out cold before the morning shift. I didn't want to miss the morphine regimen, so I set my phone alarm.

I woke up suddenly that night. No alarm. I was just wide awake, as if a kind passenger had gently shaken someone who had fallen asleep on a train so that they wouldn't miss their stop.

For a moment, nothing was wrong. The room and the house were still, I knew. I didn't check the clock because I didn't need to.

Not the full-room brightness of day, just that private glow, the kind you get when everyone else is still asleep, and the world hasn't started demanding anything yet. The lights pulsed softly in the dark. Still, the room's quiet and coldness gave me pause. I slowly pivoted in bed, grabbed some clothes, and quietly opened the door. The time was early. I walked carefully, because the old house's floors creaked.

I went downstairs. The narrow stairwell that had blocked Nancy's hospice bed from ever coming upstairs now served as a brace as I eased my weight down the stairs, one careful step at a time, until I reached the front-door landing and turned toward the living room.

The Christmas tree was lit, softly illuminating the room as if it were a Christmas morning of our younger days.

Nancy was there, but she was gone.

The realization hit, passed peacefully and quietly, just now, by the tree I knew immediately.

Her eyes were still open.

Open, but not seeing. As the last muscle that had been holding the day shut had finally let go, her face was still. Her mouth was still with a gentle smile, as if she were seeing something that made her very happy. The air in the room felt different, thinner, as if the house had exhaled and hadn't taken the next breath yet.

For a moment, I couldn't move. Death is always shocking in its stillness, and I recalled the shock of finding my mother suddenly dead many years before. It stayed with me for a lifetime. I knew that Nancy wouldn't want that for Chelsea.

I had one last duty for Nancy before I could yield to the moment's rising emotional reality.

I stood beside her for a long moment before sitting down. I took her hand and just stayed like that for a moment, letting the room catch up to me. I fixed her blanket, as I had done so many times. I checked her, following hospice teachings. I sat very still as the reality caught up with the emotion.

I leaned down, kissed her on the head, then gently closed her eyes. I said a prayer I knew by heart, Nancy's passage of Psalm 27, verses one to three.

"The LORD is my light and my salvation—Whom shall I fear? The LORD is the strength of my life—Of whom shall I be afraid? When the wicked came against me to eat up my flesh, my enemies and foes, they stumbled and fell. Though an army may encamp against me, my heart shall not fear. Though war may rise against me, in this I will be confident."

Not wanting to break the silence, I texted Chelsea to come down. She came to the foot of the bed. I sat in the chair beside her. There was silence as she walked in.

I waited a beat before gently breaking it.

"Your mom has passed away."

Chelsea looked at her for a moment, then said quietly,

"Mama wanted to live. Her body just failed her."

She reached out and stroked her mother's arm, tenderly, as if finishing something her body no longer could. We waited for the nurse to arrive so we could make it official. There were steps now, procedures, calls to make, a sequence Nancy would have appreciated. That was when we realized something was wrong.

We didn't have anything for her to wear. The only gown in the house was a Christmas one, a red festive one. It said "Ho-Ho-Ho" across the front.

Chelsea looked at me, and I looked at Brian, who had just said that. For a moment, none of us spoke. Then Brian shook his head and laughed softly.

"There's a school bus stop right outside," he said. "If Nancy goes out like that on a gurney in front of those kids…"

It was absurd, tender, and completely on-brand.

Of course, this would happen.

The funeral home solved it with a body bag. Practical, quiet, no drama. Nancy would have approved. She had gone the way she lived, without spectacle, but not without humor.

23

The Last Word

I wrote the eulogy by taking things out. Anything that sounded like performance went first. Anything that tried to soften the truth for comfort followed. What remained had to be enough to hold Nancy, but not so much that it drew attention to me. Nancy would have hated excess.

The church was small and full. People filled the pews and stood along the walls. Family. Friends. Former students. People who had briefly crossed their lives and been changed by them anyway. It had snowed. Nancy loved the snow. Some people worried about traveling, but they came anyway. The church was whole despite the storm.

My best friends, Bill and Seb, were there, having come all the distance from the Cape to New Jersey. They sat close enough that I could catch their faces without having to turn my head, steady, present, the kind of presence that doesn't ask anything from you.

My wife and girls were there too, as were Chelsea and her husband, of course. I spotted former coworkers and friends of mine. Even estranged relatives who were reunited at the wedding a year or so ago. People I never expected to see in the same room again gathered because Nancy had been the common denominator in all of it.

At the front of the church, Nancy's urn sat where you couldn't avoid it. The one she had picked out with us in those early hospice days when she could still speak clearly and decide what mattered. It looked heavier than it should have, and lighter than it had any right to be.

Chelsea, her husband, and my girls had prepared a memorial picture display. I stood before it for a long moment, scanning Nancy's life in photographs. I knew the backstory behind each one, the context, the struggles, the quiet victories that never showed in pictures.

Looking at them, I thought of something Nancy once said to me in hospice.

"I'm sixty now," she said. "That's enough living for a full life."

It was a shorter life than either of us had wanted or expected. But she was right; it had been a full one.

I stood at the lectern and waited for the room to settle. The church was so small that everything felt more intimate, no place to hide. People overflowed into the side room. The door stood open, and I could see faces there, too, half-lit, listening. Snow fell outside the windows in slow, steady sheets.

I put my hands on the lectern and felt the wood under my palms. I looked once at the urn. Then I looked out.

I began with something simple and told the congregation about the diner. A booth. Coffee that had gone cold while two siblings talked the way they always had. I just described how Nancy spoke clearly when clarity mattered, and how she refused to pretend when pretending did no one any good.

Tears and silence filled the congregation as I spoke. Not because they knew the story, but because they knew her. I talked about how Nancy taught, not just in classrooms, but everywhere. She taught by noticing people. By anticipating what they needed before they asked. By quietly holding things together so others could move through their lives without stumbling. I said she wasn't loud about it. She didn't claim credit. She adjusted herself to the world and, somehow, made it better.

My voice broke once. It surprised me. It happened when I spoke about how Nancy asked for help, not because she doubted it would be given, but because she respected the weight of asking. Nancy never assumed. She always chose.

I paused. Let it pass. Then I finished.

I didn't speak for long. Nancy would not have wanted that. I said what needed to be told and stopped.

Chelsea spoke after me. She stood where I had stood and held herself together as Nancy had taught her to. When she said "Mama," her voice caught, and the sound moved through the pews like a single breath turning into tears. Chelsea braced herself at the podium. Someone in the first row offered a tissue, subtly, should she need it, without looking up. Steady. Well poised, she completed her tribute to Nancy's life as a mother.

Even the service itself had been Nancy's work. The hymns had been chosen in advance. The urn placement. The flowers. The order of things. All of it had been written down in the funeral binder she put together when she first came home to hospice, when she could still plan and still insist on getting it right. The structure was hers. The details were hers.

Only our words weren't scripted. Afterward, people thanked me. They told me it was beautiful. That it helped. That it captured her. I accepted their words politely and understood that what mattered most had already happened.

The eulogy wasn't for me. And it wasn't even for the congregation. It was a final act of alignment. Nancy had spent her life teaching people how to live with care and intention. That day, she taught us how to say goodbye the same way.

As the service ended, people queued to greet us on their way out of the church and across to the fellowship hall for the repast. Chelsea, Brian, and I stood together receiving them, the line moving slowly, friends, relatives, former coworkers, and people I had not seen in years offering condolences, small memories, and the kind words people reach for when there is nothing large enough to say. Somewhere in the middle of it, my wife stepped in close and put a gentle arm around me, letting the moment pause for a breath before the line carried on.

Downstairs, the church basement had returned to its other job. Folding chairs. Paper plates. Coffee and cookies set out on long plastic tables. Coats draped over the backs of chairs. A temporary, borrowed feeling of spaces meant only for the aftermath. People spoke in the low, polite tone we use when we are trying not to step on grief, but still have to talk.

Brian stood a little apart from the cluster, a Styrofoam cup in his hand, looking out through the small window near the back. The snow had stopped. Outside, everything was covered, smooth and unmarked, the street and the grass erased under a clean white sheet. A strip of sun had broken through, sitting on top of it like a seal.

I walked over and followed his gaze.

"It makes everything clean and new again," he said. "A blanket, smoothing it all out. It's pretty to see."

Behind us came a sound that felt out of place for half a second, and then didn't. My girls laughed quietly, as if they'd surprised themselves. Not loud. Not careless. Just alive.

They caught it and softened it, a glance exchanged, the way you do when you remember where you are. But the sound had already landed. To me, it wasn't out of place at all. It was like birds singing after the rain, small, instinctive, and honest, a sign that something had passed and the world could start making its ordinary music again.

I watched them for a second longer than I needed to. Chelsea and my girls were just talking, like nothing to carry between them. I let it sit for a moment.

Brian finally turned and took a sip from his cup. The room's volume rose a notch, as if someone had turned a dial. We watched the light hold on the snow while the room around us kept humming with small talk.

Chelsea watched from a few feet away. When she saw me turn back toward the room, she smiled, the way you smile when you've been holding something for someone and you've waited for the right moment to give it. Only then did I notice the envelope in her hand.

Chelsea came toward me, holding the envelope.

"I have something for you," she said.

I stared at her. She read the question on my face and answered it with, "Yup, it sure is."

The envelope was addressed in Chelsea's careful writing. Inside was a folded letter. I recognized the paper immediately. I unfolded it. It was dated the day after Thanksgiving. Nancy had written it before she died. It was the last thing she did for us.

239

Nancy's Letter
11/24/23

Dear Billy,
My sibling through thick and thin. You helped me through so much turmoil in life, and I know that God ordained you to be my brother. We had typical sibling rivalries as kids, but I knew that if I yielded to what you were showing me, everything would be okay. You worked so hard to keep us together as a family, and it is so appreciated. You worked so hard to combat the trials and tribulations, and because of you, we made it. I hope you know how much God inspired you because I see it all from here. God bless you. God keep you. God give you his peace. That is my prayer for you until you and I meet again. I love you, Bill.

Love,
Nancy

About the Author

William Ledbetter is a New Jersey–based writer and business executive. Over the course of his career, he has worked as both a CPA and an IT executive in large, complex organizations. *Six Weeks* is his first book. He wrote it to fulfill a final promise to his sister Nancy, as a reflection on meeting hardship with a blend of duty and grace, and as a testament to the quiet, devoted love of those who surrounded her in hospice—the kind that shows up, stays, and does the work.

He lives in New Jersey with his family.